D0832131

GRAYSON HARTER ENSIGN, B.A., M.A., M.Div., president at one time of Central Christian College of the Bible (Moberly, MO.); twice professor of Bible, theology, hermeneutics, and apologetics, The Cincinnati Bible Seminary; preacher; missionary to Jamaica; first director of the Bible Chair of the Southwest (Amarillo, TX.); presently a pastor-teacher of Christ's Church Cincinnati; author of *You Can Understand the Bible* and *Letters to Young Christians*.

EDWARD HOWE, M.E., P.E., graduate work, The Cincinnati Christian Seminary; extensive counseling with church professionals, emotionally disturbed persons including alcoholics, drug addicts, and potential suicides; 1980 recipient of the General Electric Foundation's Gerald L. Phillippe Award for Distinguished Public Service; currently manager of B.F. V. Systems with the FMC Corporation, San Jose, California.

BOTHERED?

BEWILDERED?

BEWITCHED?

*Your Guide
To Practical Supernatural Healing*

Grayson H. Ensign, B.A., M.A., M.Div.

and

Edward Howe, M.E., P.E.

RECOVERY PUBLICATIONS
CINCINNATI, OHIO 45223

Published by Recovery Publications
4334 Pitts Ave.
Cincinnati, Ohio 45223
Cover design by Dr. Carol Ensign Bradshaw
Manufactured in the United States of America

Library of Congress Cataloging in Publication Data
Ensign, Grayson Harter and Edward Howe, 1984
Bothered? bewildered? bewitched?
Your guide to practical supernatural healing

Library of Congress Catalog Card Number
84-60177
ISBN 0-9613185-0-3

DEDICATION

We gratefully dedicate
this volume to
the Lord Jesus Christ
for the victories given
and to
Christ's Church
for her spiritual
warfare.

SUGGESTION

Please skim the table of contents
and
find the chapters that are of
the greatest value and interest
to you.

Contents

Foreword

By Kurt E. Koch

This is a wonderful book! It is the best American book which I have read on this subject. I hope that it can be read widely in the USA, and I hope that it can be translated into German. The authors are following a line similar to that which I followed for half a century. They do not go to the dangerous extremes characteristic of so many who write on the occult and work with the demonically oppressed.

When I was asked to look at the manuscript for this book, I began by reading a few selected chapters, especially the chapters on tongues, nutrition, and James 5:14ff. I found myself in strong agreement with the main thrust of this material and with most of the details.

Turning to the subject of James 5:14ff., I can say that I am enthusiastically happy about these pages! The authors confirm my own opinion and practices. I have followed James 5:14ff. since 1932 and have had it applied to myself in at least two specific cases of illness. I am quite surprised that these American brothers were led to understand this passage just as I was. They give a wonderful explanation of this important part of the Bible.

For an example from my own counseling experience, a woman and her two daughers came to me while I was holding a meeting in Brazil. They each had sicknesses which the doctors had not been able to help. They confessed their sins, and along with the believing minister I prayed for them and laid hands on them. Eight years later I visited the same town. The lady came and asked me, "Do you remember my case?" I said no. Then she reminded me of what had been done, and she reported that all three had experienced healing. The honor goes to Jesus alone!

Well, after reading the sections commented on above, I knew I would have to read more of this manuscript. I do not like to recommend just *some* chapters when there may be errors in the chapters not read. But as I continued to read (I invested four or five days reading most of the book), I did not find any mistakes. The authors exhibit an exact knowledge of the Holy Scriptures and good experience in counseling. Their experiences with demonically-oppressed people and with deliverance are almost exactly the same as my own. I agree completely with them that believers can be controlled, attacked, or possessed by Satan.

Again I say, this is a good book, and I hope that it can be widespread in the USA.

Professor Dr. Kurt E. Koch, Th.D., D.D., S.Lit.D.,

author of

Christian Counselling and Occultism

and many other books

Aglasterhausen,
West Germany
December, 1982

Thank You, Dear Reader, For Giving Us A Minute

Thank you for picking up our book, because you were in our minds when we wrote this book. Our concern is to share with you all the wisdom and lessons learned from our experiences in helping people like you. Our commitment is to share with you whatever insights the Lord God has given us relative to the healing of the *whole* person, and we invite you to remember carefully the things presented to see if you can gain from them. Of course, it is not necessary for you to agree with all of our reasoning or conclusions.

Much of our book is based on our experiential knowledge of God's working with and through us over a period of many years but especially involving more than one hundred and fifty cases of serious and often extended counseling in the past five years. We know this approach to healing the *whole* person truly works. It will be effective for you if you follow the principles and practices that we have written for you. We have wanted this to be like a handbook on healing and health with broad applications to every one in need.

Chapters one and seven through fifteen deal with the practice and outworking of the principles of our methodology. Our methodology is firmly grounded in principles that are true, because they are revealed in the Word of God. These foundations for our procedures and practices are found in chapters two through six. According to your interest you may select the chapters you want to begin your study with, though we hope you will end up by reading all the chapters to get the total picture of healing the whole person.

It is our earnest hope that you will find encouragement and assistance either in working with people with their problems to bring healing to them or in finding those who can help you with your own problems by following this book. God can and will do remarkable things as we allow Him, yes, even "impossible with men" results (Matt 19:26).

Please let us hear from you as you interact with our writings, concepts, and conclusions. By sharing with us your own insights and experiences relative to this vital work of meeting real human needs in natural and supernatural ways you will enable us to become more effective in our own ministry. Thank you so much.

Grayson H. Ensign
Edward Howe

Acknowledgements

How grateful we are for all those who have made it possible for us to offer this book to the public for its healing. Most of all, we thank the Lord Jesus Christ who gave us both the wisdom and the experience so that we could compose this book. All glory and praise belong to the triune God for the truth and value of this work, while we take responsibility for whatever is imperfect and inadequate.

Our special thanks go to the members of Christ's Church Cincinnati for giving us the time to write this book as one of our ministries for the whole body of Christ. We appreciate their unselfishness and concern for others.

Gratefully we acknowledge the valuable suggestions made by Dr. Jack Cottrell and Tim Hudson in regard to theology and the supernatural after critically reading our manuscript. Gary Albrecht gave us most useful suggestions in regard to psychological areas.

Hal and Anita Cory were used of the Lord to introduce us to the whole area of deliverance ministry. We thank God for the valuable instruction and work that they gave us in those early days.

Gladly we acknowledge the contribution of Kim Adams, our secretary, for her professional work of typing the manuscript through its various revisions. She did much of the proofreading. Along with Diane Albrecht, she is responsible for the extensive indices.

The book could not have been written without the grand support of Alma Howe and Grayce Marie Ensign. They stood by us through the many months of writing the text, gave us encouragement, and made important editorial suggestions to improve the manuscript in its content, its clarity, and grammatical style. We thank God for these women who have been our faithful and committed partners in our counseling through these years. We dub them "true yokefellows."

Finally, we express our deep appreciation to the following publishers who gave us permission to quote from their publications.

"The Epistle of James" by Burton Scott Easton in *The Interpreter's Bible*. Copyright © 1957 Abingdon Press. Reprinted by permission of Abingdon Press.

"Lawyer Says Multipersonality Man Has Relapse" from *The Cincinnati* [Ohio] *Enquirer,* Sept. 28, 1980. Copyright © 1980 Associated Press. Reprinted by permission of Associated Press.

From *Psychobabble* by Richard D. Rosen. Copyright © 1975, 1976, 1977 by Richard D. Rosen. Used with the permission of Atheneum Publishers.

Healing by Francis MacNutt. Copyright © 1974 Ave Maria Press. Reprinted by permission of Ave Maria Press.

Counterfeit Miracles by B. B. Warfield. Copyright © 1972 (reprint) Banner of Truth Trust and used by its permission.

Help! I Believe in Tongues by K. Neill Foster. Copyright © 1975 Bethany Fellowship Inc. and used by its permission.

How to Save Money on Almost Everything by Neil Gallagher. Copyright © 1978 Bethany Fellowship Inc. and used by its permission.

The Psychological Way/The Spiritual Way by Martin and Deidre Bobgan. Copyright © 1979 Bethany Fellowship Inc. and used by permission.

War On The Saints by Jessie Penn-Lewis and Evan Roberts. Taken from copyrighted material used by permission of the Christian Literature Crusade, Fort Washington, Pa. 19034.

"Do It Yourself Health Care" by Jane Heimlich. *Cincinnati Magazine,* May 1980. Reprinted by permission of *Cincinnati Magazine.*

The Authentic New Testament, edited and translated from the Greek for the General Reader by Hugh J. Schonfield. Copyright © 1955 Dennis Dobson Ltd. Permission granted by Dobson Books Ltd.

An Introduction to Christian Apologetics by E. J. Carnell. Copyright © 1948 Wm. B. Eerdmans Publishing Co. and used by its permission.

Theological Dictionary of the New Testament, Gerhard Kittel, Editor. Copyright © 1964 Wm. B. Eerdmans Publishing Co. and used by its permission.

Psychology as Religion by Paul Vitz. Copyright © 1977 Wm. B. Eerdmans Publishing Co. and used by its permission.

Orthomolecular Nutrition by Abram Hoffer and Morton Walker. Copyright © 1978 Keats Publishing and used by its permission.

(continued on page 314)

"And when evening had come, they brought to Him many who were demon-possessed, and He cast out the spirits with a word and healed all who were ill" (Matt 8:16).

"You know of Jesus of Nazareth, how God anointed Him with the Holy Spirit and with power, and how He went about doing good, and healing all who were oppressed by the devil; for God was with Him" (Acts 10:38).

"Is anyone among you sick? Let him call for the elders of the church, and let them pray over him, anointing him with oil in the name of the Lord; and the prayer offered in faith will restore the one who is sick, and the Lord will raise him up, and if he has committed sins, they will be forgiven him. Therefore, confess your sins to one another, and pray for one another, so that you may be healed. The effective prayer of a righteous man can accomplish much" (James 5:14-16).

* All Scripture quotations are from the New American Standard Bible, © The Lockman Foundation 1960, 1962, 1963, 1968, 1971, 1972, 1973, 1975, 1977 and are used by permission. Exceptions to this rule are specified.

1

"Mine! He Is Mine! I Am The Prince of Darkness!"

"CAN YOU HELP ME? I really need your help because nothing in my seminary training prepared me to deal with anything like this," the minister said over the telephone. "This man in my congregation is undergoing peculiar and frightening experiences which he cannot handle, and I simply do not know what more to do for him. Of course, we have prayed and read the Bible; but things are getting worse not better. He is being tormented, especially at night, with visions in his room, by moving objects, and by terrible thoughts of murder, devil worship, and denying Christ."

"Is this man a Christian who really believes in God and manifests a genuine walk in the Holy Spirit?" I asked.

"I have no question about his relationship to God. He is a sincere and devout follower of Christ and has shown a real earnestness about becoming more Christlike. Indeed, I almost think that some of these weird experiences began soon after he started seriously praying for God to take total control of his life," Minister Zane* replied. "For the past months I have counselled with this brother, and he appears rational and can pray though sometimes with difficulty. Recently he seems to go deaf as I talk with him, especially when we read the Bible. Also I notice that his eyes are often glazed over, and he seems to be going into a trance. It appears to me that he is coming

---

* This is a true account of an actual deliverance session though names and identifying characteristics have been changed protecting confidentiality.

under the control of some power so that he is confused and troubled. Of course he is frightened and wonders if he is going insane. Yet he keeps telling me that he thinks it is the devil who is attacking him.''

''From what you have told me the symptoms point to a possible case of demonic oppression,'' I commented. ''It appears to be a spiritually grounded conflict, and it is very likely that this Christian has been invaded by evil spirits. Does he hear voices?''

''Yes, he thinks that he has heard voices at times, yet he can't be sure that he is really hearing them. He wonders if he is only imagining it or dreaming it. He is hearing the word 'kill' most often.''

''Have you been able to get him to confess some recent actions he has taken which he knew were sinful and clearly forbidden by the Lord?'' I inquired.

''He is rather evasive about those questions but seems to be indicating something about Satanism and involvement with Satanists. It is obvious that he is terribly embarrassed and frightened about what he has done,'' Zane stated.

''Then I would suggest that you explain that you want to bring him to me for counseling and that we will pray for the Lord Jesus Christ to heal him of these evil thoughts and frightening apparitions that he has been experiencing.'' I went on to explain the procedure that is set forth in James 5:14ff. authorizing elders to pray and anoint the sick. In some detail I described how we would proceed in this first exploratory conference.

Zane was very happy to know that I would work with him. He said that he thought the man would be willing to submit this problem to Christ, because he had stated that ''only God can help me.''

We set a date for the conference and agreed to be much in prayer for the man and for Zane. I warned Zane that he must take full precautions in meeting this man, because he might attack him physically or attempt to do something to him that would compromise him morally. We had experienced such things especially in the early months of our work with people with evil spirits, for we had been physically attacked by them or in driving had them snatch the wheel and attempt to wreck the car.

An awestruck, concerned but courageous minister agreed to do all that I had instructed him to do. My wife and I began to pray regularly for Zane and Smitty.

Three nights later about 11 p.m. the ringing telephone jarred us awake. Picking up the phone I heard an excited voice, "Help, you've got to help us. We're having a terrible time with Smitty." It was my friend Zane breathing heavily as from exertion. "We have Smitty in my house, and it is taking five men to hold him down. He is so strong and is writhing and crying out to Satan to come and help him. What are we to do?"

(I realized that it was the day before our appointment and so was not surprised, because often an invaded person will suffer an apparent counterattack of the demons to keep from being confronted in a deliverance session. The demons are quite aware of what is going on and can learn from our words if not from our thoughts as to what we are planning to do. They also know the power of the Lord Jesus Christ in casting out evil spirits through the elders.)

"Get an elder as quickly as you can," I said, "and have him pray over Smitty in the name of the Lord Jesus Christ, binding all the evil spirits into helplessness and remission by the blood of Christ, and then anoint him with olive oil. We will be praying fervently here for the Lord Jesus Christ to bind those demons and keep them inoperative until we can get together."

With all our hearts we prayed for these brethren who were getting a baptism of fire in a direct confrontation with evil spirits without teaching or preparation for it. (We have written this book so that does not have to happen to you, for such "on the job training" is difficult and dangerous.) We were still praying when the telephone began to ring at 12:30.

"Pastor, we are in real trouble and don't know what to do next. We got one of the elders who came and prayed and anointed with oil as you instructed us to do. It helped quiet Smitty for a time, but now he is getting more violent and ferocious. We are getting worn out trying to hold him down. What super-human strength he has for a small guy! Please, please help us."

"Oh, Zane, my wife and I have been praying for you, for we know how terribly difficult these first experiences can be when you have no preparation for it. They are frightening and require experienced workers. We believe that the Lord wants us to come to you and go into a full deliverance since Smitty is demonized. It is clear that we do have a case of demonic oppression; but praise God, we have seen His infinite power setting Christians free from the most powerful of demons! As servants of God whom He has taught through many hundreds of hours of deliverance work, we are willing to be used by Him to meet your great need. As soon as we are dressed we will come to your house. Keep on praying, reading Scriptures, singing hymns, and trusting our Almighty Father.''

When we drove into the yard of the preacher's house, Smitty became violent and shouted out that he did not want us in the house, we were told by those present. We rushed in and with brief prayers for God's perfect protection and for His infinite power to be at work against those evil spirits in control of Smitty, we began in the name of the Lord Jesus Christ to bind the evil spirits into helplessness. As I looked into the eyes, the person looking at me clearly was not Smitty. There was cunning, hatred, and contempt in the glaring eyes which matched the obscene and mocking words pouring out of the mouth, words that no devout Christian would utter. There was a hard set to the face and an evil, scornful smirk on the lips. The hands reached out toward me in strangling motions in spite of the full force of the strong men holding the slight figure of Smitty on the couch.

"In the name of the Lord Jesus Christ, your Conqueror, I command all you evil spirits in Smitty to be bound into inoperativeness immediately. The blood of the Lord Jesus Christ breaks your power over Smitty; and in the awful name of Yahweh, the Almighty God, we command you demons to be in total remission! Leave the face, eyes, and mouth of Smitty and go down into remission in his body! By the authority of the Lord Jesus Christ you cannot go anywhere except down into his body, totally bound in subjection to the Son of God. Go down now in the name which is above every name, the Lord Jesus Christ. Go down!''

Suddenly Smitty is back with us, wide-eyed, exhausted from the enormous exertion of hours of being forcibly restrained yet unaware of the full extent of the takeover of his body by the demons. As quickly as I could I explained the procedure God had honored over and over again in scores of Christians, and Smitty agreed that he believed in Christ as Lord and Deliverer and wanted all these demons out of his body.

Even as we talked there was some glinting in the eyes and some twitching of the limbs which indicated to me that the evil spirits were not far from coming into manifestation again, i.e., seizing control of the body. Earnestly we prayed against the evil spirits and implored the Father to keep them in remission until we laid the spiritual groundwork.

Smitty was able to read the statement, "My Renunciation and Affirmation" (cf. Appendix C), but he stumbled over the words and stopped at times, breathing heavily. My wife and I were both suspicious of the person who was reading this and who signed it, for in the past we have seen persons subtly demonized so that the statement was invalid as it was made and signed by a demonized person. (At a later date Smitty signed another such statement.)

I suggested to the men that they take firm hold of Smitty, because I was ready to begin commanding in the name of the Lord Jesus Christ for Him to force the demons into manifestation to be expelled from this child of God. It was well that I did because the body was taken over swiftly in a great surge of raging power, and I stared into the eyes of a crafty, fiendish personality who exuded evil.

"How dare you call me up! Who do you think you are? I will destroy you, you stupid mortal!" With blazing eyes that beamed hatred and rage the battle was joined. *But be absolutely assured that this was not a battle between the pastor with Bible, prayer warriors and anointing oil; it was between the Lord Jesus Christ, the living Lord and Savior of Smitty, and the usurpers of the mind and body of Smitty. No man is an exorcist or a conqueror of demons save the Man, Jesus Christ of Nazareth. Forget this and you are in terrible peril.*

"Evil spirit," I commanded, "in the name of the Lord Jesus Christ, your Conqueror, what is your name?" "David." "Will that stand as truth before the Eternal God?" "Yes." "Are you there in your entirety with all your network of demons bound to you?'' ''Yes/no.''

''The Lord Jesus Christ rebuke you. You must speak only the truth before Almighty God. Will it stand as truth before Yahweh that all of your demonic associates are now bound to you without exception?'' ''Yes.'' (Hereafter the test of truth will be abbreviated as S.T. G.)

''What is your function in Smitty?'' ''To kill.'' ''S.T. G?'' ''Yes.'' ''Kill whom, Smitty?'' ''Yes.'' ''S.T. G?'' ''Yes.''

''How were you able to invade Smitty; what did he do?''

''He went to and participated in a Satanic meeting where a blood sacrifice was made to Lucifer.'' ''S.T. G?'' ''Yes.''

''Do you now have any ground or legal right to remain in Smitty as he claims forgiveness in the blood of Christ?'' ''No.'' ''S.T. G?'' ''Yes.''

''Who do you answer to; who is the highest demon over you in authority?'' ''Jason.'' ''S.T. G?'' ''Yes.'' ''Then, David, you go down into remission bound by the blood of Christ; and you, Jason, in Christ's name come up to full attention before your Lord and Conqueror!''

Immediately we observed a change in personality and even the quality of the voice as an evil being took over the face and eyes of Smitty who was barely conscious or aware of all of this as he later testified. He simply knew that none of these actions or words were done by his spirit or mind.

''Will it stand as truth before Almighty God that you are the evil spirit Jason?'' ''Yes, it will.'' ''Will it stand as truth before God the Father that you are now bound entirely with all your network of demons that have invaded Smitty and that the evil spirit David is also bound to you in entirety?'' ''Yes.''

''Who do you answer to in the demonic hierarchy?'' ''Lucifer.'' ''S.T. G?'' ''It will.'' ''Is that a demon named Lucifer?'' ''Yes/no.'' ''Is Lucifer the same as the Dragon, the evil one?'' ''Yes.'' ''S.T. G?'' ''Yes, it will.''

''Do either you, your network, and David and his network have any grounds, rights, or blocks to enable you to remain in Smitty when commanded to leave in the name of the Lord Jesus Christ?'' ''No.'' ''S.T. G?'' ''Yes.''

"Then you must renounce Satan, the devil, as your lord and god." "No, I will never do that. He is my lord and god!"

"He is not your lord or god but a liar and deceiver. Only Yahweh is Eternal Lord and God. I command you in the name of the Lord Jesus Christ, the Son of God, to confess as the eternal truth—Jesus Christ is my Lord and God." "No, I will not. I hate his name. Ugh! blah! Satan is my lord!"

"Holy Scripture which cannot be broken declares that only Jesus Christ is Lord, and every knee must bow before Him, and every tongue must confess that Jesus Christ is Lord to the glory of the Father. You must confess this as truth. Do you want us to read it to you?"

"No, I know what it says." With much reluctance and dejection Jason finally says, "Oh, all right. . . . Jesus is lord."

"That will not do. You must say, I confess that Jesus Christ, the Son of God, is my Lord and Conqueror."

Again there is a struggle and resistance, but finally Jason says with a disgusted expression on the face, "Jesus, the Holy One of God, is my Lord." "S.T. G?" "Of course, you know it is true."

"Hallelujah! Thank you, Lord God Almighty! Amen!" our team cries.

"Did you make that confession without getting Smitty to do it for you?" "Yes." "S.T. G?" "Yes."

"Now you must renounce Satan, the devil as your lord and god." After considerable commanding in Christ's name, Jason with great effort declares, "I renounce Satan, the devil, as my lord and god." "S.T. G?" "Yes."

Once more I pray the Lord Jesus Christ to bind all the evil spirits of David and Jason with all their demonic associates, place-takers, and no-name demons by the blood He shed on Calvary's cross and to please remove them from Smitty, to send them to Gehenna without any stopping. My assistant reads James 5:14ff., and I take up the bottle of olive oil. At once the eyes are opened wide and stare at the bottle; the body begins to recoil and to thrash about as I move forward to apply the oil to the forehead.

"In the name of the Lord Jesus Christ, I anoint this body with this oil and claim all of this body and this person for the sole lordship of Jesus Christ. This blood-bought body belongs to Jesus Christ alone! In the name of your Lord and Conqueror all of you demons leave this body immediately and go directly to Gehenna! Out! Keep moving out, be gone! In Christ's name you are driven out of this body. Leave the body. The blood of Christ expels you from this body." This commanding continues as my wife reads Scriptures and all the team is praying fervently.

After several minutes the body goes limp; the eyes change and are clear and calm. We all recognize Smitty the child of God is back with us. We pray that God will fill Smitty with His Holy Spirit.

"Is that you, Smitty, true child of God?" "Yes." "S.T. G?" "Yes! yes! Oh, thank you Lord Jesus Christ. Oh, how different, how wonderful I feel." And tears of joy and relief well up in the eyes of the Christian now set free from the evil spirits.

The hour is 3:15 a.m., and all of us are exhausted, especially Smitty. We cannot do more though I know that more needs to be done. All of our past experiences with such cases convince my wife and me that a lot more work of deliverance will be required. This is just the first battle of a war that must be fought until all the layered networks of demons are removed by the Lord Jesus Christ.

Since we know that evil spirits are very deceptive, I begin a time of testing to seek the Lord's assurance that all these demons are out of the body and in hell. "Evil spirits, David and Jason, if you or any of your network exist outside of hell, you must return immediately to the eyes and face of Smitty that he and I may know you are there. In the name of the Father, the Son, and the Holy Spirit you have to be in manifestation in the eyes and face of Smitty if you are not in hell now!" I keep this up for several minutes as others are praying, and I am watching intently to see if there is any indications of demonizing.

There is no visible sign of any demonic activity such as the glinting of the eyes or squinting, twitching of the limbs, the mouth drawn up, or hardened features on the face. Smitty says that he does not feel any movement in his body or any sense of some power or person in him. Great rejoicing and praise to God is offered, and we close with prayers that the Holy Spirit will control and protect Smitty as never before. Also we pray that Smitty will be protected from all the harassing attacks of the devil and his hosts.

Then with great praise and thanksgiving to God for all He has done and what we have witnessed, some for the first time in their lives, we head for our homes and some rest. My wife remarked, "Do you realize what date this is? It is October 31, the most powerful day in the calendar for all occultists and witches. No wonder Smitty suffered such a terrible attack of demons."

Two days later the telephone call came from Minister Zane, "Pastor, we are having more trouble. Smitty is being harassed so that he is very fearful and confused. After you left the other night the word 'kill' started up in his head again. Now when I read the Scriptures his eyes glaze over, and he sinks into a trance-like state. What are we going to do?"

"Zane, I knew that we would have to do more work with Smitty even when we quit the other morning too exhausted to continue. Don't be dismayed because sometimes we have had to work many hours to see the Lord Jesus Christ set people free, but He always does it. Never doubt that for one moment! He is always the Victor! You will have to bring Smitty to my office. It is much better and safer than your house where we may get interrupted or someone may call the police to find out what all the noise is about."

That night at 8 o'clock as the five men came with Smitty he became increasingly violent as they turned off the highway and neared my office. They had to literally wrap themselves around him, burly men that they were, to keep him from punching them and climbing out of the car. My wife and I had been praying and watching suspecting what was in store for all of us. Upon their arrival I rushed out to the car and began praying for the Lord Jesus Christ to bind all the demons in Smitty into inoperativeness. The sturdy men literally carried Smitty into the office and held him in a chair. (So many times God has graciously provided the darkness to keep neighbors from observing what was going on and in their alarm to call the police. The protection of our Abba, Father, is awesome and incredibly great.)

All of us are praying fervently to the Lord Jesus Christ to put the unclean spirits into remission and to break their attack on Smitty. He is twisting, struggling, and pulling to get free. His eyes are flashing; his face is flushed and sweaty, and his mouth wears a sardonic grin.

Suddenly all is changed. The body is quiet, and the personality of Smitty is clearly seen. "How did I get here?" Smitty asks in a quiet tone. We explain to him that his friends had brought him to the office even though he was violent. He says, "The last thing I remember is getting into the car with these brethren."

Christ, our Lord, is much more in charge of Smitty than the other time, and as a rational person Smitty understands now that he needs to confess all his major sins that have given grounds for invasion and in particular the willful sin of attending a Satanic worship service when he knew it was forbidden by God.

After hearing his in-depth confession alone, the other team members came around Smitty with me as we offered up strong prayers to our Lord Jesus Christ to take over the whole meeting and do whatever He wanted to do in answer to our desperate needs (cf. Appendix D). Taking leadership and as always praying in the name of the Lord Jesus Christ, I commanded, "All evil spirits in Smitty are bound in their entirety by the blood of the Lord Jesus Christ and by His absolute authority must obey all His commands through His servants. Come up to full attention before the Lord Jesus Christ, the King of kings, and bow your knees before Him now!"

Instantly the body was convulsed as demons took control of the body, and I looked into the eyes to see an alien personality of hatred and intense bitterness. I knew that it was not Smitty but a power of darkness, evil and gross.

"In the name of the Lord Jesus Christ," I called out, "you must tell the truth, the whole truth, and nothing but the truth. What is your name, demon?"

"I am Jason." "S.T. G?" "Yes, it certainly will." "Where is the evil spirit David?" "He is gone." "Where has David gone?" "He has gone to hell . . . and I'M GOING THERE TOO!"

"Amen. Praise the Lord Jesus Christ!" I shouted.

"Do you have any legal right or block to remain in Smitty?"

"Yes/no." "The finger of God Almighty strike you down for trying to lie to us. Tell the whole truth and only the truth. Do you have any right or block to remain in Smitty now that he is under the blood of Christ."

"No, there are none." "S.T.G?" "Yes." "Then how were you able to stay in the body when commanded to leave the other morning? Are you the same Jason that was commanded to leave?" "No, I am another Jason." "S.T.G?" "Yes."

I had slipped up as it is easy to do when dealing with demons with their super-intelligence and great though finite skills in deception. In the excitement of the deliverance and the lateness of the hour, I had forgotten to check out, as we regularly seek to do, the *number* of demons with the same name in the person. In this case there were two more demons called Jason in Smitty besides the Jason that the Deliverer had cast out previously. We have experienced from two or three to as many as twenty evil spirits having the same name in the same person.

After asking the Lord Jesus Christ to bind with His blood all the evil powers with the name Jason and their entire networks, I asked, "Will it stand as truth before Abba, Father, that all the demons with the name Jason and all their networks have been bound in their entirety?" "Yes," was the reply.

"Who do you, Jason, answer to as the highest ranking evil spirit, the number one demon, in Smitty?" "Monitor." "S.T.G?" "Yes." "Then all Jason spirits are bound into helplessness and put into remission by the Lord Jesus Christ; and Monitor, you have to come into full manifestation only in the eyes, face, and mouth of Smitty temporarily for your Conqueror to cast you out. In Christ's name, come forward into the eyes and face of Smitty."

Instantly there was a definite change in the features of the face and a menacing, powerful presence was in charge of the body. Through commands in Christ's name, Monitor was forced to admit that Lucifer, a demon, was protecting him. Further questioning revealed that Satan, the devil, was protecting both Jason and Monitor. Earnest prayers broke the power of Satan; and after reading James 5:14ff. I anointed Smitty's body with oil while commanding in the name of our Lord Jesus Christ for

Jason, Monitor and Lucifer (how many there might be in Smitty) to be put into Gehenna completely. Great resistance was encountered, but after several minutes of praying and commanding, the demons left. We prayed for the Holy Spirit to fill and control Smitty through his entire being.

Yet even as we prayed, a voice said, "I can't." "Who said that?" I asked. "Steven," was the reply. "Are you an evil spirit?" "Yes." "S.T.G?" "Yes." "Where are Jason, Monitor, and Lucifer and their networks?" "They are in Gehenna, hell." "S.T.G?" "Yes."

Next another demon called Steven was uncovered, and then one named Rachel. When these had been bound in their entirety to the evil spirits Steven by Christ's sovereign authority, I asked, "Are there any other high ruling demons in Smitty?" The reply was, "No more." "Is No More the name for an evil spirit?" "Yes." "S.T.G?" "Yes."

All of these evil spirits were bound together, forced to confess that Jesus Christ was their Lord and Conqueror, to renounce Satan as their lord and god. Smitty's body was anointed with oil, and commands were given for all of these demons to be driven out by Christ the Victor and into hell. The body, even though restrained by strong arms, was contorted and tortured for several minutes as we kept on praying. Then Smitty was back with us again, worn out, but oh so happy, free, and smiling radiantly. Some of the most beautiful faces we have ever seen in our lives are those of Christians set free from demonic control, for their faces glow with a loveliness that is heavenly.

This session lasted about two hours, and now we left rejoicing, praying for Smitty's full protection.

Yet our victory seemed short-lived because two days later we received a call from Zane who said with some desperation in his voice, "What can we do, Pastor? Smitty is completely demonized and is so wild that it is taking five men to hold him down. He is really worse than before. These demons seem more powerful in their control, ferocious and savage. They are trying to bite us and are calling out to Satan to come and protect them so that they can keep Smitty. It is awful, and we are at our wits' end. Some of our workers are getting discouraged and quitting, because they don't think any deliverance is taking place. Oh, won't you come and help us? We can't take Smitty in the car as the neighbors would see the struggle and hear his screams."

"Zane, my dear brother," I said, "I am so sorry that you are having such a heartbreaking experience with a brother who has been heavily invaded by multiple demons. Of course, we will come at once. Keep on praying to Christ, and don't lose heart. The Lord Jesus Christ is still absolute sovereign and all powerful. All deliverances are in His hands and in His own time. We have had to go through as many as twenty-five deliverance sessions with some people. This is a part of the cosmic war between Satan and Yahweh, but Christ has broken the back of Satan! Hallelujah! No evil spirits have been able to hold on to a single Christian who wills to let the Lord set him free in the more than one hundred cases we have dealt with. We know that Smitty can be set free. Trust our Risen Lord and keep binding the evil spirits in His name."

Smitty was quiet and in rational control of himself when we arrived. He was able to make confession of sins though we found out later that he did not confess all sins that he should have confessed. As I prayed for the Lord Jesus Christ to bind all the evil spirits in Smitty and force them into manifestation under the control of Christ Jesus, there was an immediate demonization so that the men holding on to Smitty were almost shaken off. The kind face of Smitty was changed into a twisted face of rage, wild eyes flashing defiance, and a snarling mouth with teeth bared like an animal when attacked.

"In the name of the Son of God, Jesus of Nazareth, we command you to tell the whole truth and nothing but the truth. What is your name?"

"I am Lucifer." "S.T. G?" "Yes." "Are you the same Lucifer that we dealt with the other night?" "No." "S.T. G?" "Yes."

"Have you recently come into Smitty?" "Yes." "When?" "Today!" "S.T. G?" "It certainly will." "How did you get in; what was the ground of your invasion?" "I didn't have any ground. Andrew pulled me in, for he wanted me to help him." "S.T. G?" "Yes."

At this instant Smitty's whole being was dramatically transfigured into another personality, the most powerful, haughty, and commanding manifestation we had seen. He roared, "HE IS MINE! ALL MINE. YOU CANNOT HAVE HIM. I WANT HIM! MINE! MINE!" The fierce, sinister countenance, the burning eyes, the powerful voice with the contemptuous, mocking and evil smirk was terrifying to behold.

He was gloating as I shouted back, "You are bound by the blood of the Lord Jesus Christ, your Conqueror. Get out in the name of the King of kings and the Lord of lords!"

"No, I do not have to leave. He is MINE, MINE. He came to me."

"What is your name, evil spirit?"

"I am the prince, the prince." "S. T. G?" "Absolutely, and I am going to destroy you, all of you."

"Are you a prince of Satan?" "NO, I AM THE PRINCE OF DARKNESS!"

"Will that stand as truth before Yahweh Elohim?" "Of course!"

"Then are you Lucifer, the father of lies, the devil?"

"I AM, and you have no power over me."

"Will that stand as truth before Abba, Father?" "YES, and you cannot cast me out! I am going to stay. He is MINE, ALL MINE!"

There was no need for me to verify Lucifer's statement, because it was true that *I* had no power over the devil to cast him out. Yet I believed in my heart that it was *not* true that Smitty belonged to the devil forever. Nothing is impossible to our Almighty God, Yahweh.

For the conclusion of this literal and startling confrontation with Satan, the devil, turn to page 194 in the chapter on the results of our deliverance experiences as instruments of our Lord Jesus Christ.

2

An Answer to Devastating Sufferings

ALL EXPERIENCE PAIN

The serious observer and the involved Christian know much about our devastating sufferings and pain in our world. It does not require a great deal of time to accumulate convincing evidence of the desperate plight of millions of people today, and right at our hand, hundreds of lives that have been ripped and torn by cruel affliction. Indeed, the evidence of human agony and suffering is so patent that the whole area of human pain is used as an argument against Almighty God, His existence, love, and goodness.[1]

Surrounding us are multiplied thousands of people who because of sin are broken and wounded in various aspects of their life and personality. But, as startling and grievous as it may seem, it is a fact that many professed believers in Almighty God, earnest Christians, also find themselves deeply wounded and scarred by the effects of sin. Christians, though related to God, are not immune to the pressures of life, to the reality of psychological breakdowns that can bring about depression and disorder even as they are not immune to the effect of viruses and germs. Christians are in spiritual warfare and face the unrelenting hostility of the devil. His attacks are powerful and often effective against Christians, especially those who are weak or who foolishly open themselves to the assaults of Satan through their own sinful actions. Various aspects of these difficulties which Christians encounter will be discussed in the succeeding chapters in sufficient detail, we hope, to enable you to relate these things to your own spiritual betterment, to waging a victorious warfare against Satan, and to a gracious and powerful ministering of healing in its various dimensions to those around you especially in the congregations.

THE REASONS FOR PAIN

People suffer because they are guilty of sin and live among sinful people in a fallen world. The world is fallen because of the sin and rebellion against God by Adam and Eve (Gen 3); and their sin brought evil, affliction, pain, and death upon the human race. It is not because God is cruel that these things have happened but because we live in a moral world ruled over by God who is morally perfect. God justly gives to those who sin against His loving, disciplinary action seeking to warn them against further sin and to recall them to His grace and forgiveness. C. S. Lewis has observed, "No doubt Pain as God's megaphone is a terrible instrument; it may lead to final and unrepented rebellion. But it gives the only opportunity the bad man can have for amendment. It removes the veil; it plants the flag of truth within the fortress of a rebel soul."[2] There are purposes and values in suffering that remove it from being viewed as a negative and wholly objectionable aspect of human life.

It is a simplistic and ignorant view of reality that assumes to know that there is absolutely no value derived by human beings because of suffering, that asserts it is wholly unlike God to allow just punishment to take place to discipline man. Those who believe they know everything about the world and its functioning so that they can question God's goodness or will at work in human lives should carefully read the book of Job and learn its lessons. How little we know and understand what all of human life is about. The conviction of Christians is that apart from God's own revelation we cannot know or have any adequate understanding of the meaning and purpose of human history.

Because we are sinful and weak people living in a sinful and flawed society, many disasters and painful conditions are found and experienced regardless of who we are. Job was right that "man, who is born of woman, is short-lived and full of turmoil" (Job 14:1). It is a part of life and will be until men and women humbly accept the lordship of Jesus Christ, have their sins taken away through His blood, and live in harmony with His will. Only through the resurrection will the last enemy, death, be defeated. In heaven there is no sin, pain, suffering, sickness or death (Rev 21:2-7). So much of human suffering is brought upon us by ourselves that we have only ourselves to blame and hold responsible. For those who have difficulty in understanding the reason for pain and suffering among people today and want more information than we can give, we recommend the reading of C. S. Lewis' book, *The Problem of Pain.*[3]

THE FINAL ANSWER TO PAIN

The final answer to the problem of pain, when it can be understood and accepted by us, is the death of the perfect and sinless Son of God upon the cross of Calvary for the salvation and restoration of every suffering person. There is revealed the love of God in sending His only begotten Son to remove sin and its effects and the full participation of God in the pain of rejection, grief, and death which we endure. God knows all about our suffering and agonies for He has gone through them. George MacDonald declared, "The Son of God suffered unto the death, not that men might not suffer, but that their sufferings might be like His."[4]

The ultimate answers to our individual cases of suffering and affliction must wait upon the judgment day of Almighty God when all things are disclosed. Those who trust in Him as the All-Sufficient One with self-sacrifice and love for wretched wrongdoers expect confidently that at the judgment many of the questions that we had often voiced upon this earth will not even be necessary to ask. Those questions that we might ask in that day of full disclosure will vindicate God entirely and satisfy us beyond any question of doubt that God's actions were for His glory, the perfect and only consideration in God's universe. With all of our hearts we believe that the distressing and perplexing questions that have been asked on this earth will be answered "to the praise of the glory of His grace" (Eph 1:6). No doubt thanks will be given by all of us that God did not answer some of our prayers that we so urgently and insistently presented to Him on this earth.

THE AREAS OF PAIN

The needs of individuals have their personal aspects; and, of course, there are diversities of experience of brokenness, injury, and sickness. As the nature of man has been divided generally into the areas of the mental, physical, psychological/ emotional, and spiritual, it is convenient to approach the need of healing within the four areas. All sickness, hurt, and disorder can be put under one of these headings. The magnitude of the affliction naturally varies from person to person.

Mental

By mental sickness we mean the various afflictions and disorders of the mind. This particularly refers to thought processes and irrational responses of a man to his environment. The mind of an individual can be affected through a brain injury, disease, or drugs. Warped and distorted thoughts resulting in illogical and irrational actions are particularly an area which we believe the Lord Jesus Christ can heal and overcome within the person who opens himself up to the Maker of the mind.

Psychological

Alongside the mental sicknesses are found the psychological disturbances. These may be difficult to distinguish as to which areas—mental or psychological—they belong to as there is an overlap, we believe, which must be left unresolved because of its great complexity. The work of the counselor is not affected thereby. Looking at psychological illness and difficulty, we are thinking of the human psyche, the soulishness of man and its various workings. Particularly we deal with the psychological in the healing of the emotions of the individual, the deep underlying attitudes and the repressed traumas affecting relationships. No one doubts the emotional scars and psychological wounds that many have received from childhood or later experiences. These are subject to Christ's healing power, and there can be healing of memory or psychological healing. Psychological healing has to do with the psyche and the personality of man as distinguished from the thought processes, the "gut level" from the brain level.

Physical

The next area is physical injury or biological problems. This includes all of the illnesses, diseases, and afflictions of the body. As we have noted before, it is impossible to segregate these interacting parts of man's life from one another in actual function; but it has been found useful for discussion of the various aspects as one may be predominate in needing the attention and help for the individual. Is there a single one of us who has not experienced in our own body a weakness when physical disease and illness has struck, whether chicken pox or cancer? Such being the case, there is no need to prove that we human beings can become biologically ill, run fevers, ache in all parts of our being, and urgently need relief.

The Lord has graciously provided a great deal of relief for us through the natural strength of the body and its power to resist various diseases. Medicine has been discovered in God's world and has been applied to men and women to assist the body in its fight against the attack of destructive organisms. Doctors have functioned with the wisdom that God has given them to understand a great deal about disease and to heal the body by therapy and surgery. The Christian physician is one who happily acknowledges that he is working with God to bring wholeness and healing to the individual.

The Christian counselor recognizes the value of doctors and medicine and is glad to be able to use these to the fullest extent possible in the restoring of health to the individual who is ill. At the same time, the Christian counselor realizes that many illnesses involve the mental, psychological, and spiritual aspects of the individual. He recognizes that sin is often involved in the illness which afflicts the individual, and he believes that God is the one who does the ultimate healing whatever the means used to accomplish that end. As will be presented in the next chapter, the Christian worker is convinced by the teaching of James 5:14ff. that there is a power of God which can be released in the lives of sick individuals for the healing of those individuals. It is not an either/or but a both/and situation. The power of God along with doctors and medicinal arts should be employed for the restoration of the individual.

Unfortunately there are those who do not actually believe in the power of God to heal people of various physical sicknesses with and without medical means. We need to affirm that God is in charge of everything and that His power is needed above all else. Apart from God's will and power no medicine or doctors on earth can heal our diseases. When God's power is brought to bear upon human illnesses, the results are often astonishing to doctors and beyond their ability to have produced. Remarkable answers to prayer have been received in the past and the present. They are a strong encouragement to God's people to pray without ceasing for His will to be done in every individual's life, especially those having critical illnesses or afflictions.

Spiritual

Finally, there is the area of spiritual sickness which in its first condition must be dealt with in the area of salvation, the removing of all sins by the blood of the Lord Jesus Christ. The redemption of the person is accomplished by the finished work of the Lord Jesus Christ on Calvary's cross and the empty tomb. Because Christ has died and cancelled all our sins by the power of His blood, there is spiritual cleansing from guilt and deliverance from the just retribution of God against all rebels against His will.

This initial cleansing takes place in the conversion experience when a person is brought into a saving relationship with the Lord Jesus Christ. This is done by obedience to the gospel, the good news that Jesus Christ is Lord and Savior. Submission to Christ as Lord is a necessity if one is to become cleansed and freed from sin. According to the book of Acts (the book of conversions) we find that people had to believe in the Lord Jesus Christ as their Savior with all of their hearts, to repent of their sins, turning away from their past life to surrender themselves wholly to the Lord Jesus Christ, and to be baptized into the Lord Jesus Christ. When they did this they were set free from sin, filled with the Holy Spirit, and adopted into the family of God.

This initial spiritual healing cuts the person off from Satan, brings him into the family of God, and cleanses him of spiritual guilt and condemnation. There may be other spiritual problems, for there are spiritual powers of darkness which have Satanic power to attack, harass, or invade Christians in a very real way (Eph 6:10-12). This will take a great deal of explanation and development which we prefer to take up in chapter nine.

The point that we want to make here is that there is an area of spiritual warfare in which the children of God may be deeply wounded and perhaps even controlled to some extent. A child of God now suffering from spiritual attack, harassment, or defeat usually does so because of sins or the consequences of sins in his past life *before* he became a Christian. We ask you to reject the prejudice concerning the possibility that a child of God can have some area of his life under the control of the devil. Please consider the strong evidence that a child of God can do those things which permit Satan, the devil, to control *some* part of his mind, will, or body that we will share with you in chapter nine.

THE POWER SOURCE FOR WHOLENESS

You can see we are working with Christians, seeking to allow the power of the Lord Jesus Christ to be released in their lives for healing of mental, psychological, physical, or spiritual illnesses. The major exception to this is the spiritual healing of non-Christians to whom we present the good news of the Lord Jesus Christ and, trusting in the convicting power of the Holy Spirit, seek to lead them to the obedience of faith in the Lord Jesus Christ (Rom 16:16). This is the greatest work of healing that can be accomplished for the *unbeliever* through a process in which he becomes a believer and is adopted into the family of God by his baptism into the name of the Father, the Son, and the Holy Spirit (Matt 28:18-20).

It is a debated question as to the extent the Lord will answer the prayers of those who are not believers. There are those who claim remarkable healings through various aspects of their lives before they became obedient followers of the Lord Jesus Christ. Granting such cases as possible in the remarkable providence of God and His amazing grace, they are exceptions. Almost all of our work in healing within the power of the Lord Jesus Christ has been directed to those who are children of God and can call upon Abba, Father, for His healing power in their lives. This seems to us to be the way shepherds of the flock should work with their people.

Even in working psychologically with individuals for inner healing or in clearing up personality conflicts and difficulties, full dependence always has been placed on prayer for the power of God to work in the individual's life. The Word of God is always the chief reference and resource for instruction leading to healing. According to our experience, if the person is not in the Lord Jesus Christ and the Holy Spirit is not in him (Rom 8:11), then the psychological healing will only be temporary and will not accomplish the restoration to wholeness the Christian receives through God. All true healing of the whole person must involve complete surrender of the person to the Lord Jesus Christ in obedience of faith and a continuing life of faith in and submission to the Lord Jesus Christ.

Does God have anything to say to these desperate situations of anguish and profound affliction in the lives of His children? We definitely say, yes, and reject the position of many that God has very little to say about this, that He is really only interested in redeeming the spirits of people. This is much too narrow for us in our understanding of God, His nature and revelation. We are thankful that we believe that God is very gracious, is lovingly concerned, and has taken forthright action to relieve his children of much of the suffering, pain, and misery of the illnesses which afflict us according to His permissive will.

Through the death of the Lord Jesus Christ and His absolute victory over death through His resurrection, His power has been released within the church that is more than sufficient to deal with all kinds of illness and affliction which children of God experience. Paul prays "that the eyes of your heart may be enlightened, so that you may know what is the hope of His calling, what are the riches of the glory of His inheritance in the saints, and what is the surpassing greatness of His power toward us who believe. These are in accordance with the working of the strength of His might which He brought about in Christ, when He raised Him from the dead, and seated Him at His right hand in the heavenly places, far above all rule and authority and power and dominion, and every name that is named, not only in this age, but also in the one to come. And He put all things in subjection under His feet . . ." (Eph 1:18-22a).

The care of Christ for His bride, the Church, is far more than that of any earthly husband, for He has infinite resources and is perfect in love. From Paul's analogy we can draw strong support of Christ's enormous compassion and active sustaining of His body, for He is "the Savior of the body" (Eph 5:23). He not only has cleansed the Church that He might "sanctify her," but as the husband "nourishes and cherishes it" (the body, his wife), so "Christ also does the church, because we are members of His body" (Eph 5:29-30).

Christ's loving nourishment of the body, that is, all Christians, entails the forgiveness of all of our sins though we may be battling for a long time, even a lifetime, to overcome the practice of sin and to be freed of the consequences of sin. It entails provision for His providence working in our lives in response to the amazing power of prayer. There is far more power in prayer than we have ever imagined. "Now to Him who is able to do exceeding abundantly beyond all that we ask or think, according to the power that works within us, to Him be the glory in the church and in Christ Jesus to all generations forever and ever. Amen" (Eph 3:20-21).

God answers our prayers and does amazing things for us whether in the spiritual, mental, emotional, or physical areas of our lives because we are His beloved ones. In some of the most critical sicknesses He has provided the power through the prayer of faith and the anointing with oil (James 5:14ff.). Nothing here is automatic, mechanical or absolute but rather must involve the most sincere faith and humble submission to God's will.

Thus God in Christ and through the Holy Spirit has moved powerfully to help us overcome many of our sicknesses and afflictions, our critical and desperate conditions. Where it is His will, as in the case of Paul not to remove the affliction or disease, He always does so for a purpose and provides the essential strength and grace to bear the burden.

NOTES

1. John Hick states well the critical nature of the problem of evil for the Christian faith. "The fact of evil constitutes the most serious objection there is to the Christian belief in a God of love. It is also probably the hardest objection to write about . . . . it will not do to remain passively silent in the face of so grave a challenge to one's faith—a challenge that was bitingly summed up in Stendahl's epigram, 'The only excuse for God is that he does not exist'! The enigma of evil presents so massive and direct a threat to our faith that we are bound to seek within the resources of Christian thought for ways, if not of resolving it, at least of rendering it bearable by the Christian conscience" (*Evil and the God of Love*. Great Britian: Collins, The Fontana Library edition, 1968), p. ix.

E.J. Carnell writes, "Epicurus, Lactantius, and others have given what has come down to us as probably the most succinct statement of the problem of evil yet conceived. Either God wants to prevent evil, and He cannot do it; or He can do it and does not want to; or He neither wishes to nor can do it;

or He wishes to and can do it. If He has the desire without the power, He is impotent; if He can, but has not the desire, He has a malice which we cannot attribute to Him; if He has neither the power nor the desire, He is both impotent and evil, and consequently not God; if He has the desire and the power, whence then comes evil, or why does He not prevent it?" (*An Introduction to Christian Apologetics,* Grand Rapids: Wm. B. Eerdmans Publishing Co., 1948, p. 277.)

This gives you a sharp understanding of this most serious objection to the God of the Bible. It is something that needs careful study and preparation for meeting the argument as it is presented time after time to Christians. C. S. Lewis testifies that when he was an atheist he considered the evil and pain in the universe as the most complete answer that he could give as to why he did not believe in God. After stating his case, he concludes, "If you ask me to believe that this is the work of a benevolent and omnipotent spirit, I reply that all the evidence points in the opposite direction. Either there is no spirit behind the universe, or else a spirit indifferent to good and evil, or else an evil spirit" (*The Problem of Pain,* London: Geoffrey Bles, 1940, p. 3). Cf. end note 3 for recommended books on this problem.

2. C. S. Lewis, *The Problem of Pain* (London: Geoffrey Bles, 1940), p. 83.

3. Besides this excellent book by C. S. Lewis, there are others that give valuable assistance to the Christian in understanding the problem of evil and in helping sincere unbelievers overcome this major objection to the God of the Scripture. E. J. Carnell, *An Introduction to Christian Apologetics,* "The Problem of Evil," (Grand Rapids: Wm. B. Eerdmans Publishing Co., 1948), pp. 276-314. Norman L. Geisler, *Christian Apologetics* (Grand Rapids: Baker Book House, 1976), pp. 217-229. Norman L. Geisler, *Philosophy of Religion* (Grand Rapids: Zondervan Publishing Co., 1974), pp. 311-403. John Hick, *Evil and the God of Love* (Great Britain: Collins, The Fontana Library, 1968). George I. Mavrodes, *Belief in God* (New York: Random House, 1970), pp. 90-111. John W. Wenham, *The Goodness of God* (Downers Grove, Il: InterVarsity Press, 1974).

C. S. Lewis notes the self-defeating nature of the argument of the atheist against the good God of the Bible (as Geisler also does): "There was one question which I never dreamed of raising. I never noticed that the very strength and facility of the pessimists' case at once poses us a problem. If the universe is so bad, or even half so bad, how on earth did human beings ever come to attribute it to the activity of a wise and good Creator? Men are fools, perhaps; but hardly so foolish as that. The direct inference from black to white, from evil flower to virtuous root, from senseless work to a workman infinitely wise, staggers belief. The spectacle of the universe as revealed by experience can never have been the ground of religion: it must always have been something in spite of which religion, acquired from a different source, was held" (op. cit., p. 3).

4. George MacDonald, *Unspoken Sermons,* First Series. Quoted by C. S. Lewis, *The Problem of Pain,* p. vi.

3

Viable Answers for Your Health Needs

As one studies the Scriptures of the Old and New Covenants he is impressed by the fact that God ordinarily works through means and available resources of His creation rather than directly and miraculously. The high miracles of the Old Covenant and the unique miracles of Christ and the apostles accompany new revelations from God establishing new covenants. These are truly miracles because of their extraordinary power, direct action without means, instantaneous results, and magnitude. Biblical evidence leads us to believe that God uses miracles sparingly and that their primary purpose is to authenticate and credential revelation.

GOD'S USE OF MEANS

Prayers for God to give us "daily bread" still require us to use various means to receive the bread. Prayers alone are not enough. When God works miracles He often requires the use of means as in the saving of Noah through the building of the ark. We find that in the healing of Hezekiah's boil God honored a fig poultice although He had announced a miraculous extension of the man's life by fifteen years (2 Kings 20:1-7). In various cases God has expected His people to do their part in securing their healing even when miracuously given.

Jesus commanded people to go to the priest (Matt 8:4) or go wash in the pool of Siloam (John 9:7). In the feeding of the

5,000 and the 4,000 Jesus required the disciples to use the available food though it was totally inadequate. The first recorded miracle (turning water into wine) found Jesus requiring the filling of the present jars with water (John 2:7-8). In the miraculous catch of fish, the disciples had to put out into the deep and let down their nets (Luke 5:4-5). The fish did not miraculously jump into the boat.

Out of the thirty-five miracles recorded as performed by Jesus on individuals, ten required some action or use of means to be done while twenty-five did not require means or acts from the person. From this evidence there appears to be a clear presumption that the Lord generally uses available means to secure the restoration to wholeness of the person in whatever parts of his nature he is experiencing disease or distress.

God can achieve health with or without means. Some of the means involve human beings with their wisdom and skills as well as the use of organic materials and medicines. God may use the participation of the members of the congregation in prayer or even the procedure of the prayer of faith and anointing of oil by the elders per James 5:14ff. These actions are not said to be dependent upon a miraculous power resident in the congregation or the elders. They are only acts of faith and humbly used means as available for God's power to be manifested as He pleases.

PHYSICIANS AND SURGEONS

We believe it is appropriate for children of God to use the means that God has put at their disposal, and such use does not mean a lack of faith or an attempt to bypass our dependence on God. It is quite right that people of God with prayer and great trust in Him at the same time use what is available. It is our conviction that children of God should honor Him in everything, give Him first place, and that God can sovereignly use means if He so chooses. All encouragement is given to those with sickness of any kind to go to those who have ability and skill to assist them. This involves the use of physicians and surgeons. We reject as false the denial of the reality of bodily sickness and disease. Sickness is not all just in the mind or even in the spirit although these can play an important part in any sickness that people experience.

God has provided doctors in the sense that He has given them the skill and ability they have, and those with physical ailments and difficulties should go to the doctors for help. The doctors may prescribe medicine or chemical compounds found in creation, for these have been placed there by God for judicious use by men for His creatures. There can be misuse of these as seen by the widespread use of tranquilizers and narcotics by our society. As dependence upon the Lord has diminished the use of the drugs has increased so that American society especially is a drug functioning society. Such use is quite contrary to God's will.

PSYCHOLOGISTS AND PSYCHIATRISTS

Beyond the area of the help of doctors and medicine is the area of those skilled in understanding the working of the human mind and psyche. The psychologist and psychiatrist are those who deal with the inner conditions which may give rise to the hurt and damage to the personality. Psychology and other sciences have a contribution to make to many people and are able to give insight into why people think and act the way they do.

Naturally, we believe that the most helpful psychologist is the one with the Christian theistic orientation because he is working with God and His power.[1] Prayer and the Word of God are needed very much to enable the healing to be successful and permanent. Those without faith in God are able to offer helpful insights; but the greatest good results, we believe, will flow from those who trust in the Lord Jesus Christ to work in and through them for the healing of individuals.

It is necessary to caution those seeking the help of the psychologist or psychiatrist that the mere nominal allegiance to Christ or the profession of a Christian commitment may not be sufficient to insure that the treatment received will be of a Christian nature. A Christian may use a secular psychology with only a light coating of Christian imagery or terminology. This does not change the essential nature of the discipline as it may stand in its non-theistic form. Certainly, it is our conviction that the Christian psychologist or psychiatrist should be distinctly Christian in his use of the techniques and concepts of psychology. His therapy will not stand in the human strength but in the wisdom and strength of God. We agree with Jay Adams, "If the counseling is in essence one aspect of the work of sanctification (as I have argued elsewhere), then the Holy Spirit, whose principal work in the regenerated man is to sanctify him (cf. also Ezekiel 36:25-27), must be considered the most important Person in the counseling context. Indeed, He must be viewed as the Counselor. Ignoring the Holy Spirit or avoiding the use of the Scriptures in counseling is tantamount to an act of autonomous rebellion. Christians may not counsel apart from the Holy Spirit and His Word without grievously sinning against Him and the counselee. Any counseling context that disassociates itself from these elements is decidedly a non-Christian context, even though it may be called Christian or may be structured by a counselor who is himself a Christian but who has (wrongly) attempted to divorce his Christian faith from his counseling principles and techniques."[2]

PRAYER AND THE CHURCH

Turning to the most spiritual grounded means, one would immediately think of the great promises of God concerning prayer and its power in achieving remarkable results in the lives of those who trust God our Father. The Word of God is implicit that God hears and answers prayer. He does this in His own providence, of course, and according to His will and wisdom. Prayer changes things and conditions when used with trust in God's power. It really works for we have experienced it for ourselves and in others. Prayer is turning from self to God for His work and will to be performed. God honors those who trust Him and put their needs in His hands.

The fact that God answers prayer does not mean that He answers the way we want Him to or precisely at the time we requested. As God answers prayer we realize the answer may be "No" as well as "Yes." Delay may occur due to the lack of readiness of the person to receive the request. Often the delay is because other conditions or other people are not completely prepared, or the person is not ready for the positive answer to be given. Only God knows when the timing is appropriate. Prayer is dynamic, effective, and very powerful indeed. Earnest Christians can testify from an empirical basis that prayer works. All that the Bible states about the powerful implementation of God's will through earnest supplication and petition has been borne out repeatedly in our experience. It is definitely true that "more things are wrought by prayer than this world dreams of,"[3] and we are called to a ministry and a perseverance in prayer for God's will to be achieved.

The essence of prayer is always, "Your will be done!" God always honors that prayer offered by His children in faith, because prayer is seeking God's good and perfect will. It is not an assault upon God in seeking to bend Him to our way of thinking which would be ridiculous. It is a humble submission to God and an active desire that only His will be done. There is the element of mystery in the way our prayers affect the will of God and part of this comes about because it is very difficult for us time-space creatures to understand the total knowledge of the I AM THAT I AM (*Yahweh*). There is no past, present, or future with our Heavenly Father. Thus He knows already all the actions we are going to take and the prayer requests that we are going to make and has allowed for these in His infinite wisdom and providence.

Some real help on this difficult subject of the impact of our prayers upon God is given by C. S. Lewis. He says, "But then to God (though not to me) I and the prayer I made in 1945 were just as much present at the creation of the world as they are now and will be a million years hence. God's creative act is timeless and adaptation meets our consciousness as a sequence of prayer and answer."[4] He goes on to state that our prayers do have significance before God in what actually occurs: "The event has already happened and one of its causes is your present prayer. Thus something does really depend on my choice. My free act contributes to the cosmic shape. That contribution is made in eternity or 'before all worlds'; but my consciousness of contributing reaches me at a particular point in the time-series.''[5]

God does hear and answer all prayers because He knows all and is totally in charge. The Christian, says Lewis, ''is rather to believe that all events without exception are *answers* to prayer in the sense that whether they are grantings or refusals the prayers of all concerned and their needs have all been taken into account. All prayers are heard, though not all prayers are granted. We must not picture destiny as a film unrolling for the most part on its own, but in which our prayers are sometimes allowed to insert additional items. On the contrary, what the film displays to us as it unrolls already contains the results of our prayers and of all our other acts. There is no question *whether* an event has happened because of your prayer. When the event you prayed for occurs your prayer has always contributed to it. When the opposite event occurs your prayer has never been ignored; it has been considered and refused, for your ultimate good and the good of the whole universe.''[6]

Somehow unknown to us the immense power of prayer in the lives of the children of God is increased when the whole body of Christ prays together. A particular congregation of believers will find its effectiveness in prayer multiplied when with one heart and mind the people pray for the will of God to be done in meeting a particular need.

It is not altogether clear why God chooses to honor in a remarkable way the consecrated prayers of the body of Christ even beyond those of individuals, but continuous prayers of the body have been answered in tremendous ways (Matt 18:19-20). Perhaps God honors the prayers of a body of Christians because it underscores that the body of Christ is an extremely precious, unique, and powerful part of His plan of human redemption. Perhaps it is to de-emphasize the individualistic efforts which may develop into the sin of pride that He honors the body's prayers above the individual's prayer. Yet God does not discount the prayers of any single person. The examples are numerous in the Scriptures, and James cites Elijah as one of these cases which motivate us to pray. "The effective prayer of a righteous man can accomplish much. Elijah was a man with a nature like ours, and he prayed earnestly that it might not rain; and it did not rain on the earth for three years and six months. And he prayed again, and the sky poured rain, and the earth produced its fruit" (James 5:16b-18).

THE ELDERS

Christians need to recognize the authority and will of Christ in praying earnestly together for those things they believe are the will of God and in sincerely asking that God provide the answer according to His will. As we shall prove in chapter five, God has provided a means for those who are desperately sick to appeal for special help from the spiritual leaders, the elders, of the congregation: "Is anyone among you sick? Let him call for the elders of the church, and let them pray for him, anointing him with oil in the name of the Lord" (James 5:14). And it works! We have witnessed remarkable restorations to health. This does not exclude the power of prayer of the body or that of individuals. It is not supposed to replace those intercessions. All it does is to provide a special and distinct power from God for peculiar and difficult cases of sickness, especially originating in the spiritual area and in a person's relationship to God. The following chapters will give a full explanation of this means.

In all of this discussion of the means of healing that God has provided and the assumption that God is able to use such means to restore the sick to health we must not forget that the outcome is dependent upon God's good will for those we pray for and for all His creatures. There is no guarantee that the use of any or all of these means will cure the sick and restore him to health. Our experiences as human beings indicate that there can be a strong expectation that the use of God-given means will return us to health. We have a strong majority statistic in our favor, and we have every reason to believe that God is not against us but ever working for our good. All of us live in hope.

Yet day after day some folk become worse in their health, and funerals occur every day of the year. No one lives forever physically. Our bodies are dying while we live. Accordingly we see God's will for each of us to be the determinative factor in whether or not the means we use result in a restoration to health.

In summary we can say that God has graciously provided various means for the healing of people who become sick. All of these are appropriate and may be used—physicians and surgeons, psychologists and psychiatrists, medicine, Christian prayers, and prayers and anointing by the elders. God has used these through the ages to restore people to health and especially those who trust Him and seek His will.

NOTES

1. How gratifying it is to be able to refer many skeptical readers who think that Christian truth is almost the antithesis of psychology/psychiatry to the outstanding writing of a notable psychiatrist, Dr. M. Scott Peck. Dr. Peck, graduate of Harvard University and Case Western Reserve, was Assistant Chief of Psychiatry and Neurology Consultant to the Surgeon General of the Army. He is a practicing psychiatrist and even more, an unabashed, practicing Christian who declares his total commitment to Christianity is the most important fact in his life.

Be sure to read Dr. Peck's valuable contribution to our understanding of evil in human beings, *People Of The Lie: The Hope For Healing Human Evil* (New York: Simon and Schuster, 1983).

2. Jay Adams, *The Christian Counselor's Manual* (Grand Rapids: Baker Book House, 1973), pp. 6-7.

3. Alfred, Lord Tennyson, "Morte d' Arthur," *The Works of Alfred Lord Tennyson* (New York: The Macmillan Co., 1913).

"More things are wrought by prayer
   Than this world dreams of. Wherefore, let thy voice
   Rise like a fountain for me night and day.
   For what are men better than sheep or goats
   That nourish a blind life within the brain,
   If, knowing God, they lift not hands of prayer
   Both for themselves and those who call them friend?
   For so the whole round earth is every way
   Bound by gold chains about the feet of God."

4. C. S. Lewis, *Miracles* (New York: The Macmillan Co., 1947), p. 213.

5. Ibid., p. 214.

6. Ibid., p. 215-216. To anyone interested in learning more about prayer, we recommend C. S. Lewis' book, *Letters to Malcolm,* (London: Collins, 1963).

4

Foundations: Sand or Rock?

You have a right to know, so we will introduce you to some fundamental concepts which are our presuppositions concerning the subject of counseling and healing. We use the word *healing* in this book to indicate the restoration of people to wholeness as they were created by God to function, without any necessary implication that this is *miraculous* healing equivalent to that instantaneous healing done by Christ and the apostles. Counseling is an effort to help persons understand themselves and their problems, conflicts, emotions, and failures so they can cope with them and lead wholesome lives as God planned.[1] Making people well and whole is done, we believe, with full reliance upon the authority and power of our Lord Jesus Christ and the use of the best skills and techniques of psychology with genuine love for the person as a child of God or a potential child of God. Only when a person is submissive to the Lord Jesus Christ and striving faithfully to carry out God's will can he expect to lead a contented and healthy life.

OUR FOUNDATION IS SOLID ROCK

Without apology and with grand confidence that the Christian theistic world view is the only world view that has any rational validity as a truth system, we affirm that this is the context for all of our thinking. The ultimate reality of the universe is the God revealed in the Bible, *Yahweh Elohim*; and He is Triune—Father, Son, and Holy Spirit. He is the eternal, self-existent, self-consistent, perfect God, Creator and Sustainer of the universe. Because He is the God of truth, because He is the God of love and revealed to be a Father-God whom we are to address as "Abba" (that is, personal and loving father), it is altogether reasonable to believe that He has graciously revealed Himself and His will to His creatures who were brought into existence to share in His life and fellowship.

This reasonable probability of a Father God who loves His children and so communicates with them is established as a fact by the existence of a written revelation from Him. This book, the Bible, claims to be given by the authorship of God and communicated by the power and inspiration of the Holy Spirit of God to human writers. The highest witness to this revelation is the living Word of God Himself, the Lord Jesus Christ. All who accept Him as the Son of God and the ultimate revelation of God to man by the incarnation also accept His authoritative statements that the Holy Scripture is the revelation of *God* to man and not a merely human book. The Scripture is extremely clear and explicit in its declarations to be the inspired Word of the Almighty God given through men but by the inspiration of the Holy Spirit protected from error and falsehood. If you have questions in this area, you are referred to the standard books by conservative and scholarly writers in this field, particularly to Carl F. H. Henry in his outstanding works on *God, Revelation and Authority.* [2]

To those who have difficulty accepting the fact of the Lord Jesus Christ and His all authority as the Son of God and/or the fact of an authoritative and infallible revelation given to men, we earnestly ask that you consider the alternatives to the Christian position for rational and logical probability. It is our premise that the test for truth is systematic consistency, which is the consideration of all facts and evidence available to us tested by logic with a view to integrating all these things into a cohesive, functioning explanation. [3] That which is able to assimilate, integrate, and explain the greatest number of facts with the fewest presuppositions and *ad hoc* assumptions has to commend itself as the truth to the logical, intelligent, and earnest seeker after reality. He does not accept it blindly nor by coercion. He does not accept it as the last word above question and investigation; but he does accept it as the very best, most rational explanation for all the evidence which we have from experience and testimony of mankind. Thus it is our conviction that to repudiate the Christian world view and its tremendous, holistic explanation of most of the facts more reasonably than any other world view is illogical for the sincere seeker after truth. There is no better beginning point for exploring reality.[4]

WHO IS WORKING DYNAMICALLY?

As Christian theists, we write with an unshaken belief in the existence of the Triune God as the only true and living God of the universe. Therefore, we accept without difficulty or apology the view that God is dynamically involved with His creation and is actively working with people who are willing to trust Him to bring about His purposes. There is no question in our minds that the promises of God are true and realized, not only in our experience but that of millions of Christians over the past 1900 years. We have seen in a remarkable way the working of God to bring about enormous changes for good in restoring people to wholeness and usefulness according to His plan.

The deistic and rationalistic position that God is incapable of doing mighty works and of engaging powerfully in ministry with His people for salvation, sanctification, and healing is rejected by us as a complete misrepresentation of scriptural teaching and of the actual work of our God in human lives. Our God is not an absentee God who has retired to a distant heaven to sit and watch how the creation that He has made will work itself out. The Holy Spirit of God is not a retired member of the Godhead who does not forcefully work in God's people today. The Holy Spirit is alive and well, powerful and very active among all those who desire His creative force in their lives.

Yes, there are excesses in the thinking of many good people about the Holy Spirit and His work today; but such excesses and distortions of truth do not invalidate truth. Every teaching and every experience related about the Holy Spirit and His activity today must always be brought to the severe test of Holy Scripture and must be seriously investigated hermeneutically[5] to determine if, indeed, the statements are in harmony with the inerrant revelation of God. We are convinced that various excesses and exaggerated claims about the work of the Holy Spirit will be exposed by Scripture and that the good judgment of believers in the God of the Bible will be able by the help of the Holy Spirit to sort out those things that are distortions and counterfeits. We have a great confidence in you as an intelligent person created in the likeness of God and endowed from your creation with the capabilities of intelligent and logical discernment to find yourself, in both your teaching and experience, in harmony with biblical teaching.

We are convinced that Almighty God, existing as a loving and caring Father with infinite power under His sovereign control, is able to effect whatever is according to His will and His glory with or without the assistance of mere human beings. There is no limitation upon God's power except that which He chooses to place upon it Himself. Thus, we are convinced that men today must trust Abba, Father, to do according to His word, to keep His promises. This is decisively confirmed in our experience.

OUR DIFFERENCES AND THE NEED FOR UNITY

There are those differences in interpretation among sincere followers of Christ which will not be overcome in any easy manner or in a short time. Though these exist (and we would prefer that they did not exist among Christians believing in God and the Bible), yet we are not at all afraid to admit that they are there. After all, people are only human, fallible creatures. All of us are finite creatures, and all of us are in process of learning more about God and His will in His Word for us. We must be patient with one another, learn from each other, and be as open and honest as we possibly can in subjecting ourselves to the lordship of Christ and the authority of His Word.

The more we are able to do this, laying aside our prejudices and our inherited traditions, the more we will find ourselves drawing together in our understanding of God and His will.

It is not necessary for all of us to understand everything exactly the same way; and, indeed, it would be asking the impossible for us to do so in this present fallen world. We certainly must have unity in accepting Christ as the Lord, the Son of God and our Savior. We must be in submission to Him and His authority. We must allow the Holy Spirit to convict and lead us in the paths of righteousness, humility, and love of the truth. If we are one in Christ Jesus and have the Holy Spirit of God living in us, and if we accept the authority and finality of Holy Scripture as the revelation and standard of truth, then we are bound together in Christian love to accept one another and move forward together while seeking further understanding in difficult areas of revelation. Our unity is in our obedience to the Lord Christ Jesus as the son of God not in doctrinal agreement or in uniform interpretation. The closer we all draw to the Lord Jesus Christ, the closer we will draw to one another as brothers and sisters in the family of God.

Truly the greatest need of healing among Christians today is the removal of the divisions and schisms that are visible to the public among the professed people of God. Without a doubt, it is the perfect will of our Abba, Father, and Jesus Christ, the Head of the Church, to have unity among all the disciples of Christ in the world. We should not stop until this has become reality, and we experience the love and acceptance of one another even as taught by the apostle Paul by the Holy Spirit (Rom 15:7).

WHO IS FOR US?

Another presupposition that you should recognize and we hope find valid and understandable is that God is for us and not against us, that He is for our health and well-being as a gracious, loving Heavenly Father naturally would be. It is our conviction that God will do all that is *according to His will* for the restoration, cleansing, and healing of His people. Forced to deal with the seriously hurt and oppressed people, we have been confident that God in the overwhelming number of cases desires and will give wholeness and restoration to His own children.

We want to make it very clear that we do not *demand* anything of God or try to instruct Him as to how or when He is to heal people. Healing is not inevitable or automatic, nor is it universal. We feel that it is a serious error to dictate to God what He should do in any particular case of need. It is a presumptuous sin and is fundamentally rebellion against the sovereignty of Almighty God. It is a ridiculous and preposterous action insulting to the ultimate wisdom and goodness of God that we short-sighted, selfish, and sinful human beings presume to know more than God as to what should be done in any particular case.

The only right approach is to go to God in praise and deep humility and ask for His will to be done in each particular case to His glory and according to His will. It is putting it entirely in His hands with ultimate trust that our Heavenly Father does all things well; "all things work together for good to those who love God and are called according to His purpose" (Rom 8:28). [6] Everything that we have experienced, especially in the past five enlightening and astonishing years, has confirmed this. The power belongs to God, the timing is His, and the means to be employed are within His gracious providence. Thereby all glory, honor, and praise go to our Heavenly Father and never to the mere human instruments which He is willing to use.

We wish to affirm again that we are not making any claim or affirmation as to the miraculous healing of Almighty God parallel to that which He did in the New Testament period. This has not been our experience and is not our understanding from an examination of the Scriptures. We hold that miracles recorded in the New Testament were basically signs and wonders done for the confirmation of the person of Christ as the Son of God and done by the apostles to confirm their message as from God (Heb 2:1-4). We do not deny that God has absolute authority to do whatever He pleases to do according to His will now. It is not up to us to say that God could not or does not sometime work a miracle which would be equivalent to those astonishing wonders set forth in the New Testament. So far this has not been our experience nor do we have evidence to support such results. We are quite aware of the presence of "signs and false wonders" which are the result of Satan's working and which may deceive the elect (2 Thess 2:9-12).

IS ANYONE CONCERNED ABOUT YOUR WHOLENESS?

Finally, it is our belief and presupposition that the Lord God Almighty is concerned about the *whole* individual, the entire person which He has created. This means that, while recognizing the practical value of designating parts of a person as emotional, mental, physical or spiritual, in the end all of a person's problems must find their answer within God and His will for the individual. To us God does not work with isolated parts of our being. Certainly we reject the idea that God is *only* interested in redeeming the spirit of an individual and making the person spiritually whole apart from other considerations. Equally we reject as false the idea that God is only concerned about the psychological or physiological healing and does not have anything to do with man's spirit. We take a holistic view of man's nature that it is in every aspect or part to be brought under the authority of the Lord Jesus Christ. Bringing every aspect of man's nature under the control of God will bring about a health that will permeate more and more the entire person and make the weak or sick individual everything that God Almighty in His love expects that person to be.

In later chapters you will find us reasoning in depth that the teaching concerning healing in James 5:14ff. is not restricted to the days of the apostles and miracle workers or to the healing only of physical sickness. Since our God loves the whole person and Christ died to redeem the entire nature of man, then it is reasonable to suppose that any deficiency or defect caused by a person's sin in his human body or personality may be overcome by the power of Almighty God. It depends upon God's will. Healing is available in God's providence for sickness whether it be mental, emotional, physical, or spiritual and is generally given. This is the position which we believe honors God, is scripturally true, and is being empirically verified by ourselves and others. Yet carefully note that our prayers may receive an answer of "no," and our faith must accept it gladly.

It is our sincere hope that these presuppositions will lead you to a sincere and diligent examination of the evidence which we will present in the following pages in hope that they will bring encouragement and help to you in your ministry for Christ. If you find yourself reacting to any of these presuppositions, we implore you to proceed to a careful examination of what we have said for the sheer challenge to your thinking from a source that is not of your tradition or mind-set, believing as we do that God can use all things to His glory and even overrule our mistakes and inadequate judgments to His praise. Perhaps it will be only one chapter that will stimulate you to some further consideration of the will and the working of God today. Maybe it will only be a paragraph, but to God be the glory for whatever He chooses to use these simple words of ours to accomplish.

NOTES

1. Dr. Gary Collins has an excellent treatment of counseling, "The Church and Counseling," in his first-class work, *Christian Counseling* (Waco, Tx: Word Books, 1980), pp. 13-21. He effectively refutes the contention of some that counseling is not an appropriate work for a pastor and points out the vital role of the congregation as a healing power in the lives of people.

2. Carl F. H. Henry, *God, Revelation, and Authority* (Waco, Tx: Word Books, 1976), 4 vols. with a fifth and sixth to be published. Other valuable books are: Clark H. Pinnock, *Biblical Revelation—The Foundation of Christian Theology* (Chicago: Moody Press, 1971); Rene Pache, *The Inspiration and Authority of Scripture* (Chicago: Moody Press, 1969); Edward J. Young, *Thy Word Is Truth* (Grand Rapids: Wm. B. Eerdmans Publishing Co., 1957); Norman Geisler, *Christian Apologetics* (Grand Rapids: Baker Book House, 1976).

3. The classic treatment of the question of the nature and test of truth is by Brand Blanshard, *The Nature of Thought* (New York: Macmillan Co., 1939), 2 vols. More recently Norman Geisler has offered some cogent remarks on the matter of the nature and test of truth in *Christian Apologetics* (Grand Rapids: Baker Book House, 1976), pp. 117-147. He is favorably impressed by systematic consistency as a test of truth *within* a world view but believes

that it is an inadequate test of the truth of the world views themselves. He states that "more than one system might be equally systematically consistent and that the facts within a system are given meaning by that system" (p. 145). He believes that systematic consistency can show the falsity of a world view (or its inadquacy in comparison with the Christian world view), but that it cannot show the *truth* of a world view. Geisler proposes a test for the truth of a world view in the principle of *undeniability* and *unaffirmability* as the test for the falsity of a world view. His excellent book is an exposition of these principles.

4. Edward J. Carnell, *An Introduction to Christian Apologetics* (Grand Rapids: Wm. B. Eerdmans Publishing Co., 1948); Colin Chapman, *Christianity on Trial* (Wheaton, Il: Tyndale House Publishers, Inc., 1972); Norman Geisler, *Christian Apologetics* (Grand Rapids: Baker Book House, 1976); Norman L. Geisler, *A Philosophy of Religion* (Grand Rapids: Zondervan Publishing House, 1974); John Hick, *Arguments for the Existence of God* (New York: Seabury Press, 1971); John Warwick Montgomery, ed., *Christianity for the Tough Minded* (Minneapolis: Bethany Fellowship, Inc., 1973); Clark H. Pinnock, *Set Forth Your Case* (Nutley, NJ: Craig Press, 1967); Rousas J. Rushdoony, *The One and the Many* (Nutley, NJ: The Craig Press, 1971); Dorothy L. Sayers, *The Mind of the Maker,* second edition (London: Methuen and Co. Ltd., 1941); Francis A. Schaeffer, *He Is There and He Is Not Silent* (Wheaton, Il: Tyndale House Publishers, 1972); Francis A. Schaeffer, *The God Who Is There* (Chicago: InterVarsity Press, 1968).

5. Hermeneutics is the science of interpretation of language, verbal or written. To secure a proper understanding of the correct method of interpretation, we recommend that you read Grayson H. Ensign's book, *You Can Understand the Bible* (Joplin, Mo: College Press, 1978).

6. All Scripture quotations are from the New American Standard Bible, © The Lockman Foundation 1960, 1962, 1963, 1968, 1971, 1972, 1973, 1975, 1977, and are used by permission. Exceptions are specified.

5

A Spiritual Plan
for Healing the Sick

The most serious omission in most modern day counseling is the power of God Almighty, the God revealed in the Scriptures. God is the most essential part of any work that is done; and He is essential in the restoration to health of those human beings, His creatures, who have been wounded and injured by sin and its effects. There is no real power to effect lasting healing in any part of our human personality or body except God. True, there is occult healing, and there are pseudo-miracles that are wrought by demonic powers; but these leave the person with a far more serious spiritual illness than anything they had before. We hold that the foundation of all successful healing must be in the dependence upon the working of God which is wrought through the use of the Word of God and prayer through our mediator Jesus Christ. This position is grounded in the teaching of the Word of God and has been confirmed in our experience.

The key passage which teaches the church to carry on a ministry for restoration to health of those who are in Christ is set forth by James in his letter, chapter 5:14-16. The passage has fallen into wide disuse and is either ignored or sometimes rejected as not being in effect today. It is a very sad thing that those who are given the privilege and responsibility of taking care of the sick have not practiced that responsibility to the glory of God.

It is even sadder to realize so many Christians live lives of distress, disease, and despair when these could be largely taken care of according to the will of God by the appeal to and the practice of the teaching of James 5:14ff. That passage sets forth in simple language authoritative teaching of the Holy Spirit without difficulty of interpretation. James simply states, "Is anyone among you sick? Let him call for the elders of the church, and let them pray over him, anointing him with oil in the name of the Lord; and the prayer offered in faith will restore the one who is sick and the Lord will raise him up, and if he has committed sins they will be forgiven him. Therefore, confess your sins to one another, and pray for one another, so that you may be healed. The effective prayer of a righteous man can accomplish much." In the following pages we want to offer a clear exposition of this teaching to enable you to see the truth as taught by Almighty God, to encourage elders to practice this, and to encourage the sick to call the elders to them in times of serious sickness. The benefit will be mutual, and God will get the glory. Then, hopefully, the unbelieving world may become aware of the fact that the Most High God is still at work in His universe.

To remove the question of some that this passage is not correctly translated by Christians we submit the translation of the Jewish scholar, Hugh J. Schonfield: "Is any of you ailing? Let him summon the elders of the community, and let them pray for him after anointing him with oil in the name of the Lord. And the request in faith shall save the sick, and the Lord will raise him up. If he has committed sins they will be forgiven him. Confess your sins to one another therefore, and pray for one another, that you may be cured. The heart-felt petition of an upright man has great force."[1]

AN EXAMINATION OF THE PROCEDURE: JAMES 5:14FF.

There are no real problems in regard to this text written by James through the inspiration of the Holy Spirit. No questions can be raised of any merit against the wording of the text as now accepted in the latest Nestle Greek New Testament. The various translators of the Greek text into English have been in almost identical agreement in their choice of words. It stands as an authentic teaching of Scripture.

Though the text enjoys integrity that is not in question, yet Burton S. Easton is willing to attempt to get rid of this teaching in James by a gratuitous assumption of a "Jewish original" behind the present Greek text. Then with this mythical and non-existent text "before him" he declares, ". . . the suggestion may be hazarded that the Jewish original of vs. 14 read, 'Is any among you sick? Pray over him.'" He argues, "The continuation of this teaching by vs. 15 makes not only good sense but certainly smoother sense than the present text; it is really plausible to argue that here the purely Christian directions about the elders and the anointing have been inserted into a passage that originally appealed to the universal Jewish (and Christian!) belief in the universal efficacy of prayer."[2]

There is nothing to support Easton in his assumption of a supposed Jewish original text. It is unknown to the ancients, and the only reason for the rewriting of the established text without any textual evidence is found in Easton's imagination. It is a clear illustration of how men will fabricate something to their own liking even when the text is well supported. If men do not accept the high view of Scripture which the Lord Jesus Christ taught, then the words are only those of men and can be manipulated to become what wisdom demands.

Easton's attempt to eliminate the action of the elders in anointing with oil is without merit. He affirms, "And then a second and distinct method of relief is directed: *anointing him with oil in the name of the Lord* . . . 15. The emphasis shifts from anointing to prayer as the medium of healing."[3] This is untrue for the anointing is in the context of prayer and faith. On the one side the anointing is grounded in prayer—"let them pray over him"—and on the other side it is "the prayer offered in faith" that will heal the sick one. Prayer is definitely there but so is the oil of anointing as a minor yet not meaningless part of the procedure. There is no way to remove from the text what the Holy Spirit has written about an anointing with oil of the sick by the elders of the congregation. All must confront honestly the text and find the meaning intended by the Holy Spirit.

THE INTERPRETATION OF KEY TERMS

Certainly key terms need to be analyzed to clarify their meaning in this context. First, the word *asthenei* (sick) is from *astheneo* and is used thirty-six times in the New Covenant writings.[4] It is translated as sick in reference to physical conditions or as weak when speaking of moral, spiritual conditions. In the James 5 context it indicates sickness of a physical nature, but this would not exclude spiritual or mental sickness.

The term *aleipsantes* (anoint) comes from *aleipho* and is used nine times in the Greek New Testament. Beside the James 5 usage, one other reference to the specific use of oil in connection with the healing of the sick is Mark 6:13: "And they were casting out many demons and were anointing with oil many sick people and healing them." In James *aleipsantes* is a first person aorist, active participle which indicates that the anointing is an action that is completed and not continuously carried on. This does not prevent a sick person from being prayed for and anointed with oil more than once on different occasions of need. The exact action in applying the olive oil to the person of the sick is not indicated nor the amount of oil to be used. This allows flexibility in the action as deemed appropriate by the elders. In some cases the oil could be applied to the head or in other cases to specific parts of the body that are affected.

The oil used in the anointing is a translation of the noun *elaio,* a neuter noun from *elaia,* olive. This would be olive oil without a doubt.[5] The oil used by the elders was olive oil and should be today as it is available and called for as most appropriate to the solemn and scriptural act in which it is used.[6]

The prayer of faith (*euke pisteos*) is unusual for this is the only time *euke* is translated prayer in the New Covenant Scriptures (it is translated vow in Acts 18:18; 21:23). *Pistis* is used 244 times in the New Covenant writings and refers to faith that is trust and confidence. Thus the comment of Macknight that this phrase, prayer of faith, points to spiritual gifts or the gift of working miracles is not supported by the evidence.[7] Also, it is our view that it is not supported by the context of James. There is no implied connotation that this "prayer of faith" is some exceptional or unique type of prayer or faith. It is a prayer offered in utter trust to the God who answers prayer according to His grace and goodness.

James writes that the prayer of faith will *sosei* (save or heal) the sick. The word *sosei* comes from *sozo,* whose root is *sos* (safe). In 111 usages in the Greek Scriptures it is overwhelmingly translated saved. In eleven cases it is translated be whole, in three cases, be healed, and in one place, will preserve. James 5:15 is translated, shall save in the King James Version. This is generally the translation with the exception of heal (*Living Bible Paraphrase* and *Today's English Version*), well (*New International Version*), and restore (*New American Standard Bible*). Perhaps translators have felt that there was more to the use of the term by James than just making a sick person physically healthy. Thus the term in the James context seems to allow the thought of bodily healing plus spiritual healing through forgiveness of sins. This is strengthened by the Hebrew concept that a person is a whole person not separable into compartments of physical, spiritual, or mental.

In verse 16 the word *iathete* (from *iaomai*) is translated healed as it is in twenty-six out of the twenty-eight occurrences in the New Covenant Scriptures (King James Version). In one instance it refers to the healing of those "oppressed by the devil" (Acts 10:38), and in five places it is used metaphorically for spiritual healing (Matt 13:15; Luke 4:18; John 12:40; Heb 12:13; and I Pet 2:24). Its basic significance is healing, usually physical but sometimes spiritual.

Summarizing the interpretation of the text in its key terms reveals that the sick person is in no condition to go to the elders but must call them to him. It is the critically sick who are to receive the action of the elders. He may be sick physically, but in other cases his sickness (weakness) may be spiritual; or the physical sickness may be rooted in spiritual problems, hence the necessity of the confession of sins and forgiveness.

Strong emphasis is placed upon prayer bringing the power of God to effect the restoration and healing of the sick person. It is *praying with faith* in the all-sufficiency and goodness of God that is powerful and effective; so the result will be the saving of the sick person by the Lord, not man. The sick one includes the entire person with all of his needs, for the healing is connected with forgiveness of sins which has to do with man as a spiritual being.

THE MEANING OF THE PHRASES AND CLAUSES

What is the meaning of the action which is set forth in the words of James 5:14ff.? It has been shown that the terms are not in themselves difficult to understand, yet certain significant questions remain which need to be answered by applying the correct method of hermeneutics to these verses. This method is the grammatical-cultural-critical-inductive-spiritual method which is fully described in the book, *You Can Understand the Bible* by Grayson H. Ensign.[8]

Dr. B. B. Warfield, great Princeton scholar, was as much opposed as we are to the fanaticism of so-called "faith healing," basically a belief in a miraculous healing of individuals and a rejection of any use of means such as doctors or medicine. Warfield gives a summary of the James passage and the admission which he is willing to make about its meaning: "We allow, of course, that the presumption is, 'that the passage refers to an established and perpetual usage in the church'; we should not find it difficult to believe that 'the oil is applied as a symbol of the communication of the Spirit, by whose power healing is effected'; we agree that 'the promise of recovery is explicit and unconditional'; to the prayer of faith. But we see no indication in the passage that 'a peculiar miraculous faith' is intended; no promise of a healing in a specifically miraculous manner; and no command to exclude medicinal means or proof of their exclusion. If we read the passage with simple minds, free from preconceptions, I think we shall find in it nothing but a very earnest exhortation to sick people to turn to the Lord in their extremity, and a very precious promise to those who thus call upon Him, that the Lord will surely hearken to their cry . . . . Is there anything here that is not repeated before our eyes every day, whenever any Christian is sick—except that we have allowed the formal churchly act of intercession to fall into desuetude . . . . Apart from this failure, we have nothing in the passage that transcends universal Christian experience. Where is there any command in it to exclude the ordinary medicinal means? Where is there any promise of a specifically miraculous answer?"[9]

We find ourselves in complete agreement with Warfield at this point in setting forth the essential meaning of the teaching of James, though we will disagree subsequently with him in regard to the use of the anointing of oil.

Why Call the Elders?

The elders are called or summoned to come to the sick person which seems to eliminate the public performance of this ministry. The elders are clearly the overseers (pastors, elders) of the local congregation where the sick person is a member. This strongly speaks against any traveling "healer" who comes to town and puts up a tent or rents a hall for a "healing meeting." Also it rules out those who are not pastors according to the teaching of the Scriptures (1 Tim 3:1-7; Titus 1:5-9). These elders and overseers are the ones to be called and not others who are ministers, deacons, or evangelists according to a strict hermeneutic. The sick person is too critically ill to come outside to get help so minor illnesses are not really covered by the procedure in James.

Why does James by the Holy Spirit restrict this ministry to the *presbuteroi* (elders) of the local *ekklesia*? The simple fact seems to be because they are the leaders of the body of Christ and fit representatives of the body in its ministry to the sick through the power of the Lord Jesus Christ. Since it is the prayer of faith that the Lord will honor in healing the sick person and the prayers of a righteous man can accomplish much, it would be expected that the elders have both faith and righteousness in a high degree. If they do not, they are not scripturally qualified elders and should not expect answers to their prayers on behalf of the sick person. Correctly Scott comments, "Doubtless within the body of 'presbyters' were found (though not exclusively) all the miraculous gifts of the Spirit, and especially that of healing. But the words point not to certain gifted individuals, as such, but to a solemn visit of the Body, as the representatives—in ecclesiastical language, the 'Persons'—of the Church of which they are the ministers.''[10]

The elders are not called because they have the gift of healing, for there is no reference to this gift. If that was the intent, then anyone could be called who had the gift, and it would have been written, simply, "Is anyone among you sick? Let him call for the elders or anyone else in the congregation who has the miraculous power of healing to pray over him." But this whole matter of a special gift and of miraculous healing is left out and cannot be imported into the text even though we know that there were persons in first century congregations with the gift of miraculous healing.

The contrast between this procedure in James and the charismatic healing is drawn by Leahy: ''. . . the following points are important with regard to the substantial identity of what James is here recommending with the sacrament of Anointing of the Sick in the Church: the distinction from mere charismatic healing (1 Cor 12:9, 28, 30), as evinced by the cultic role of the *presbyteroi*; the anointing with olive oil; the invoking of the name of the Lord and the prayer of faith; the ensuing recovery and forgiveness of sins.''[11] It is an assumption without any evidence in the text that the elders are called because they have miraculous power to heal.

Again the elders are not called because they are skilled in medicine and can treat the sick person. Nothing in the text implies this, and Plummer says, "Of that there is not only no hint, but the context excludes the idea. If that were in the writer's mind, why does he not say at once, 'Let him call for the physicians'? If the healing art is to be thought of at all in connection with the passage, the case is one in which medicine has already done all that it can do, or in which it can do nothing at all.''[12] As there were physicians in those days available to the public,[13] it is not reasonable to suppose that James is teaching that the elders are to be called because they are physicians or better physicians. The thing James is affirming is that the sickness is to be dealt with by prayer and God's intervention.

Why Anoint With Oil?

What is the purpose of the "anointing him with oil in the name of the Lord"? Among the answers that have been given to this question are: 1. a cosmetic use preparing the sick one to return to his daily life in public, 2. simply an aid to faith, 3. medicinal, 4. symbolic of the power of the Holy Spirit in the life of the person, or 5. a means of God's grace and power being released in the life of the believer. It is possible that all five of these answers may have some value and validity. No doubt each reader may be drawn to one above another because of his own convictions about the teaching of the passage and his view of the anointing.

The suggestion of the cosmetic use of the oil would be along the line of an aid to faith, an encouragement to believe that the sick person is going out of the house and into society again. But the cosmetic purpose appears to be too insignificant a use of the oil in this serious context in which healing of the critically sick with prayer and forgiveness of sins are prominent. More likely the oil would convey the symbolic meaning that the power of the Holy Spirit is involved in the healing of the sick because oil is sometimes used in Scripture as a symbol of the Holy Spirit.[14] Christians would quickly sense the appropriateness of anointing with oil indicating the presence and power of the Holy Spirit with dynamic spiritual and psychological effects. Helmbold notes the anointing in connection with the gift of God's Spirit in both Old and New Covenants and comments, "Perhaps James 5:14 should be included here, with oil as the symbol of the presence of the Holy Spirit, the Lord and Giver of Life."[15] Leahy agrees, "Thus the anointing is not a mere medicinal remedy, but as in Mk 6:13, it symbolizes the healing presence of the Lord, i.e., of Jesus Christ."[16] With this a number of scholars would agree.[17]

The possibility that the oil is used as a medicinal remedy finds both advocates and opponents. To A. T. Robertson the medicinal value in the use of oil is very clear: "The use of olive oil was one of the best remedial agencies known to the ancients . . . . It is clear both in Mark 6:13 and here that medicinal value is attached to the use of the oil and emphasis is placed on the worth of prayer . . . . It is by no means certain that *aleipho* here and in Mark 6:13 means "anoint" in a ceremonial fashion rather than "rub" as it commonly does in medical treatises."[18]

Warfield also favors the idea: "The circumstantial clause, thrown in almost incidentally [we do not believe that this is incidental] 'anointing with oil in the name of the Lord,' is susceptible of two interpretations. The reference may be to the use of oil as a symbol of the power of the Spirit to be exercised in the healing; or it may be to the use of oil as a medicinal agent. In neither view is the employment of a medicinal agent excluded; but in the latter view the employment is distinctly alluded to. The circumstance of oil as well nigh the universal remedy in the medical practices of the day favors the latter view as does the employment of, as Archbishop Trench puts it, 'the mundane and profane' instead of the 'sacred and religious word' for the act of anointing. [But Trench is not correct in his assertion.] The lightness of the illusion to the anointing points in the same direction. It scarcely seems that so solemn an act and so distinct an act as ceremonial anointing would be alluded to so cursorily. If, on the other hand, the allusion is to the use of oil as a medicinal agent, everything falls into its place. The meaning then is in effect, 'giving him his medicine in the name of the Lord.' The emphasis falls not on the anointing, but on its being done 'in the name of the Lord,' and the whole becomes an exhortation to Christians, when they are sick, to seek unto the Lord as well as to their physician—nay, to seek unto the Lord rather than to their physician—with the promise that the Lord will attend to their cry."[19]

Much of what Warfield and Robertson say is quite true in the sense that there is no prohibition of Scripture to the use of doctors and medicine. We also agree that there is no major emphasis upon the anointing of oil which would lead to a view of some kind of magical application or miraculous power in the oil itself. The anointing of oil is a minor part of the whole procedure but is nevertheless an integral part of it. W. E. Vine specifically refutes the distinction made by Trench between the word *aleipho* as a mundane and profane use while the word *chrio* is the sacred and religious word. Vine declares that the evidence will not support this, and the word *chrisis* in a papyrus document describes "a lotion for a sick horse."[20]

This is upheld by Schlier who notes that the Old Testament Septuagint used *chrio* with religious and theological significance in anointing. "This is confirmed at once in the NT where *aleiphein* is used only of external, physical anointing and *chriein* in the figurative sense of anointing by God. Yet the external action has its own inner meaning."[21] He goes on to elaborate, "In the NT anointing with oil is used on the sick for the purpose of both medicine and exorcism. In Mk 6:13 the apostles heal in connection with their preaching of repentance and their expulsion of demons, and in this regard they are messengers and bearers of the inbreaking kingdom of God. In Jm 5:14 the same kind of anointing is carried out by Church officials, and in the situation of the Church it brings healing of the body and soul, i.e., the remission of sins, as in Mk 6:13 health is mediated to make fit for the kingdom of God. The whole action is envisaged in Jm 5:14ff. Anointing takes place in invocation of the name of God and is enclosed by prayer, which as the *euche tes pisteos* brings healing and forgiveness. Here the oil has the character of the matter of a sacrament."[22]

Our conclusion is that the oil is not principally or primarily used as a medicinal substance. The elders are not called to administer medicine, as Stoesz underscores, "There is no suggestion of medicinal use of the oil, since this might have been administered by anyone beside the elders. The use of oil symbolized sanctified commitment of the sick body to the operation of the Holy Spirit's ministry of quickening the mortal bodies of believers that they might be enabled and led to fulfill the ministry He has purposed for them as fellow heirs with Christ (Rom 8:11-17)."[23]

We agree with Plummer that the mere medicinal use of the oil is not the meaning, "but it is obvious that St. James does not recommend the oil merely as medicine, for he does not say that the oil shall cure the sick person, nor yet that the oil with prayer shall do so; but that 'the prayer of faith shall save him that is sick,' without mentioning the oil at all . . . ."[24]

The anointing of oil does not refer, then, to a natural remedy for the sick; but when used with the prayer of faith and the name of the Lord, it is a factor in the healing. The anointing of oil does not rule out or forbid the use of any medical means then or now; but the use of the oil in James does not carry the meaning, let them administer medicine to the sick. "Some suggest 'medicated oils,' but common sense shows us that something is described here utterly different from the ordinary blessing of God or medical applicances," says Robert Scott.[25]

Plummer favors the idea that the anointing with oil would be an aid to faith and "a channel of Divine power" because the oil ". . . was believed to have healing properties. It is easier to believe when visible means are used than when nothing is visible, and it is still easier to believe when the visible means appear to be likely to contribute to the desired effect."[26]

A sacramental factor already referred to by Schlier is noted by Easton: ". . . something more than a merely medicinal effect is assumed; that the oil, when applied by the duly authorized elders of the church, in conjunction with their prayer, is believed to have a quasi-sacramental (or even wholly sacramental?) healing effect is unmistakable and never should have been denied."[27]

Considerable evidence supports the idea of the anointing of oil as a means of grace. Many evangelicals reject the idea of a means or channel of divine power because of the extremes of Roman Catholic teaching and practice of sacraments which are definitely in error.[28] Yet there may be as much damage done by denying the idea of a *proper* sacred means as there is in overdoing it through priestcraft and connotations of miraculous infusion (*ex opere operato*) apart from personal faith in the Triune God. The word sacrament does not occur in our English translation of the New Covenant Scriptures but does come through the Latin Vulgate into ecclesiastical use. Protestants generally have held that both baptism and the Lord's Supper are channels of divine action or power without either magical or miraculous connotation and in that sense sacramental.

We believe that the whole procedure described by James when done in accordance with the Scripture by the elders of the congregation can be a means of grace used by God. This grace can only be received by faith in the Lord Jesus Christ. The anointing is symbolic (Macknight says, "a sensible token") but with real significance because it is prescribed by God, done in the name of the Lord, with positive faith in Christ, the Healer, and with the results of forgiveness of sins (always) and physical healing (expected). Thus the term "means of grace" is descriptive of more than a mere symbol. Horne notes the difference between the Roman Catholic view (realism) and the Protestant view (symbolism) yet correctly comments, "It should be clearly understood however, that symbolical does not mean without real efficacy. Symbol is not opposed to reality."[29]

Those of us who have been practicing the exact form of James 5:14ff., which includes the anointing with oil, have seen God's power in action for the believing person who has met the conditions verified over and over. The anointing with oil is a minor feature, but it is commanded to be done. While the oil is not magical or having some special miraculous power of God, it is a means of bringing God's grace (favor) to the person when it is combined with the prayer of faith. The whole action has been used of God to provide remarkable, providential answer to prayer.

Surely there is value in doing exactly what the Holy Spirit teaches regardless of any ignorance, fear, or prejudice on our part. When done it underscores one's faith and submission to God and His Word. When done it allows God to do with it as He pleases and intends whether Christians understand anything about it at all. We are very much in agreement with the statement by Greeven, ". . . believing prayer will save the sick (v. 15). This excludes any magical operation of the oil with which the sick is to be anointed by the elders."[30] Believing prayer is the greatest means in the healing of the sick; but the conditions of faith, confession of sins, and the anointing of oil are not to be ignored or denied their proper place when elders pray for the seriously ill Christian. There is no magical power in the oil. Some may ask, "How can the rubbing of olive oil on the body of a Christian have any value or power in healing that person of sickness?'' Yet these same people have no difficulty answering the question, *''*How can the baptism of a person into *mere water* have any power in canceling all of a person's sins, imparting to him the gift of the Holy Spirit, and clothing him with Christ?'' (Acts 2:38; Galatians 3:27).

The Power: Miraculous or Providential?

A key issue remains to be discussed. Is this healing of the sick in James a miracle and thus guaranteed to take place always without fail? At first glance it appears there is an absolute assurance that there will be a healing and therefore a miracle because of the direct action by God. Reference to a miracle in this passage is found by Calvin, Tasker, Manton, Macknight, Huther, and others. But there is no statement that there is a miracle involved, and it is not necessary to assume that the act is done by those capable of doing miracles.

As both sickness and the eldership could be expected to continue until the Lord Jesus Christ comes again, and it was not the intention of the Lord to continue miraculous gifts through all time,[31] it appears that the teaching of James 5 is not something restricted to the elders of the first century. Since sickness is so prevalent and Christ still has the power to grant healing and restoration of the sick to take place, it is apparent why Christian elders need such teaching as James 5 to learn how Christ's healing in grave illness can be provided through the centuries.

It is granted that at the time James wrote this message there were and could be widespread miraculous healings due to the many who had the miraculous gifts through the laying on of the hands of the apostles. But there is no convincing reason why this means of grace disclosed by the Holy Spirit should not continue to be used even after the miraculous power was no longer available. God's arm is not shortened even when He does not choose to give direct, miraculous actions. It is our faith that has shriveled. Prayer is still heard and answered by God and in far greater measure than people lacking strong faith and concrete experiences imagine. Paul makes no appeal to miraculous intervention of God in our prayers when he says, "Now to Him who is able to do exceeding abundantly beyond all that we ask or think, according to the power that works within us, to Him be the glory in the church and in Christ Jesus to all generations forever and ever. Amen" (Eph 3:20-21). Christians must give up their rationalistic *inferences* that the Holy Spirit, having completed His work in the first century, has retired to be seated at the right hand of God along with Jesus Christ and does nothing now but watch Christians struggling alone on the plains of sin.

Our experience is that God will work powerfully through ordinary elders without *supernatural gifts* in answer to our sincere prayer of faith coupled with the anointing of oil. Experientially we can say it actually takes place and brings glory to God.

But are not the words in verse 15 absolutes and guarantee the restoration of the sick? Several writers have noted that the very strong assurance of healing expressed by James does not mean to imply inevitable success in healing all and so require a miracle. Huther is right when he says James' words are ". . . founded on his confidence in the Lord, who hears believing intercession, so that it is not in vain. It is certainly surprising that James gives this assurance without any restriction . . . on the other hand, it is self-evident that true *pistis* [faith] includes the humble *plen ouk hos ego thelo all hos su* [yet not as I will but as thou] (Matt xxvi.39); and, on the other hand, it is to be observed that although James here evidently speaks of bodily sickness and its cure, yet he uses such expressions as point beyond the sphere of the corporeal to the spiritual, so that even when the result corresponds not to the expectation in reference to the bodily sickness, yet the prayer of faith does not remain unanswered in the higher sense."[32]

Plummer amplifies this thought, "That St. James makes the promise of recovery without any restriction may at first sight appear to be surprising; but in this he is only following the example of the Lord, who makes similar promises, and leaves it to the thought and experience of Christians to find out the limitations to them. St. James is only applying to a particular

case what Christ promised in general terms, 'All things, whatsoever ye pray and ask for, believe that ye have received them,
and ye shall have them' (Mark xi.24. Comp. Matt xvii.20) . . . .
The apostles themselves had no indiscriminate power of healing.
St. Paul did not heal Epaphroditus, much as he yearned for his
recovery (Phil ii.27). He left Trophimus at Miletus sick (2 Tim
iv.20). He did not cure his own thorn in the flesh (2 Cor xii.7-9).
How, then, can we suppose that St. James credited the elders
of every congregation with an unrestricted power of healing?
He leaves it to the common sense and Christian submission of
his readers to understand that the elders have no power to cancel
the sentence of death pronounced on the whole human race.
To pray that any one should be exempt from this sentence would
be not faith but presumption."[33]

There is no valid reason or compelling evidence that the terms
"will save the one who is sick" and "the Lord will raise him
up" are to be construed as absolutes. Strong, confident faith
in God's power and a definite belief that God wants His children to have health as a general principle led James to write
the statements which anticipate affirmative answers to the
prayers of the elders. That is the right way to approach a matter
of prayer, the trustful commitment of everything to the Lord's
gracious will. Strong encouragements to pray expectantly are
spelled out in the Word of God, but the mature disciple knows
that prayer is "not what I will, but what Thou wilt" (Mark
14:36).[34]

God's perfect and specific will for individuals is not known,
yet all pray in confidence that their petitions and requests may
be granted to the glory of God. Such prayer is what James is
talking about, and the results are left to God's perfect knowledge of what is best for His kingdom as well as for the individual.
We conclude that the idea of a miracle healing—instantaneous,
direct, and guaranteed—is not taught by the strong words that
James uses. (Of course we acknowledge that God can act
sovereignly any way and any time He pleases.) His teaching
has relevance and application today when miraculous gifts are
not available, and we depend on prayer and its remarkable
power. We rejoice in the sufficiency of God's working and the
results which have brought praise to Him.

NOTES

1. Hugh J. Schonfield, *The Authentic New Testament* (London: Dennis Dobson Ltd., 1955), p. 435.

2. Burton Scott Easton, "The Epistle of James," *The Interpreter's Bible,* ed. George Arthur Buttrick (New York: Abingdon Press, 1957), XII, p. 71.

3. Ibid., pp. 70, 71.

4. Much of this information has been derived from *The Word Study Concordance* by George V. Wigram and Ralph D. Winter (Pasadena, Ca: William Carey Library, 1978).

5. Gerhard Kittel, ed., *Theological Dictionary of the New Testament,* trans. Geoffrey W. Bromiley (Grand Rapids: Wm. B. Eerdmans Publishing Co., 1964), II, 470.

6. It is always best to adhere as strictly as possible to the elements prescribed by Scriptures in the performance of those acts commanded by God. This is true of using water in baptism and the unleavened loaf and fruit of the vine in the Lord's Supper. Obedience to the Word of God in these matters may seem small, but the simple conformity to what the Holy Spirit has written may be very significant in the eyes of God. Human pride is a great evil; and religious persons led by pride can too easily assume, "What difference does it make?" To Jehovah God it may reveal the difference between humble submission and sensual presumption.

7. James Macknight, *Apostolical Epistles* (Grand Rapids: Baker Book House, 1949), p. 602.

8. Grayson H. Ensign, *You Can Understand the Bible* (Joplin, Mo: College Press, 1978).

9. B. B. Warfield, *Counterfeit Miracles* (London: Banner of Truth Trust, 1972), pp. 169-170.

10. Robert Scott, "James," *The Holy Bible with an Explanatory and Critical Commentary,* ed. F. C. Cook (New York: Charles Scribner's Sons, 1904), New Testament IV, p. 147. (These are scripturally qualified elders, mature, experienced men obedient to Christ in everyday living.)

11. Thomas W. Leahy, "James," *The Jerome Biblical Commentary,* eds. Raymond E. Brown, Joseph A. Fitzmeyer, and Roland E. Murphy (Englewood Cliffs, NJ: Prentice-Hall Inc., 1968), p. 377.

12. Alfred Plummer, "The General Epistles of St. James and St. Jude," *An Exposition of the Bible* (Hartford, Ct: The S. S. Scranton Co., 1908), VI, p. 634.

13. ". . . there were many physicians in Israel . . . every city had its own physician . . . ." R. H. Pousma, "Physician," *The Zondervan Pictorial Encyclopedia of the Bible,* ed. Merrill C. Tenney (Grand Rapids: Zondervan Publishing House, 1975), IV, p. 788.

14. 1 Sam 10:1, 6, 10; 16:13; Isa 61:1; 2 Cor 1:21-22.

15. A. K. Helmbold, "Anoint, Anointed," *The Zondervan Pictorial Encyclopedia of the Bible,* ed. Merrill C. Tenney (Grand Rapids: Zondervan Publishing House, 1975), I, p. 171.

16. Leahy, op. cit., p. 376.

17. Cf. S. J. Stoesz, "Gifts of Healing," *The Zondervan Pictorial Encyclopedia of the Bible,* ed. Merrill C. Tenney (Grand Rapids: Zondervan Publishing House, 1975), III, pp. 53-54, and A. J. Gordon, *The Ministry of Healing* (Harrisburg, Pa: Christian Publications, Inc., n.d.), p. 31.

18. A. T. Robertson, *Word Pictures in the New Testament* (New York: Harper and Brothers Publishers, 1933), VI, p. 64.

19. Warfield, op. cit., pp. 171-172.

20. W. E. Vine, *An Expository Dictionary of New Testament Words* (Westwood, NJ: Fleming H. Revell Co., 1920), p. 59.

21. Kittel, op. cit., I, p. 229.

22. Ibid., I, pp. 231-232.

23. Stoesz, op. cit., pp. 53-54.

24. Plummer, op. cit., p. 635.

25. Scott, op. cit., p. 147.

26. Plummer, op. cit., p. 635.

27. Easton, op. cit., pp. 70-71.

28. The sacrament of Extreme Unction grew out of the procedure in James 5 although the Roman Catholic sacrament of Extreme Unction is far removed from that teaching. It appears that over the years this prayer of faith and anointing more and more was directed toward those desperately sick and expected to die. So Extreme Unction practically became a formality connected with death rather than any anticipation of life and restoration to health. This sacrament has now been changed by the Second Vatican Council to an Anointing of the Sick and is not to be called Extreme Unction any longer. This is a most welcome change back to the scriptural purpose of the anointing of the sick with prayer for their recovery according to the will of God. Francis MacNutt describes in his book, *Healing,* (pp. 275-285) the use of anointing and the development of the sacrament of Extreme Unction through the past centuries.

29. C. M. Horne, "Sacraments," *The Zondervan Pictorial Encyclopedia of the Bible,* ed. Merrill C. Tenney (Grand Rapids: Zondervan Publishing House, 1975), V, p. 193.

30. Heinrich Greeven, *Theological Dictionary of the New Testament,* ed. Gerhard Kittel (Grand Rapids: Wm. B. Eerdmans Publishing Co., 1964), II, p. 776.

31. It is the understanding of the authors in line with much of Protestant thought that the miraculous gifts, though not the special providences of God through prayer, ceased sometime after the death of the apostles. When those died upon whom the apostles had laid their hands to impart miraculous powers, there was no continuation of this miraculous power. This position is particularly based on the purpose of first class miracles which is to credential and attest to the fact that the messengers and the message came from God (Heb 2:1-4; John 5:36; 10:37-38; Rom 1:4; Exod 7:3-5; etc.). The meaning of miracle is diluted and nullified if miracles are happening all the time around

people for they are extraordinary works of God's power. Actually miracles are clustered around the giving of the Mosaic Covenant, the prophets in mortal combat with false religions, and at the coming of the Lord Jesus Christ and the New Covenant.

32. J. E. Huther, *Critical and Exegetical Handbook to the General Epistles of James, Peter, John, and Jude* from *Meyer's Commentary on the New Testament,* trans. Paton J. Gloag, D. B. Croom, and Clarke H. Irwin (New York: Funk and Wagnalls, Publishers, 1887), pp. 158-159.

33. Plummer, op. cit., p. 625.

34. Ps 91:15; Isa 65:24; Matt 18:19; Luke 11:9; John 15:7; 1 John 3:22.

6

The Practice of Spiritual Healing

Let us assume that you have accepted the exposition of James 5 offered in the previous chapter. We are sure that your next question would be, How shall we go about doing it? In a very practical way we must say, "Do it very slowly and cautiously with a great deal of teaching within the congregation to head off serious misunderstandings and conflict." People who have been reared in certain traditions and who have accepted a false interpretation of James 5 which has rendered it largely meaningless have to be educated as to its true meaning. After the education has been given we do not doubt that people will begin to approach the elders for the practice of James 5 in their lives.

It is our position that those who are sick should become aware of their condition; and when they are ready to let God have control of their healing, they will come to the elders for help. We believe that the use of James 5 in congregations of Christians can be restored, but there must be the thorough explanation and a clearing away of the questions and doubts of the past. In this chapter we shall point out some contemporary views in regard to carrying out the procedure of James 5 along with a description of the way we have used it in our counseling thus enabling you to prepare to use it. The details of using the procedure of James 5 in the specific areas of physical, psychological, and spiritual sickness will be taken up in later chapters.

CONTEMPORARY APPROACHES TO SPIRITUAL HEALING

In this last quarter of the twentieth century several interesting developments have taken place in regard to understanding and practicing the teaching in James 5:14ff. As the Lord Jesus Christ has graciously brought a renewal to His Church through a practice of the truth of His Word and the recognition of the power of the Holy Spirit in the body, there has been a new interest in a restoration of the procedure for healing set forth in James. The necessity of such a ministry of healing has reached staggering proportions in the midst of the existential despair which is so devastating to many. With utmost confidence in the love and power of the triune God to remove despair and to heal the broken-hearted, many believers have turned to the Lord Jesus Christ for the answer. His teaching in the synagogue at Nazareth has strengthened our belief in the all-sufficiency of God to deal with the tragic sins and sicknesses of this day: " 'The Spirit of the Lord is upon Me because He anointed Me to preach the gospel to the poor. He has sent Me to proclaim release to the captives, and recovery of sight to the blind, to set free those who are downtrodden, and to proclaim the favorable year of the Lord' .... And He began to say to them, 'Today this Scripture has been fulfilled in your hearing' " (Luke 4:18, 19, 21). While recognizing the peculiar miraculous power released through the presence of Jesus Christ in the flesh to bring about these remarkable results, we also believe that through the power of prayer God will graciously continue this work of Christ which He began by providential means.

Startling and pleasing is the change in the Roman Catholic Church from the old view of James 5 as a Sacrament of Extreme Unction to a Sacrament of Healing the Sick. On January 1, 1974, a new official view went into effect. "The 'Anointing of the Sick' is now for the professed purpose of healing the whole man and is no longer primarily a preparation of the soul for death. In line with this reorientation of the sacrament's purpose it is to be administered not just to those in danger of death, but to anyone suffering from a serious illness," according to Francis MacNutt.[1] Thus there has been a dramatic shift back to the exegetical meaning of James 5:14ff.

This view is reinforced by the new prayer to be offered for the blessing of the oil to be used in the anointing by Roman

Catholics: "Lord God, all-comforting Father, you brought healing to the sick through your son Jesus Christ. Hear us as we pray to you in faith and send the Holy Spirit, the Comforter, from heaven upon this oil, which nature has provided to serve the needs of men.

"May your blessing come upon all who are anointed with this oil, that *they may be freed from pain, illness, and disease and made well again in body, mind, and soul.*

"Father, may this oil, which you have blessed for our use, produce its healing effect, in the name of the Lord Jesus Christ."[2]

We are happy to see the lessening of the emphasis upon absolution of sins and preparation for death which gave rise to the Sacrament of Extreme Unction and the emphasis upon the healing of the whole person. This remarkable change in returning to this teaching of Scripture on the part of the Roman Catholic Church is a challenge to Protestant Churches.

Among Protestants some changes also have taken place. Four schools of thought continue to have their advocates. First, there is the traditional and wide-spread view that the James teaching calls only for prayer for the sick. Occasionally this has been expanded in an effort to involve the whole congregation in such praying for the sick. The actual procedure in James 5:14ff. has been ignored and has not been used. It is not applicable to our day according to this school of thought.

Second, there has been a minority of Protestants who, having lost confidence in the Bible as the Word of God and consequently the reality and power of the risen Christ, do not believe in any value in prayer for any purpose and especially for healing. These people are essentially rationalists and are unable to pray a "prayer of faith." For these liberal Protestants the teaching of James 5:14 has no relevance.

A third approach involves a growing number of Protestants (and Roman Catholics) who believe in the restoration of all the miraculous gifts to the church "in the last days" and who believe that James 5:14ff. indicates miraculous healing for those that are sick. These people are usually designated as charismatics or neo-pentecostals. They agree with the earlier Pentecostal movement in the miraculous healing of the sick by the laying

on of hands and prayers of faith. The actual requirements of
James 5 are sometimes not carried out precisely among these
people. Perhaps scripturally qualified elders are not involved.
Often the sick are brought to a healing service rather than the
elders going to the sick. In some cases there is no confession
of sins before the prayers and no anointing of oil by the elders.

We believe failure to follow exactly and carefully the biblical
teaching may have a negative result even though healing may
be experienced. There may be physical healing but with spiritual
problems afterward because healing carelessly done may be
achieved by occult or Satanic power, in our opinion. Satan is
the deceiver and master counterfeiter.

A fourth school of thought encompasses Bible-believing Christians who are strongly convicted by the promises of God in
the Scripture and proceed to take Him at His Word in a *non-
miraculous* way. These Christians believe in the awesome power
of God and the working of the Holy Spirit but do not believe
the Scriptures teach the existence of miraculous gifts in the
Church of the Lord today. They certainly believe that God can
and does operate powerfully and effectively through prayer,
through the Word, and through the Holy Spirit to accomplish
His will. Many of these follow the procedure laid down by
James precisely, while others would be less exact in the procedure. There has not been a wide dissemination or publication
of the results of this ministry contrasted with that of the neo-
pentecostals, but there are increasing testimonies that underscore and verify James' statement, "The effective prayer of a
righteous man can accomplish much" (James 5:16c).

The new Roman Catholic emphasis upon James 5 accords
well with the understanding of the Protestant Christians in
this fourth grouping and somewhat overlaps the neo-pentecostals
in the third group with some individual differences. We, of
course, want to believe that we are in "the golden mean" between the extreme of the rationalistic rejection of James 5 and
the misinterpretation by the neo-pentecostals of a *miraculous*
action. It is our experience that Almighty God does work remarkably through prayers of faith by "non-charismatics" and
gives results equal or superior to "charismatic" results in their

holistic and permanent value. As Christians sincerely search the Scriptures for God's answers to the overwhelming problems of people today, we believe an increasing number of Bible-believers will take up the practice of James 5 apart from pentecostal emphases.

REQUIREMENTS FOR SPIRITUAL HEALING

As Christians get back their confidence in the teaching of the Word of God and believe the Lord Jesus Christ has the power to heal the sick, two major factors must be brought up to the scriptural standard. The first is a confident faith and whole-soul trust in the triune God to do what He promised in His revelation, for "without faith it is impossible to please Him, for he who comes to God must believe that He is, and that He is a rewarder of those who seek Him" (Heb 11:6). All who offer "the prayer of faith" must pray in full commitment to God's will being done whatever that may be. It is true faith that submits the decision to God and does not tell God what He must do, for that is presumption, not faith. Yet we are to pray with strong confidence that in most cases it is God's will and to His glory that His children be whole and in good health.

Elders who pray for the healing of the sick need to pray with all the faith that Paul expressed in his prayer, "I pray that the eyes of your heart will be enlightened, so that you may know what is the hope of His calling, what are the riches of the glory of His inheritance in the saints, and what is the surpassing greatness of His power toward us who believe. These are in accordance with the working out of the strength of His might which He brought about in Christ when He raised Him from the dead and seated Him at His right hand in the heavenly places, far above all rulers and authority and power and dominion, and every name that is named, not only in this age, but also in the one to come. And He put all things in subjection under His feet . . ." (Eph 1:18-22a).

Second, when godly men have supreme confidence in God and His workings through prayer we need scripturally qualified elders to carry out the procedure of prayer and anointing of the sick. It appears plain to us that God emphasizes the vital service of the overseer to shepherd the flock of God. The office of pastor, elder, or overseer is a tremendously important one in the eyes of the head of the *ekklesia*. He has given both high responsibility and significant power to qualified elders (Acts 20:17-35; Eph 4:11-16; 1 Tim 5:17; Heb 13:17; 1 Pet 5:1-5). The high responsibility of the office calls for the highest quality of righteous character and gifts of leadership, teaching, and administration. The Holy Spirit has spelled out in plain terms the essential qualifications for the office of overseer (1 Tim 3:2-7; Titus 1:5-9). When men are genuinely qualified to be elders by the work of the Holy Spirit in their lives, we believe that Abba, Father, will honor their prayers of faith in a remarkable way.[3]

As the people of God and the elders grow in their commitment to God and laying claim to the promises of God in the immeasurable greatness of the power of prayer, brothers and sisters will begin to experience the full force of God in their lives for healing. Christians will begin to call upon the elders to counsel with them and in many cases carry out the procedure defined by James. As the good news travels among the members of the congregation that there is a "wonder-working power in the blood of the Lamb" for the healing of the afflictions and infirmities of the saints, more and more members of the church will come for restoration to health and wholeness in the Lord as He pleases to provide.

SUGGESTIONS FOR CARRYING OUT THE PROCEDURE FOR SPIRITUAL HEALING

Let us assume that you are in a counseling situation with a Christian and have developed a mutually strong basis of acceptance, love, and dependence upon God for His help in overcoming the difficulties or sickness of the person. It may become obvious to you that there is a real need for a healing or removal of spiritual barriers in the life of the counselee. At such a time you may suggest a consideration of the teaching of James 5 and share your experiences with the person relative to God's use of the procedure of prayer and anointing. On the other hand the person may become increasingly aware that he has need of an action of God involving forgiveness of sins and cleansing the effect of sin in his life. It has been our custom to allow the Lord to set the timing as much as He will in regard to the person's readiness for the very serious action of the individual in calling the elders.

It is always best, though not absolutely required in cases of emergency and exceptional nature, for at least two elders to be involved with the prayer and anointing. Enough time must be set aside so that it is done in an unhurried, serious, and gracious manner. Usually the time required has been from an hour to an hour and a half. Sometimes a longer period is needed. We strongly suggest that you have the counselee (except the physically sick) come at a time when he/she is most relaxed and not pressured by time or having some appointment which might interfere with the completion of this God-blessed procedure. The elders will go to the home or the hospital to deal with those physically sick.

The elders meeting with the counselee should begin with earnest prayers and reading of the Scripture to allow the Lord Jesus Christ to be in full control of everything that is done and to allow only the power of the Holy Spirit to operate through the entire action. Great passages of Scripture which exalt God the Father, the Son, and the Holy Spirit, which tell of His sovereignty, lovingkindness, and His covenant mercies should be used.[4] If any good is going to be accomplished, all have to agree that it is going to be done by the power of the triune God and for His glory according to His will alone.

The elders need to explain carefully what is going to take place, what is expected of the counselee and why. One should explain the fact that God is in charge, and there must be total submission to the will of God regardless of what that may be. We make it clear to the individual that we have no special gifts or powers and that no miraculous answer is promised by us though we do not rule out any action of God that pleases Him. We explain that the healing may be done slowly over a period of time or rapidly, with or without means such as medicine and doctors, simply as the Lord dictates. With affirmations of confidence in the Lord, His lovingkindness toward us, and in full assurance of faith, all three persons commit themselves to letting the Lord answer the prayers of faith exactly the way He wants.

Next, one of the elders should explain to the person the need for a confession of all the major sins of the past, especially those that have been addictive and compulsive by which Satan may have been enabled to get some kind of control over his life. Sins that have never been confessed or for which guilt is still experienced on a regular basis need to be articulated with true repentance and genuine contrition. Usually we suggest to the person that in preparation for the conference he should ask God to enable him to recall all the significant sins which need to be brought before Him for pardon. Often these are sins committed since the person has become a Christian but not always. Note well that this is a work of God in sanctification and not salvation / justification.

Various Scriptures having to do with the confession of sins and the forgiveness of the Lord along with the involvement of sin as a cause or a related factor to sickness of any kind are read and explained.[5] Especially it is necessary for the individual to forgive those who have sinned against him so that he may be forgiven according to the requirement of Christ (Matt 6:12, 14-15). This is one of the biggest areas of need in the lives of many Christians who, in spite of their baptism into Christ and their progress as Christians, still harbor bitterness, resentment, and hatred toward various persons. We have found it necessary to remind these people we counsel that they may easily overlook their bitterness or resentment against God and their hatred of themselves. We have encountered many who have never faced these profound sins which can so terribly hurt the individual and allow sickness. All the interpersonal relationships need to be searched for bitterness, resentment, and hatred to be sure that the individual is not holding out anything on God; because sins that are not repented of and forgiven usually block the healing.

Also, it is important to get the counselee to ask the heavenly Father to be forgiven for all the sins against other people that he has committed and, as far as possible, to agree to apologize and ask the forgiveness of such persons as he is able to reach if he has not done so already. Following all these acts of confession, prayers for forgiveness through the blood of the Lord Jesus Christ by His saving grace are offered by the counselee and the counselors. Since the confession of sins needs to be thorough and involves, in many cases, the most intimate details of a person's life which can be embarrassing to tell to another human being, we have allowed the person to select one of the elders to hear the confession as we find it easier for some to make full disclosure of sin before one person rather than two. Sometimes those who are preparing to confess their sins are overcome by a great feeling of their guilt and the tragic violation of the holiness of God and the sacredness of human life. It is often a time of careful teaching of genuine repentance and the full, total forgiveness of Almighty God through the blood of the Lord Jesus Christ. Some people preparing to confess their sins have indicated that we will end up hating them or rejecting them because of the enormity of their sins or the vileness of their transgressions. The elders must know the grace of the Lord Jesus Christ in their own lives and be truly able to express their love and acceptance of the individual in spite of anything that is confessed; because they, too, have been forgiven by the atoning work of the Lord Jesus Christ. Genuine reassurances must be given to the counselees that all that is said will be kept in perfect confidence.

It is interesting in this connection to note the fact that even though we have heard all kinds of sins confessed, almost every sin that we read about in the Bible, we have never had the experience of remembering those sins in connection with a person so it jeopardizes our relationship or causes some kind of barrier to our acceptance of one another. Indeed, the very opposite has occurred in that when the James 5 procedure has been completed the counselee and the counselors experience the greatest personal closeness and *koinonia* in the Spirit which they have ever had. The practice of James 5 throughout the membership of our congregation has strengthened the unity of the body in a tremendous way and has developed the closest, most personal inter-relationship of leaders and members that we have ever experienced. The love of God is truly shed abroad in our hearts as we go through the experience of James 5 and lead others to that experience also. All of our elders and counselors have gone through the procedure offered by James.

Following the confession of sins and the prayers for the forgiveness of sins confessed, the counselee is prayed for by the elders for healing or restoration and then anointed with oil, the oil being smeared or rubbed on the forehead and sometimes the mouth, ears, or hands of the individual. This is a matter of discretion and decision by the elders involved as to the suitability of anointing various parts of the body. Since a great deal of overt sin is done with the ears, mouth, and hands these may be anointed to indicate the cleansing of the blood of the Lord Jesus Christ and the consecration of all parts of the body to the control of Almighty God. After the anointing, the elders usually place their hands upon the head or shoulders of the individual as prayers are offered for the power of God to completely remove all sin and the consequences of sin from the life of the individual along with the sickness, pain, or disability in the life of that person.

The results have uniformly been of a wonderful release from all the sins and heartaches of the past and an experience of joy, peace, and acceptance by Almighty God. Some people have indicated that it has been one of the most significant, happiest days in their lives. Others have indicated how clean, whole, and pure they now feel by the healing power of the Lord Jesus Christ. We make it clear that this work is not for salvation, for those who have been baptized into the Lord Jesus Christ have had their sins forgiven by the blood of our Savior. It is an experience of growth in the Lord and a sanctifying work of the Holy Spirit in the life of the child of God through his surrendering to his heavenly Father more completely than he ever has before. Spiritual cleansing and sanctification are remarkable outcomes of this procedure, even if no immediate or even future improvements in health are experienced.

This service of prayer and anointing which we have just described is foundational, and we believe must be done before specific counseling and action can be taken toward the healing of other areas of sickness, especially the mental, emotional, or spiritual. Frequently when physical sickness is clearly the need, the action described is carried through and specific prayer is immediately given for the Lord to relieve the individual of the physical ailment that he is experiencing. Again (we find it worth repeating) providentially given changes have been observed and sometimes remarkably special providences so that in the face of contrary medical opinion, people have been restored to health. We have not experienced an immediate, instantaneous, and direct restoration to health so that any seriously ill person in the hospital has arisen from the bed, put on his clothes and left the hospital with us. But we certainly do not rule out the possibility that if God wants it that way, He will do it that way. He is sovereign; and the rebuke of Paul must not apply to us in our finite theology, "On the contrary, who are you, O man, who answers back to God? The thing molded will not say to the molder, 'Why did you make me like this,' will it?" (Rom 9:20).

Generally we have found it best in counseling about mental, emotional and spiritual sickness to take these up at a period of time after this foundational phase has been carried out. It is important not to overburden the individual with the extreme pressures that come about through such in-depth counseling and yielding up to God of the whole person. In most of the counseling situations using James 5 as the foundational action of forgiveness of sins and in later sessions in healing of the person of sickness we have tried to think in terms of an hour and a half up to two and a half hours. We emphasize that God is in charge and not us. Some of these sessions can become extremely exhausting as we will describe in some detail in the later chapters.

Christian counselors have heard it before, but because we are sinful and often err we must underscore the necessity of complete confidentiality in regard to this whole procedure. It is important not to talk to others about the people with whom we are counseling or who are receiving the procedure of James 5. Above all, never mention the sins that have been confessed to the elders. Any betrayal of trust in this regard will be used by the devil to destroy the use of this valuable procedure among the children of God, something he is most anxious to do.

In summary, we have outlined the way we believe that the procedure in James 5 can be carried out. These ways are those that have been learned by us to be most effective, and we feel that they are very useful. No doubt others will find certain variations which are more acceptable to them and which they feel are more effective in the Lord. We are sure that the words we say and the ways we act are not the important thing, but the tremendous power of God Almighty that is released through our submission to Him and allowing Him to work through this method of healing is everything. To God be the glory, great things He has done!

NOTES

1. Francis MacNutt, *Healing* (Notre Dame: Ave Maria Press, 1974), p. 9.
2. Ibid., pp. 276-277.
3. Dr. Koch commented about Germany. "Call the elders! Do you not know the situation in Germany? There are big towns with five churches and twenty ministers and not one minister and not one elder is willing to use James 5:14. In most cases they are not believers. You see I come from the State church, but we have among one hundred ministers five or six believers. In most of the churches there are no believing ministers or elders. In such a situation a sick person cannot wait thirty or forty years but has the right to call a believer from an evangelical free church or a missionary. That was my situation too" (Personal letter from Dr. Kurt E. Koch, December 12, 1982, p. 3).

How tragic is the desolation of unbelief, and it is not confined to Germany unfortunately. We agree that when a person cannot secure a qualified elder-pastor to pray the prayer of faith and to anoint, then a prayer of faith without anointing can be done by some mature, godly person of faith.

4. We suggest you consider these Scriptures among others: Ps 18:1-19; 23; 25:1-22; 31:19-24; 32; 40:1-4; 46:1-7; 59; 69:1-15; 73:21-28; 84; 89:1-10; 91; 103; 106:1-12; 116; 118:1-18; 121; 136; 139; 145; 147; 148; 149; 150; Isa 40:21-31; 41:9-13; 44:24-28; 55; Jer 10:6-16; 17:7-14; 32:27; Hos 6:1-3; Mic 7:18-20; John 6:41-58; 8:31-36; 14:1-18; Rom 8; Eph 1:15-23; 6:10-18; Rev 5:9-14; 11:15-18; 12:7-11; 19:1-21.

5. We suggest these Scriptures among others: Jas 5:14-18; Ps 32; 51; Job 33:16-28.

7

Guidelines for
Your Physical Healing

The words counseling and physical healing are in the minds of many people two widely separated subjects of discussion because counseling generally refers to mental, emotional, and personal problems. The word healing is most often used in connection with physical maladies and illnesses. Yet the two terms belong together when the Christian worker begins to deal with the person who comes to him with various problems. It is increasingly verified (as has been pointed out in other places in this book) that the physical condition of the individual as affected by bad health whatever its cause can have a very significant bearing upon the psychological problems encountered and vice versa. For example, good nutrition must be of major importance to the counselor who wants to see an effective change in the life of the client. This is very elementary, but it is often ignored with the result that many people who could experience major improvements in their psychological health are prevented from doing so by lack of careful attention to the physical health problems.

The Christian counselor, especially recognizing that the individual is a whole person as created by God, knows that God is most willing to restore physical health to people as much as their mental, emotional, and spiritual health. It is quite obvious from reading the gospel accounts that Jesus Christ spent a considerable amount of time in helping needy people with their physical problems. Physical healing was a ministry of the early church as recorded in the book of Acts; and while it must not be made a major emphasis in the work of the Lord's ministers, yet it definitely has a significant role. While the wholly miraculous healings which the Lord Jesus Christ and the apostles did were especially for the authenticating of the divine origin of the new revelation which they were bringing into the world, nevertheless these established the interest of God in the whole person and in the physical well-being of the person.

Tragic mistakes have been made in the past by a forced division between the spiritual and the physical. At one extreme some men have been "saving souls" as the one and only concern of Christ with almost a complete neglect of the social and physical well-being of the individuals. On the other extreme, some have been almost entirely concerned with physical healing of the individuals or with bringing about improvement of their social conditions. This gave rise to the widespread and often questionable healing campaigns of traveling evangelists who for the most part failed to integrate the saving gospel of the Lord Jesus Christ with a physical restoration of the individual according to God's providential will.

The non-biblical faith healers have often brought the work of Christ into disrepute and a cynical rejection of the possibility that Christ is capable of healing providentially in a non-miraculous manner as well as in a miraculous way. On the other hand, disappointment and failure came through the so-called "social gospel" as men got so caught up in the sociological sufferings of people that almost all time and energy were spent upon improving people's conditions by physical means. This led to a tragic neglect of the fact that a person must be healed on the inside and experience the regenerating force of God along with physical improvement if there was to be any permanent cure.

We see a Siamese twins relationship between the physical/social impact of the teaching of Christ upon the individual and the supernatural work of God in transforming the life into a new creature in Christ through the experience of regeneration and salvation. As Christ was concerned and had compassion upon people for the healing of their bodies, even so must Christians today have that compassion mingled with their concern for their spiritual relationship to Jesus Christ as Lord and Savior.

Immediately some may be disturbed over the use of the word healing because everything they have read in the past where that word has been used in Christian circles has been used to describe the miraculous or faith-healer activities for which very strong, if not exaggerated, claims were made. Our use of the word healing does not necessarily have the connotation of miraculous in the biblical sense of that term. The healing which we are talking about and have witnessed is described properly as providential because God has used means and time to bring about the restoration to health. It also would encompass those more infrequent occasions when we have experienced extraordinary answer to prayer where all human means have proved ineffectual and God has worked supernaturally.

Everything that we have studied and everything that we have experienced gives the strongest confirmation of the fact that God is still very much interested in the physical well-being of His people in particular; and where there is a strong, spiritual relationship with God there can be highly remarkable answers to prayers for the recovery of health in the lives of God's children. Since the need is so great today, we can see no reason for anyone to neglect the very best counseling of the individuals in complete dependence upon God and in confidence in His ability to answer prayer today.

THE MEANING OF HEALING TODAY

All Bible-believing Christians affirm that the Lord Jesus Christ and His apostles along with certain members in the early Church had the miraculous power of healing people physically upon command. This miracle power was also found to be equally effective in spiritual healing in-so-far as evil spirits were expelled from human beings with a subsequent healing of their mental, psychological, and social behavior (Mark 5:1-15). The great question for so many Christians today is whether or not an equal power from Almighty God continues to be available to the Church today. We answer the question with a firm yes with qualifications.

On the one hand, we reject as inadequate and erroneous the view that God does not answer the prayers of Christians today in a remarkable and extraordinary manner which results in the restoration to health of those for whom we pray. But we also reject as erroneous and contrary to both Scripture and experience that *miracles* of healing like those in the Bible are being done by God in the world today. This does not mean that God Almighty cannot do whatever He sovereignly wants to do. We believe miracles in a *biblical* sense are extremely difficult to document under strict research conditions.

Dr. William A. Nolen, M.D., has written a most interesting book, *Healing: A Doctor in Search of a Miracle.*[1] His conclusion after investigating patients supposedly healed in a Kathryn Kuhlman meeting was that not one was actually healed. This agrees with the testimony of Dr. Louis Rose who was for twenty years a member of the Department of Psychological Medicine at St. Bartholomew's Hospital, London. "I narrowed my quest to the search for a handful of cases—or perhaps only a single case—in which the intervention of a faith healer had led to an irrefutable cure. This must have been a cure, not in the vague sense of a patient's 'feeling better' or even in that a progressive disease had been limited, but in the sense that, as a result of the healer's work alone, a demonstrable pathological state had been entirely eliminated.

"To those who have read this book it will be clear that in that search I have been unsuccessful. After nearly twenty years of work I have yet to find one 'miracle cure'; and without that (or, alternatively massive statistics which others must provide) I cannot be convinced of the efficacy of what is commonly termed faith healing."[2]

Even cases that seem to be documented by doctors may prove to be false "miracles." Consider this retraction from the *National Courier,* a biweekly tabloid published by Logos International; "This 'Miracle' Didn't Happen": "Self-proclaimed 'living miracle' Alice Pattico never had malignant cancer, nor was she used as a 'guinea pig' in an experimental operation, as she claimed in a story on her 'miraculous healing' printed in the October 15, 1976 edition of the *National Courier.*

"Furthermore, doctors whose 'testimonial' letters Mrs. Pattico circulated as proof of her healing, denied ever having penned those letters. These and other findings culminated a two-month *Courier* investigation sparked by the complaint of a Tulsa, Oklahoma, doctor who spotted discrepancies in Mrs. Pattico's statements. The inconsistencies were first exposed in a 1975 article by Robin Witt, church editor of the *Bakersfield Californian.* Witt contacted several doctors connected with Mrs. Pattico's 'healing' and all denied writing letters on her behalf.

"Following that article, Mrs. Pattico left California. Later, however, she surfaced in Tulsa, began conducting healing campaigns and continued witnessing to the 'miraculous healing' supposedly received at a 1974 Kathryn Kuhlman meeting in Los Angeles.

. . . .

"Mrs. Pattico said her condition continued to deteriorate after the hole drilling and she was finally persuaded to attend Miss Kuhlman's meeting. During the course of that service, Mrs. Pattico claimed she was healed of cancer, and that God filled the holes in her head, restored her breasts, and delivered her from addiction to pain killing drugs. To 'prove' this sequence of events, Mrs. Pattico and her husband, Dick, provided the *Courier* with doctors' letters. One letter was 'written' by the doctor who supposedly administered the laser beam surgery, the other by a San Diego doctor studying faith healing.

. . . .

"Dr. C. reiterated that he never wrote the letter. 'Mrs. Pattico did not undergo surgery at (name of hospital) and no evidence of cancer was found by Dr. C. during the course of his examination of her or by Dr. W. during the course of his neurological consultation and the test performed in connection therewith,' Dr. C.'s lawyer wrote the *Californian.*

"The Patticos apparently took copies of Dr. C.'s stationery during a visit to his office, wrote the alleged proof, and then superimposed or forged the doctor's signature."[3]

It seems to us that in ninety-five per cent of the cases in which God is working to bring about the restoration of health in His children it comes through His gracious use of *means,* our prayers and takes a period of *time.* This removes them from being in the same category as the instant and direct miraculous cures performed by Christ and the apostles.

It is the considered experiential opinion of the authors that 35 to 40% of all purported *miracles* of healing may be medically misinterpreted, exaggerated in details, or fraudulent. Another 25 to 30% may be accounted for by the fact that the origin of the medical problem is psychosomatic and not organic. Perhaps in 15% the grace of God is given through sincere prayer to bring about supernatural healing, and from 20 to 25% of purported miracles may be accomplished by occult power from Satan. This leaves approximately 5% in which judgment has to be suspended because of insufficient evidence.[4]

Serious interpretation seems to indicate no sound basis in Scripture for the assumption that a *gift* of miracle-working is still available to people today through the Lord Jesus Christ. It is our conviction that many supernatural cures and remarkable restorations to health (and they do occur) come from the god of this world, Satan, through occult power. We believe that those who hold great healing campaigns and heal some selected people according to certain "demonstrations of healing" are often either working through the power of psychological or hypnotic suggestion, or they are doing it by the counterfeit power of Satan, the archdeceiver of the world. We do not believe that Scripture teaches us to hold great healing campaigns in tents or great auditoriums, because James 5 is very specific about the elders being called *to* the sick *person* which indicates a private gathering without sensationalism, music, psychological manipulation, and without the big money aspects of all the healing campaigns of modern times.

In a very perceptive and objective essay, Linda Coleman does an excellent job of presenting what she calls a catalog of viewpoints on the question, "Christian Healing: Is It Real?"[5] After noting that there is no consensus among Christians in regard to the subject of Christian healing today, Miss Coleman makes it clear that her use of the term "Christian healing" is equivalent to "divine healing" or miraculous healing when "God intervenes directly, by-passing the natural processes of the body and the skills of doctors and nurses."[6] She recognizes that the term "supernatural healing" is equivalent to divine healing but is quite aware that there is an *evil* supernaturalism that can be the cause of healing in some cases. So her reseach is to determine the reality of a different type of healing than we are dealing with in this chapter. We uphold the norm of gradual healing in answer to prayers and by the means which God has provided for Christians to help themselves back to health through His power, but we know that God can and does work supernaturally without means.

Miss Coleman's article is helpful in setting forth some factors that must be considered in attempting to arrive at any valid answer. She notes that besides the biblical evidence which must be taken into account there is empirical evidence which is much more difficult to evaluate. She says, "Those who deny that divine healing occurs today must explain away . . . the cases of extraordinary cure that are difficult to account for scientifically. Those who maintain that supernatural healing is the norm must account for the fact that . . . many cures turn out to have resulted from suggestions (or are not cures at all but momentary neutralizing of symptoms), as well as the fact that many patients experience no change, despite the most fervent prayer and healing efforts."[7] In discussing physical ailments Miss Coleman establishes a distinction between functional disorders and organic diseases and states correctly that functional disorders are those which can be influenced sometimes by suggestions, "particularly from someone with a forceful personality and in whom the patient has faith. So, when a claim of divine healing is made for a functional disease, it is nearly impossible to demonstrate that the cure was not merely effected by the power of suggestion."[8]

Documentation is a very difficult area, Miss Coleman declares, and subject to a great many questions in regard to the investigation and the prejudices of the individuals. Even the most sincere Christian doctors have disagreed upon the genuineness of the cures which have been claimed to have resulted from divine healing. We strongly agree upon this point and our belief is not in so-called "faith-healing" as practiced in large public gatherings or in those cures that claim to be wholly supernatural without any human means being employed. Thus we see ourselves as occupying a middle ground between the extremes.

We believe that God has chosen to work differently with different people at different periods of time in history. This position has been most thoroughly expounded by B. B. Warfield, and his book *Counterfeit Miracles* is required reading for anyone who is investigating seriously the claims for divine healing today. We believe that miracles were given primarily for the attesting to the divine nature of Jesus Christ and the fact that His revelation came from the eternal God. Since the completion of the revelation by the New Covenant Scriptures there is no longer any compelling need for miraculous signs to be given, and we find confirmation for this in Heb 2:1-4. Once a document has been notarized it does not require periodic notarizations. The extraordinary gifts of the early Church were a continuation of this authenticating work of God upholding His new revelation in a pagan and hostile world; but when the revelation was completed, there was no longer any primary use for the miraculous gifts which we also believe were given through the laying on of the hands of the apostles. Thus we believe that the teaching of James 5:14-16 is now the primary basis for the providential healing of those who are sick.

Some circumstances of our day, Miss Coleman says, may affect the impact of God's working in our lives and prevent a higher level of divine healing. She suggests that the conditions in the Church today may be so inferior to those in the first century Church that the quality of our faith is a "serious obstacle for contemporary healing."[9] And, "Perhaps God heals today mostly after a concerted, long-term prayer commitment by a group of Christians, not because He needs more prayer hours to work with than He did 2,000 years ago, but because He thinks *we* need to spend more time together in prayer."[10]

These are thoughtful suggestions, and we recommend the careful study of Miss Coleman's article as a much needed caution against accepting the view that miraculous healing on the level of the New Testament or even divine healing apart from means is the ordinary working of God today in answer to prayer. We believe that all operate on a sound basis who use James 5 with prayer power along with the body of Christ praying earnestly and in faith for the recovery of one of its members.

Another valuable essay to be read by anyone interested in the matter of faith healing or divine healing apart from means is by B. B. Warfield and entitled, "Faith-Healing."[11] Many valuable footnotes are also given in this scholarly work by Warfield. Dr. Warfield points out that God expects man to use the ordinary channels which are opened to him and not to expect a miracle. He says, "No man prays God for a good harvest and then neglects to plan and plant and cultivate. If he did he knows perfectly well he would neither deserve nor receive the harvest. Similarly God requires effort on the part of those who receive His supernatural salvation—even though there are elements in it which do not come by 'law.' 'Work out your own salvation with fear and trembling,' Paul commands, 'for it is God who worketh in you both to will and to work for His good pleasure' . . . . He who prays for a harvest and does not plow, and sow, and reap is a fanatic. He who prays for salvation and does not work out his own salvation is certainly a Quietist, and may become an Antinomian. He who prays for healing and does not employ all the means of healing within his reach—hygiene, nursing, medicine, surgery,—unless God has promised to heal him in the specific mode of precise miracle, is certainly a fanatic and may become also a suicide . . . . It is the essence of fanaticism to neglect the means which God has ordained for the production of effect."[12]

We cannot deal at length with the interpretation of Matt 8:17 which is confidently appealed to by many people today who believe in miraculous or faith-healing cures apart from the use of means. A number of scholarly works have dealt with this passage which clearly shows that it is not exegetically valid to apply it to a healing of the sicknesses and diseases of Christian people.[13] B. B. Warfield does an excellent job of refuting this misinterpretation in the work already referred to. One quotation from a footnote in Warfield will suffice to expose considerable errors of the teaching that we are healed of *all* bodily sickness and disease through the atonement. Warfield says, "A very little consideration will suffice to show that these attempts so to state the doctrine of the atonement as to obtain from it a basis on which a doctrine of Faith-Healing can be erected, betray us into a long series of serious errors. They imply, for example, that Christ having borne our sicknesses as our substitute, Christians are not to bear them, and accordingly all sickness should be banished from the Christian world; Christians are not to be cured of sickness, but ought not to get sick. They imply further that, this being so, the presence of sickness is not only a proof of sin, but argues the absence of the faith which unites us to Christ, our Substitute, that is saving faith; so that no sick person can be a saved man. They imply still further that, as sickness and inward corruption are alike effects of sin, and we must contend that sickness, because it is an effect of sin, is removed completely and immediately by the atoning act of Christ, taking away sins, so must also inward corruption be wholly and at once removed; no Christian can be a sinner. Thus we have full-blown 'Perfectionism'."[14]

SOME CASE STUDIES OF PHYSICAL HEALING TODAY

When all of the sifting out has taken place and all the spurious miracle healing has been removed along with all the occult and Satanic counterfeits which are designed to deceive God's people and the world, we still believe that there is substantial empirical evidence not only from our own experience but from that of others that God is doing much more than churches and Christians have allowed. Many have allowed a rationalistic filter from logic and a naturalistic filter from the spirit of our age to remove a *proper* recognition of the extraordinary power of prayer to bring about providential and occasionally supernatural answers in regard to man's physical as well as spiritual well-being. It is time for the church that is biblically based to return to a sane and scriptural approach of helping people with their physical problems as well as the mental, emotional, and spiritual problems. The need has never been greater than in our chaotic and calloused world where men no longer believe in the power of Almighty God to improve human lives including physical afflictions.

Laying aside all the extremes that have been used of Satan to cover up the actuality of God's answers to prayer, we believe that, according to God's gracious will, healing of physical maladies both functional and organic can take place. Always it depends upon the grace of God and His perfect will and is never *guaranteed* to us as a right nor to be given upon demand. Our own experience has brought us face to face with notable results which we define as non-miraculous but extraordinary. These cures were given gradually and not instantaneously, but those whom we prayed over and anointed with oil in the name of the Lord in almost all cases received distinct improvement in their physical condition and in some cases a complete remission of their illness.

Case 1. One of the first ones in this category was a sister who had a bad hip that caused her discomfort, weakness, and often resulted in her falling down unexpectedly. After X-rays her doctor declared that she had a disintegrating hip joint and an operation would be required. The sister requested the elders to come and carry out the procedure of James 5 and we did it. Several weeks after this another doctor examined the X-rays of the first doctor, made fresh X-rays, and declared that he was unable to find any bone deterioration. This sister has continued to be in healthy condition up to this point.

Case 2. Another example involved a brother who began to have failing eyesight and glasses did not seem to help the situation or improve his sight. After going through James 5 and specific prayers of faith being offered for the Lord to bless him with improvement in his vision, no change was noted for several weeks. We continued to pray about the Lord's will, and after several weeks he reported that his eyesight was improved. In all cases we feel that there is a very significant spiritual dimension that has to be dealt with in the lives of the individuals seeking phsyical healing and that through the confession and forgiveness of sins people are made ready for the Lord's will in their lives whether there was a significant improvement in their health, no change whatsoever, or a complete cure of their physical malady.

Case 3. Still another case of eye trouble was a woman whose vision failure was connected with glaucoma. After consulting with her doctor and receiving some medicine to use in her eyes, this sister went through the procedure of James 5 with the elders. Within a day or two her vision had improved by about fifty percent, and she continues to have good sight with a minimum of problems. She continues to use the medicine perscribed.

This may disturb some who feel that there must be always a complete healing if the work is by the Lord God Almighty who does everything perfectly. It is extremely important, in our view, for all involved in a ministry of prayer for the restoration of health to recognize that God is in total charge and will do that which is His will. We make it very clear to those for whom we pray that it is completely in God's hands, and they must be willing to accept a "no" answer from God through our prayers or a partial restoration to health as being in the will of God. As we have observed, these cures do not take place all at once and are sometimes in stages as the individual grows spiritually and learns to commit himself more thoroughly to the Lord God.

Case 4. Healing involving prayer and application of medical means was experienced by one of the elders of Christ's Church Cincinnati. This person injured his wrist in an industrial accident which was verified via workman's compensation investigation. The injury caused a form of tenosynovitis which later progressed into carpal tunnel syndrome. Diagnosis by a physician-surgeon indicated that only an operation would correct this condition. The wrist hurt so much that writing was not possible for more than five consecutive minutes.

Prior to the wrist accident the patient had been treated for a year for a painful shoulder. The pain in his shoulder became so intense that it became necessary to sleep sitting upright in a chair. X-rays revealed calcium deposits in the shoulder socket area. Recommendations were made by a physician-surgeon for surgery to be performed to remove the calcium desposits. To ease the pain occasional injections of cortisone were given, and anti-inflammatory and muscle relaxant drugs were administered orally. Though these drugs eased the pain, nevertheless the condition recurred periodically, and the patient was advised that no known cure existed other than corrective surgery.

Having pursued the best known medical advice, the patient decided to request general prayer by his congregation for God to heal his physical problems. The elder was treated by a doctor of chiropractic. He prescribed changes in diet to avoid buildup of calcium in the joints and recommended certain vitamins and minerals to dissolve deposited calcium while providing the type of calcium which the body could assimilate. He also performed a series of physical therapy treatments on the wrist and shoulder including ultra-sound massage, manual massage, electro-convulsive massage, and physical manipulative therapy of the affected joints. After eight weeks of such treatments the shoulder and wrist were healed completely. Eight months later there has been no recurrence of immobility, discomfort, or pain.

Case 5. The most outstanding instance of God's honoring the procedure for healing that *we* have observed is in the case of a brother who after having Hodgkin's disease became a Christian. After a period of time the disease became active again, and he requested the elders to pray for him and anoint him with oil. He entered the hospital and received therapy and chemotherapy for a period of time. After several weeks he was significantly improved but later suffered a relapse. Again he requested the elders to come and carry out the procedure of James 5.

There was significant spiritual maturing in his life during these periods of sickness and of the procedure for healing. Again a number of weeks went by, and gradually the brother recovered strength and health in a very substantial way. His doctor ran various tests on him and found no evidence of symptoms of Hodgkin's disease. After four years there has been no recurrence of any symptoms of Hodgkin's disease.

After the chemotherapy and the destruction of the antibodies in his system, he was in a weakened state and most susceptible to many kinds of germs. Prayer was continued by the members of the congregation on his behalf for his protection and health. After several months this brother came down with a disease which was diagnosed as Guillain Barre. This disease began to affect his nerves in the extremities of his body and gradually went throughout his entire body to the point that he had to have a tracheotomy for his survival and was on a respirator in intensive care for many weeks.

During this time he was prayed for and anointed twice at different periods by his request. Almost no therapy could be done for him from a medical standpoint to enable him to recover, but the whole congregation prayed around the clock for him day after day. Finally his condition was so bad that he was put in an isolation ward in intensive care and everything pointed toward death. However, the Lord heard and answered the prayers of His people in a remarkable way as the patient was able to leave intensive care and to gain strength so that he went into a rehabilitation program. The nurses from intensive care came to see him in physical therapy because they said he was the man who should have been dead. They stated that they had never had anyone in intensive care who was so sick and who had recovered.

His rehabilitation proceeded in a remarkable way so that he was back in the meetings of the congregation within weeks, and the Lord continued to strengthen him and give him a considerable measure of health. After two years this brother has married a wife, and the Social Security administration has declared him to be disabled no longer. He gives God the glory and thanks for his recovery and has a tremendous faith in the work of God in his life.

Many have been helped with serious infections that have not responded to medical treatment while others have had viral sicknesses which caused them to be hospitalized, and all of these responded to the procedure set forth in James 5. Now many members of the congregation call the elders when they are stricken with serious illness as the first action to take. The Lord continues to honor the prayers of the whole body as well as the prayers of faith and anointing by the elders.

Case 6. Dr. Koch gives an example from his own ministry. "A missionary was flown home from Sumatra. The ambulance car was waiting at the airport. The seriously ill missionary was taken immediately to the hospital for an operation. The surgeons opened up the abdomen and closed it right away. It was too late for metastasis was everywhere.

"His wife was desperate. She was looking for a believing minister who was willing to use James 5:14. She went two hundred kilometers to find one. . . . This lady wept and urged me to go to her husband. I took two other believers with me. The missionary confessed his sins to the oldest of us. The sick missionary had never in his life used James 5:14, and he was skeptical even in this life dangerous situation. . . .

"We anointed his forehead and prayed with him. The next day the patient asked the nurse, 'Give me my clothes.' She replied, 'I have to ask the doctor.' The doctor advised the nurse, 'Go ahead and do it. Fulfill every wish. This man goes out of the hospital only in the coffin. Perhaps he has only three weeks to live.'

"The patient got his clothes, went out in the garden of the hospital and walked there five hours. Three weeks later he left the hospital not in the coffin but healthy. He lived another twelve years and died a natural death. He was already an old man when he came home from Sumatra."[15]

Case 7. A remarkable personal testimony to the power of God in physical healing under the action of James 5:14ff. is given by Dr. Kurt E. Koch. "In 1977 a specialist discovered a tumor on my right kidney. It was tested six times by X-rays. I came January, 1978 in the hospital to be operated on. I was three weeks staying there. My kidney was out of order. My wife, without asking me phoned the missionary [from Kwa Sizabantu, Natal, South Africa] who had prayed for me in 1976.

"He travelled from South Africa at his own costs to me. He stayed five days in my home and visited me five times. He prayed again with me under the laying on of hands. Then came the decisive days. I was brought to a university clinic. They checked again, and the tumor has gone till today! Six months later they checked again. No tumor. Twelve months again. No tumor."[16]

THE DIFFICULTIES CREATED BY
"FAILURES" IN HEALING

God does not always answer our prayers in the way that we thought He would, and this gives rise to what is called a "failure to heal." However, there are no failures with God because of His perfect will and His absolute power to do whatever He pleases. Those things that we may designate as failures are simply negative answers from God in regard to our prayers and express His good will. We accept them as answers because we trust our Abba, Father, to do all things well.

Case 8. One of our members came down with serious sickness and was hospitalized. The elders were called to carry out the provisions of James 5, and the whole congregation prayed for this young mother. Her condition got worse, and in spite of our requests of God for her healing and recovery of health, she died. Yes, she died peacefully and confidently in our Lord, but she died. Everything was done, as nearly as we know, as in the earlier cases through which the Lord graciously granted a recovery; but in this case the person did not receive the blessing of health and life from the Lord. How can we account for such things?

There is no one answer and no simple, easy answer to the question why some are healed while others with great faith do not get better and may die as a result of their illness. We are forced to recognize that God is sovereign in everything, and as He sees the end from the beginning He is able to make decisions that do not fit in with our narrow vision of what would be best. Francis MacNutt has had a notable ministry in healing, and his book entitled *Healing* is a valuable reference on a number of topics associated with healing. Out of his experience and study he has defined eleven reasons that we must ponder if we are to give an adequate answer to the question of why some are not healed.

Dr. MacNutt[17] points out: 1. that there can be a lack of faith in those who are praying for the recovery of the sick one or there may be a lack of faith in the individual for whom prayer is made. 2. Redemptive suffering may be involved so that God uses the sickness for His own purposes. "Physical healing is not in itself the highest value in the world."[18] There may be an occasion when God does not heal a sickness as in the case of the apostle Paul who had to continue to bear his thorn in the flesh. This was for Paul's own benefit in spiritual ways and was used of God for significant purposes (2 Cor 12:7-9). 3. There may be a false value attached to suffering and the individual may be holding on to the illness for selfish or manipulative reasons. He may enjoy his suffering and feel that he is honoring God through it. It is probable that such a person will not request the elders to come and pray for him.

MacNutt notes that 4. sin can also be a block to the healing, for there must be forgiveness of the sins that others have committed against us and the forgiveness from God through the blood of Christ for all of our sins. 5. Healing may not occur when we do not pray specifically enough because we do not know what is required or what is God's plan. This requires getting at the specific root of the sickness where possible rather than the symptoms. 6. There may be a faulty diagnosis in that a prayer for the healing of physical illness may rather have to be a prayer for inner healing or for deliverance from the power of evil spirits. Those who are involved in the procedure for healing must ask the Lord for discernment so as to give the proper ministry to the person. If physical healing does not take place, then it may well be that there must be work done either with inner healing or deliverance.

7. Again MacNutt says one may not be healed because of a "refusal to see medicine as a way that God heals"[19] and trying to do it without any use of means. There is no teaching of Scripture against the use of means but every encouragement for it. God can certainly use whatever means He wants to and ordinarily seems to encourage the use of means.

Another reason for failure that MacNutt points out is 8. "not using the natural means of preserving health"[20] or a neglect of ordinary common sense means of keeping ourselves in a good condition for health to be realized. In other words, we may need to change our work habits, eating habits, lifestyle, or other circumstances which are under our control to prevent the onslaught of certain illnesses arising from these bad patterns or work habits. 9. God may often indicate in a person not being healed that it is not the right time. All timing is with God, and He knows the condition of the person more than any of us do. He knows whether the person is ready to be healed to the glory of God.

10. It is sometimes true that the Lord will determine that "a different person is to be the instrument of healing."[21] Simply because one set of elders or a certain person cannot at a particular time be used by the Lord to bring healing does not mean that some other persons will not be able to do so. We must avoid all messianic obsessions on our part, and often the Lord may have to humble us by refusing to heal someone through our ministry while someone else does it so that we do not become filled with pride. Always we are merely instruments that God may choose to work through or not according to His own determination.

MacNutt's final observation is that "the social environment prevents healing from taking place."[22] Healing will most often be accomplished by God through the prayers and ministry of the loving family of God. If there are sinful conditions in the home or the community of the person, there may not be healing until the conditions have been changed as much as the person is able to do so.

In a poignant and moving chapter Joni Eareckson describes her experience with others in seeking a direct miraculous healing from her heavenly Father. She notes the many Scriptures that were given to her to establish the fact that God was not only able but would definitely heal people miraculously today. With full confidence in God and great expectancy of faith she gathered with Christian elders and ministers for prayer and anointing. Then weeks went by, and no changes were observed in her body. Naturally she began to question what may have prevented her healing since she had done everything that she knew to do along with those who were a part of her request for healing. Out of the experience Joni came to this conclusion: "God certainly can, and sometimes does, heal people in a miraculous way today. But the Bible does *not* teach that He will *always* heal those who come to Him in faith. He sovereignly reserves the right to heal or not to heal as He sees fit."[23]

Miss Eareckson with Steve Estes presents some sound and helpful explanation of the matter of disease and death that came about through man's sin. Joni draws this conclusion, *"Disease is just one of the many results of sin that Jesus began, but didn't finish, dealing with when He started His kingdom while on earth.* Jesus' miracles, including healing, didn't guarantee the end of any of sin's results for those who follow Him."[24] Her discussion of the interaction of God with our illnesses and the need of healing is very helpful, and we commend it to you for your study.

Joni gives this summary of her understanding of God's answers to prayer. "Jesus gave wonderful promises to His disciples; whatever they needed to get God's work done on earth, He would give it. But Jesus' own words in the rest of Scripture make it clear that there were at least two conditions to any prayer they made—they must be remaining in Him, and their requests must be in line with God's will. Since God hasn't chosen to reveal all of His will to Christians, then we must leave our requests in His hands and wait to see what He decides to do. And if He chooses to refuse our request? Well, there is more than one way to 'move a mountain.' The New Testament stresses that God loves to use weak vessels (people) to do His work so that He, and not they, gets the glory. And in the light of all the spiritual benefits resulting from sickness and suffering, God may choose that our very sickness be His way of moving the mountains before us."[25]

NOTES

1. William A. Nolen, *Healing, A Doctor in Search of a Miracle* (New York: Random House, 1974).

2. Louis Rose, edited by Bryan Morgan, *Faith Healing* (London: Penguin Books, 1968, 1970), pp. 175-176.

3. Kenny Waters, "This 'Miracle' Didn't Happen," *National Courier,* February 4, 1977, p. 3.

4. Richard L. Mayhue has some very helpful information on the explanation of the many accounts of healing today in *Divine Healing Today* (Chicago: Moody Press, 1983), pp. 87-95. The entire book is excellent in its treatment of the whole subject of healing.

5. Linda Coleman, "Christian Healing: Is It Real?" *The Spiritual Counterfeits Project Journal,* August, 1978, pp. 42-51.

6. Ibid., p. 42.

7. Ibid., p. 44.

8. Ibid., p. 45.

9. Ibid., p. 51.

10. Ibid., p. 51.

11. B. B. Warfield, *Counterfeit Miracles* (London: The Banner of Truth Trust, 1918, reprint 1972).

12. Ibid., pp. 165-166. The exposition by Warfield relative to the James 5:14-16 passage is not on the whole a good treatment of this text although much of what he says is sound. We much prefer our exposition (in chapter 5) as more exegetically correct and theologically adequate.

13. Some references to this question are: William Edward Biederwolf, *Whipping Post Theology or Did Jesus Atone for Disease?* (Grand Rapids: William B. Eerdmans Publishing Co., 1934); Stephen Nash, "Is Physical Healing An Intended Benefit of the Atonement?" (Cincinnati: *The Seminary Review,* XXVII: no. 3, September, 1981, 111-121; Richard L. Mayhue, *Divine Healing Today* (Chicago: Moody Press, 1983), pp. 43-54.

14. Warfield, op. cit., p. 307.

15. Personal letter to the authors from Dr. Kurt E. Koch, December 1982, p. 4.

16. Ibid., p. 3.

17. Francis MacNutt, O. P., *Healing* (Notre Dame, IN: Ave Maria Press, 1974), pp. 248-261. There are some helpful and stimulating parts of this book, but the reader needs to question and sift other parts.

18. Ibid., p. 250.

19. Ibid., p. 256.

20. Ibid., p. 258.

21. Ibid., p. 259.

22. Ibid., p. 260.

23. Joni Eareckson and Steve Estes, *A Step Further* (Minneapolis: World Wide Publications, 1978. © Zondervan Publishing House), p. 127.

24. Ibid., p. 133.

25. Ibid., p. 157.

8

Healing Your Psychological Hurts and Memories

As strong believers in man's spiritual nature by the act of God's creation, we naturally believe that the psyche (soul) is an important part of man's functioning. Man's psyche has been affected by sin and is influenced by Satan as is man's spirit and body. Thus there is a place for psychology; but we have insisted that psychology, to be effective, must be a biblically-based psychology and provided by a practicing Christian. Merely to study the psyche apart from God's revelation and God's power is to end up with some information which can only be humanistically interpreted and inadequately used. Without the power of God through prayer and Scripture the knowledge of a person's psychological difficulties will not likely produce any lasting or holistic healing of the person. One may be taught to cope with his emotions and the pressures that create stress situations, but these may not be lasting and are certainly not as restorative as those which involve God and His power in the life of the individual.

We believe that James 5 and its procedure for calling the elders of the church to deal with a person who has sickness is most pertinent in dealing with the major psychological problems which people face, especially those which come from repressed emotions and traumas of their lives. There already exist a number of valuable books for psychological counseling from a Christian standpoint which we highly recommend to you for your study and use in helping people with their psychological problems. Dr. Gary R. Collins, professor of psychology at

Trinity Evangelical Divinity School, has produced a highly competent and complete book on counseling called *Christian Counseling.*[1] Dr. Collins gives excellent information in regard to preparations for counseling and then treats major areas of difficulty which the counselor may be confronted with from time to time. He attempts to give an overview of the particular issue and adequate information to enable the counselor to work with the counselee. He does not give as much background from the Scripture as Dr. Jay Adams does in his working through psychological issues. However, Dr. Collins is good in giving basic foundations from the Scripture to indicate its teaching on the problems.

This book is also supplemented by a valuable set of twenty-eight tapes, most of which are quite helpful in counseling with the individuals in a particular area for the tape involves activities for the counselee. The use of these tapes has been a help to us to discriminate between people who want to get better and are willing to undertake specific remedial efforts and those who simply want to have someone to talk to and to soothe their spirits.

Dr. Jay Adams has been a notable as well as a controversial figure in Christian counseling. He is the author of *Competent to Counsel.*[2] A number of psychologists, including some Christian psychologists, have questioned his methodology and feel it may be a simplistic approach to the complex problems that beset people today. As a discriminating reader you will have to make your own judgment in this regard. Certainly the secular psychologists and those Christians who are very strongly influenced by secular models of counseling are not too happy with Dr. Adams' emphasis upon the Word of God and the big role that sin plays in the whole matter of mental and emotional illness.

We are sympathetic with the approach of Dr. Adams, because he is specifically Christian in his orientation and recognizes that all problems ultimately go back to relationships to God which are distorted or destroyed by sin. Sin is clearly the great problem in the lives of people today as they live in a sinful environment and are themselves selfish and rebellious sinners.

Even Christians are sinful and can be self-willed individuals who often fail to make right decisions unless they act prayerfully, in the context of the teaching of God's Word, and with the help and direction of godly brothers and sisters. You will find much helpful information in psychological counseling in the various books by Dr. Adams; and you should be intelligent enough to balance his writings, because he is only an uninspired human being, with the uninspired teaching of other Christian counselors and psychologists.

One of the finest books of a modest length that we have encountered is *Effective Biblical Counseling* by Lawrence J. Crabb, Jr.[3] Dr. Crabb does an excellent work in setting forth basic information for the Christian counselor in something over two hundred pages. After treating preliminaries he presents basic concepts: What do you need to know about people in order to effectively counsel? Next he deals with basic strategy: How to understand and deal with personal problems. Then he suggests the very great value of counseling *within* the Christian community, the very thing we urged—that every person who hopes to deal successfully with the issues of life and personality problems must be an active member of a loving and caring community of Christian believers.

These books and some others like them[4] are of real value in setting forth psychological methods of counseling, and there is no reason for us to cover the same subject matter that is found in these outstanding books. What we desire to do is to go beyond what most of the books teach and recommend, for we know there is a greater power of God to be released in the lives of individuals enabling them to be healed of deep psychological problems by God as indicated in James 5.

THE NEED AND THE MEANING OF PSYCHOLOGICAL HEALING (INNER HEALING)

Many of us are aware of the fact that we have experienced along with others psychological difficulties in our development through life which have taken the form of traumas because of the very difficult emotional content of those experiences. Many are very personal, frequently unpleasant, and sometimes tragic in their sinfulness. Consequently people bear scars and continue to suffer psychological damage in their relationships because of the repressed emotions. Psychologists have done a valuable work in pointing out the reality and functioning of these memories of severe emotional disturbances and their effect upon the individual in living his life normally in the present. The beautiful part that the Christian can play within this grave problem is to bring the presence and power of God into the life of the individual to heal these memory scars and to get rid of their negative impact.

To do this the Christian worker follows a procedure which has been called "psychological healing," "inner healing," or "healing of the memories." Considerable literature on this has flowed from various sources and theologies, and we are skeptical of some of these sources. As you have already learned, we do not agree with neo-pentecostal excesses, so we reject much of the procedure that is often used in many neo-pentecostal circles for inner healing. Too much of the inner healing from or among neo-pentecostal groups tends to be open to occult power and a subjectivism which is very unhealthy and proceeds from an inadequate scriptural context and control. The devil, the archdeceiver, is quick to counterfeit where possible the genuine product that the Spirit of God produces for the children of God; and we believe that one must proceed with great caution to avoid entanglement in undesirable and even dangerous activities when it comes to healing.

Inner healing as we have seen God working among us has been along the line of the definition given by Steve Scott and Brooks Alexander in their helpful article, "Inner Healing."[5] "Its primary and spiritual objective is to extend the Lordship and healing power of Christ into our past history, affecting even our pre-conversion experience. Its secondary and psychological goal is thereby to release us from whatever emotional psychological bondage our past experiences produced. Inner healing theorists claim that emotional blocks and habitual behavior patterns (with their negative fruits of frustration, defeat and poor self-image) prevent us from moving into the abundant life that Jesus promised. Therefore, they conclude, that a special effort should be made to heal these inner wounds, so that we may be free from the many ways in which they constrict and impoverish our lives. In summary, the overall goal of inner healing can be described as a kind of 'retroactive sanctification.' Indeed, we see this matter of the healing of the memories as a cleansing action of the Spirit of God by the blood of the Lord Jesus Christ in bringing the person to a new level of spiritual freedom in Christ, purity of thought, and sanctification growth. To us it is viewed as a procedure in sanctification whereby the person is enabled to be liberated from the past and made whole in the Lord Jesus Christ.''[6]

Inner healing, then, is a work of God wrought through the ministry of some of His servants who are dedicated to letting the Lord use them with prayer power and with guidance, sympathy, and compassionate listening to the ones who have been deeply wounded. This ministry stands between the healing of physical problems and the ministry of deliverance which deals specifically with demonic intruders in the life of the child of God. It is not something mysterious and difficult and does not actually have to be restricted to a ministry of the elders under James 5 because it does not specifically require anointing with oil. It has generally been our practice as elders to follow James 5 with the individual in both the preliminary matters and in offering a prayer of faith coupled with the anointing of oil. Our Lord has honored this procedure and given significant healing to a large number of people.

Basically, the healing of memories is exercising our confidence in the Lord Jesus Christ as the redeemer and deliverer of our whole person from the bondage of sin, of human depravity, and our own tragic experiences which can bring us oppression such as is found in depression, anxiety, rejection, etc. Thus the person who is not helped by the ordinary means of grace which God has given to us and who cannot eliminate the persistent problems of his psychological life through a growing experience with the Lord Jesus Christ may now find a means of help from the Lord which can take away the memory of the repressed emotions and their consequences. Essentially, it is a submission of the person to the lordship of Jesus Christ and an opening to Him for His healing action relative to those problems which persist and continue to drag the individual down into unhealthy or unholy states of being.

THE SPIRITUAL BASIS FOR INNER HEALING

For those who want an exact description of the work of inner healing in the life of the individual, we have to point out that there is no such chapter in Scripture. It is based on the principle that the Lord Jesus Christ is set forth in Scripture as the one who can heal us from all of our sins and the consequences, to cleanse and make us whole as His recreated and regenerated people (Col 3:10). Also for us it is based upon the truth of James 5 which brings about a spiritual cleansing and psychological healing as the individuals recognize the depth of their problems and call for the elders of the church to pray with them for the power of God to come upon them. This power of God is brought forth from the Word of God, which is the foundation for the actions taken, and the power of prayer which is the most fundamental weapon that the Christian has to overcome problems through the work of our mediator, the Lord Jesus Christ. Faith is an essential ingredient to any healing, and faith claims the promises of God such as that found in Eph 3:10-21, "Now to Him who is able to do exceeding abundantly beyond all that we ask or think according to the power that works within us, to Him be the glory in the church and in Christ Jesus to all generations forever and ever."

Another scriptural foundation for the ministry of inner healing is found in the concept that man as created by God is a complete, integrated personality who should not be compartmentalized after the order of Greek thought. The Lord Jesus Christ is the redeemer of the whole person, every part, and this includes the body, the mind, the emotions, and the spirit. Therefore our Lord's redemptive love is powerful in its effect enabling the redeemed person to have unusual health in all the different aspects of his being. Of course there are some exceptions that may take place such as Paul's thorn in the flesh which, according to the will of God, was not removed by even the prayers of the apostle. It is of absolute necessity for all working in any kind of restorative and healing ministry to realize that only *God* does the healing and that it is a sovereign act of His grace, not something forced upon Him by anything that we mere mortals do. Basically there is no sickness or problem of the life which the Lord Jesus Christ cannot heal *if* He chooses. God's gracious invitation to all with wounds from the past is to seek the fullness of God's love and healing action.

Our Lord Jesus Christ recognized the central place that the heart plays in the life of the individual, for the heart is the controlling center of the inner life. The prophet Isaiah predicted that when the Messiah would come He would, among other things, bind up the broken-hearted (Isa 61:1). Although this is not quoted exactly in Christ's words in the synagogue at Nazareth, it still vividly describes a part of the ministry of our Lord Jesus Christ (Luke 4:17-19). Scott and Alexander state it well, "Our inner life is a critical part of our personal identity, so the need for a healing of emotions and memories has always been a part of our human condition. Jesus' teaching and ministry recognized implicitly this need, as did the outreach of the infant church."[7]

They go on to note that the description of the meeting of Christ on the road to Emmaus with two disciples is a form of memory healing (Luke 24:13-35). We quite agree that this is an excellent prototype or model for the healing of memories and concerns more than "emotional scars and psychological damage of childhood trauma . . . . The pivot point of inner healing in this expanded perspective is Christ's sacrificial death and resurrectional victory over sin and death, just as it was on the Emmaus road. From this viewpoint inner healing is less a goal in its own right as a preliminary step which enables the Christian to be helped toward freedom (Gal 5:1) and spiritual maturity, laying aside the ingrained, selfish, childish ways of handling life (1 Cor 13:11-12)."[8]

The apostle Paul speaks of the necessity of Christians having a transformation of their lives by "the renewing of your mind, that you may prove what the will of God is, that which is good and acceptable and perfect" (Rom 12:2). Writing to the Ephesians he declares that Christians should "lay aside the old self, which is being corrupted in accordance with the lusts of deceit, and that you be renewed in the spirit of your mind, and put on the new self, which in the likeness of God has been created in righteousness and holiness of the truth'' (Eph 4:22-24). Thus among the first century Christians and in a very vivid and full description in the case of the apostle Paul, a transformation and renewal of mind was being experienced through the power of the Lord Jesus Christ, His resurrection power.

Moreover, it is true that our Lord Jesus Christ is the Prince of peace, and He gives peace to His people, "And He came and preached peace to you who were far away, and peace to those who were near (Eph 2:17). The individual Christian who lacks peace within needs inner healing. The Lord Jesus Christ can bring inner peace and serenity that should be the mark of a Christian and enables him to function as a restored person walking in the Spirit. The fruit of the Spirit is love, joy, and peace (Gal 5:22). So the "peace of God which passes all understanding" is to "rule in your hearts" (Phil 4:7; Col 3:15). The tempest which often rages within the life of the Christian can as certainly be stilled and brought to a state of peace as the Sea of Galilee was when the Son of God rode upon its waters and rebuked the winds and the waves (Matt 8:24). We believe that the Lord uses the procedure of inner healing (healing of the memories) to bring about this peace.

Thus there seems to be an adequate and strong foundation in the Scriptures for a ministry enabling the Lord Jesus Christ to cleanse the mind of bad memories and evil experiences. He gives a much greater freedom in all personal relationships and allows the person to have more of that peace that passes all understanding. This has been our happy experience in dealing with a number of people who have had psychological and personality problems. The Lord has brought a tremendous new quality of life, a liberation, and a wholesome outlook with peace to many.

THE PROCEDURE FOR INNER HEALING

When people begin to mature in the Lord and to recognize critically the areas of their lives that are troublesome to them in interpersonal relationships and self acceptance, we believe that they should consider the teaching of James 5:14 and seek the ministry of the elders in overcoming the causes of these problems. As we counsel such people we proceed to carry them through the first major step of James 5 with a time of spiritual cleansing through their confession of the major sins in their lives, particularly in the areas that they may have overlooked in the past. They also are instructed that the Lord says He cannot forgive them and heal them unless they forgive those who have sinned against them or wronged them with the resultant bitterness, resentment, and even hatred (Matt 6:14, 15; Luke 6:36-37; Heb 12:14, 15).

Following this initial and essential first step, people are ready to consider a session for the healing of memories and the prayer for inner peace. It has been our custom to instruct these people relative to the power of God in their lives and His sufficiency for healing them in all of the scarred areas of their lives. When they are ready for such action of God in their lives, one of us usually meets with them in a very quiet and peaceful place where there will be no interruptions for whatever period of time it takes, often from forty-five minutes to an hour and a half.

There must be every effort on the part of the elder or leader to show the person the patience, forgiveness, and love of God by his own attitude and actions. The climate should be one of great acceptance and an assurance of faith that God is all-powerful and all-merciful, that He is more than willing to heal us of every condition that could be used against us. A number of scriptural readings are used to prepare the individual for the healing that the Lord is asked to give. Among these are Ps 34, 91, 103, 119:25-32; 139; 2 Cor 12:9; 5:16—6:2. Each counselor develops his own list of Scriptures which he feels are particularly appropriate for establishing the warm, loving, and restorative atmosphere between the individual and Almighty God.

First come scriptural readings and prayers (the children's prayer, commonly called the Lord's Prayer, Matt 6:9-13, is certainly a very excellent prayer to use). Next the counselee will begin (with the assurance that the Lord is enabling him to think clearly) to express those experiences which come to mind as the most traumatic. A person may desire to begin with the earliest memories of childhood and move forward to his adult life or the reverse of that. No set order is required.

As the individual recounts the experience with whatever detail he feels comfortable with in the Lord, the counselor will listen attentively and give every kind of appropriate body language encouragement. After the counselee has recited the experience, the counselor can indicate (if the counselee has not already done so) why this is a troublesome and injurious area to the life and interpersonal relationships. Then the counselor should pray very specifically to the Lord God Almighty for the cleansing power of the Lord Jesus' blood to be applied to this person's life and mind and to remove everything that troubles and hurts this individual and his functioning as a normal person.

In regard to elements of the procedure and accompanying the prayer for healing, Michael Scanlan suggests that four elements need to be involved, "1. *Be clear on the specific area of bondage or wound.* It is essential to know what specifically you're praying *for* and what you are praying *against* . . . . 2. *Encourage the person to lead or actively respond to prayer by deciding to reject evil and emotional bondage.* You may want the person to repeat the prayer after you. You may encourage him if appropriate to stand or kneel as an indication of his decision to reject what is not of God's life. 3. *Lead the person in a decision to commit the area in question to the Lordship of Jesus Christ.* As this is done all involved in the ministry need to center on Jesus . . . . 4. *Instruct the person that in the Lord he or she has the power to maintain the new freedom even though there may be a time of struggle.* Encourage the person to be faithful to praying daily and to attending gatherings of Christians where faith and feeling can be supported."[9]

The prayers are very simple, sincere, and intimate as we look to our Abba (Daddy), God for the love and power necessary for removing all the scars that have been wrought by this painful experience. Where there has been rejection, we pray for the person to experience the full acceptance of his heavenly Father. Where there has been the denial of love and hatred given, we pray for the unconditional love of God to flood the heart of the person. Where there has been the loss of security and confidence, we pray for the mighty arms of God to hold fast the individual so that he may experience the great security of resting in the arms of our perfect Father. Further prayers are offered as other particular needs of the individual are expressed and with special request that God will remove entirely the bitter memory or to neutralize it so that the individual, if he remembers it at all, will no longer have any pain, resentment, or injury from it. Also we pray for the Holy Spirit to fill more of the life and body of the believer and to continue to comfort, heal, and protect the Christian from Satan's attacks.

Then in succession the other repressed emotional experiences are recounted, and prayers of faith are offered for these in a manner similar to the prayers that have already been given for the other experiences. For the counselors who are elders the session is usually closed with a final prayer of faith and an anointing with oil in the name of the Lord Jesus Christ.

SOME CASE STUDIES OF INNER HEALING

We can report that the results uniformly have been outstandingly good and have brought peace to many people in troubled areas of their lives. It is a moving and beautiful experience of God's grace for both the counselee and counselor which often brings tears of joy and relief. The client has become more aware of the love and unmerited favor of God as He answers the prayers and removes the fears and traumas of the past. There is a new sense of freedom and of wholeness where before there was crippling distress and guilt.

Case studies of the activities and results of sessions for inner healing are not easy to give as no notes are taken during the sessions as this would distract from the needed openness on the part of the person. Also it would hurt the warm, personal involvement of both counselor and counselee in the profound, even intimate, issues of life. A couple of cases may give some detail beyond the summary of results already given.

Case 1. A young woman who had suffered a great deal of abuse and rejection as a girl and later as a wife came for a healing of these memories that affected her relationship to men, especially her husband, and to children. The repressed memories also had severely damaged her self-image so that almost all suffering, defeats, and difficulties were taken as deserved punishment.

During the session she was able to recall various times when she had been pulled out from under the bed or other places of hiding to be punished. These were vividly recited in a re-enactment of some of the scenes with tears and pleadings to her father not to hurt her, that she would be a good girl. The felt rejection and lack of love by parents were prayed about, and the Lord enabled her to realize her total acceptance by her Daddy God. Substantial improvements in her personal relationship to her parents, husband, and children took place after this time. Her self-image problem was eased as she accepted the fact that God had created her in His image and that He had thought so much of her that He allowed His only begotten Son to die for her.

Case 2. During a counseling session a client reported that at the age of five he was sent alone by bus several hundred miles to visit his grandparents. The memory of this event not only produced difficulties in being comfortable on buses (as an adult) but also contributed to his pattern of feeling rejected and worthless.

After this experience was verbalized, the brother chose to accept the love and worth given to him by his heavenly Father to replace the feelings acquired during his bus ride. Prayers were offered that all the negative and traumatic feelings associated with this episode might be removed from his memory or neutralized as the Lord Jesus Christ might choose. He was anointed with oil by the elder. Now this brother reports an emotionally neutral memory of the childhood event. The healing of this particular memory is a part of the process of his gaining victory over feelings of being rejected and worthless.

Sometimes there may be the need of other sessions to deal with other repressed experiences which may be remembered as the child of God grows in grace and knowledge. Occasionally there may be blocks that have to be dealt with such as sin that has not been repented of and confessed to God because if these exist, then God seldom heals the individual. The individual must be acting in faith and in the highest degree of submission to God of which he is capable at the time. There may be occasions when the individual will need deliverance work to free him of demonic powers which can influence the mind and confuse him in such a way as to keep him in some bondage to the experiences of the past.

Ordinarily the individual is immediately helped and set free from the oppression of the traumas of his life, and this freedom continues to abide with the individual as a new factor in his life. Instruction is given for the individual to continue in a close walk with the Lord in all spiritual disciplines. Especially prayers should be offered for the Holy Spirit to continue to bring love, peace, and confidence into his life as a humble child of God.

There is really no reason why this procedure for the healing of the memories cannot be carried out with any sincere Christian who is willing to submit his life to the Lord Jesus Christ and to work with a Christian man or woman who knows how to accept him as the Lord does, to administer the grace of God to him, and to pray for God's mighty work in his life. It is a work of faith and of prayer which honors God and allows Him to do that which He is most willing to do for His children in making them well and whole, to walk in the Holy Spirit, and not to be in fear and bondage. This ministry may be one of the earliest ones that is attempted by the elders or by other mature leaders in the congregation as they take up a healing ministry to the needy members of the congregation. Such restoration for individuals will have a wonderful impact for the Lord both upon the congregation and upon the lives of other people outside the congregation who observe those who have been set free by the Lord.

SOME CRITERIA FOR CONDUCTING A HEALING OF MEMORIES

In any working for the Lord and asking for His will to be done, our sinful, finite selves may prevent the accomplishment of this. We are dedicated to the proposition that we should follow every detail that is given scripturally or to follow the principles of Scripture with prayerful concern so that anything humanistic and occultic will be excluded from our procedures. Michael Scanlan has warned against two problems which he has seen in the healing of the memories among those in the charismatic (neo-pentecostal) renewal—superficiality and excessive emotionalism.[10]

Under superficiality he indicates that the approach, the lack of seriousness with which it is done, and the involvement of the person's own heart may be much too shallow. There may be a real need to deal with evil or sin in the life of the individual. Inner healing will not take place until root causes for the difficulties in the life of the individual have been removed. The individual must be active in determining not only the roots of the problem but in earnestly asking God to remove those roots and to renounce them as far as he is concerned. He must be willing, in other words, to get rid of the sin and the cause of the sin in his life.

Scanlan points out that there must be the corresponding responsible action and disciplined life of the individual as he grows toward maturity in his dependence upon God and spiritual resources while repudiating his sinful self. So the healing of the memories is never by any magical means or an instant guarantee of peace without the earnest commitment of the individual to allow God's continuing work and even discipline in his life (Heb 12:1-15).

The second major danger that Scanlan notes among some in this ministry is excessive emotionalism that encourages too much ventilating of the feelings and expressing dramatically the traumas of one's life. Acting out in fantasy any of the experiences of the past or changing our roles is not a scripturally approved activity. Such expressions will not in themselves remove the repressed emotional injury to the person. There must be prayer for God's healing power to be released in the life of the individual and a determined effort to let God guide him in disciplined behavior. These will bring about the needed changes in his present outlook and functioning as a Christian.

Steve Scott and Brooks Alexander also see various dangers in regard to emotionalism and faith visualization which may tend toward an occult working rather than the power of the Holy Spirit: "The overemphasis on particular techniques in the spiritual life easily becomes an attempt at psychic manipulation, an effort to *produce* an experience or encounter with God . . . . The use of the term 'faith visualization' does not semantically baptize such practices. The products of imagination can be all too conveniently brought into bondage to the will and ego, while the living Christ cannot. An extreme emphasis on the believer's spoken confession in the 'word of faith' movement is another such aberrant teaching which subtly becomes a species of borderline occultism. In its successive forms, faith visualization creates an 'inner-video Jesus' which can be manipulated to almost any end."[11]

Scott and Alexander correctly state that, "Inner healing *can* be consistently biblical," and they stress three major marks of spiritual integrity which they feel are vital to a balanced understanding of the subject. "*First*: Inner healing should touch the problem at its source. The individual should be freed from the whole of a particular memory and *the false meaning attributed to it* . . . . In fact, it is the 'continual sprinkling of His blood' that purges both the heart and the conscience from 'dead works' (Heb 9:14; 10:22) and sets us free from emotional bondage to those dead works in order to serve the living God.

"*Second*: Inner healing should break the patterns of habitual responses and behavior that are generated in reaction to an initial trauma. The person being healed should cooperate actively in this process instead of acting passively to the healer's instructions and manipulation.

. . . .

"*Third*: Inner healing should produce personal changes which are true to the Scriptural revelation of our new self in Christ. This should be combined with the stress on learning to trust what God says about us, instead of how we feel about ourselves . . . . As we understand how God sees us, as well as the provision he has made for our growth, we will begin to develop self-esteem that corresponds precisely to our reliance on Christ's righteousness rather than our own (Romans 12:3)."[12]

We are very much in agreement with their further statement, "We do not have to abandon a biblical viewpoint or compromise the Lordship of Christ in order to benefit from inner healing."[13] We, too, have many reservations about the basic theology and techniques of "the inner healing movement" especially carried on by neo-pentecostal people. Scott and Alexander have indicated, "Many of Jung's concepts have been employed in a 'charismatic' framework by people like John Sanford and Morton Kelsey."[14]

Thus we must be very careful to apply biblical evaluations to any methodology or procedures used in inner healing work. With proper safeguards there seems to be every reason to employ a ministry of healing of the memories (psychological healing or inner healing for peace) in the name of the Lord Jesus Christ and by the power of His atonement-resurrection.

We agree with Scanlan that the ministry of inner healing is a work of the Holy Spirit and should become a normal part of the life of the child of God who is growing toward maturity so, apart from a work of healing involving others, the Christian can experience forgiveness and peace. Scanlan challenges us to recognize that often the Holy Spirit is identifying areas of our lives which are not yet under the lordship of Jesus Christ and need to be brought under our Lord's control. It is not only a matter of receiving God's release from certain difficult areas of our lives relating to the past, but it is a sanctifying work of the Holy Spirit which is ongoing as we seek to grow up into Christlikeness.

NOTES

1. Gary Collins, *Christian Counseling* (Waco, Tx: Word Books, 1980). Also available from Word is *Christian Counselor's Library*, a manual and twenty-eight cassette tapes.

2. Jay Adams, *Competent to Counsel* (Nutley, NJ: Presbyterian and Reformed, 1970).

3. Lawrence J. Crabb, Jr., *Effective Biblical Counseling* (Grand Rapids: Zondervan Publishing House, 1977).

4. Cf. bibliography.

5. Steve Scott and Brooks Alexander, "Inner Healing," *Spiritual Counterfeits Project Journal,* April 1980, pp. 12-15.

6. Ibid., p. 5.

7. Ibid., p. 13.

8. Ibid., p. 13.

9. Michael Scanlan, "Inner Healing Reexamined," *Pastoral Renewal,* August 1980, p. 15.

10. Ibid., p. 14.

11. Scott and Alexander, op. cit., p. 14.

12. Ibid., p. 15.

13. Ibid., p. 15.

14. Ibid., p. 14.

"The refusal of modern 'enlightenment' to treat 'possession' as a hypothesis to be spoken of as even possible, in spite of the massive human tradition based on concrete experience in its favor, has always seemed to me a curious example of the power of fashion in things scientific. That the demon theory will have its innings again is to my mind absolutely certain."

— *William James.*

9

Overcoming Demonic Activity: The Meaning

The words of God through Paul demand grave attention and critical restudy by all Christians today: "Put on the whole armor of God, that you may be able to stand against the schemes of the devil. For our struggle is not against flesh and blood, but against rulers, against the powers, against the world forces of this darkness, against the spiritual forces of wickedness in heavenly places" (Eph 6:11-12). Many Christians have tended to accept these as words of warning about spiritual conflict and usually have spent more time with the description of the armor than with the source of the attack. Much of our warfare has been with flesh and blood, sadly sometimes with our brethren with whom we disagree. Paul declares by the Spirit that our real struggle is not with mortal beings like ourselves but with spiritual beings with supernatural power. This is a warning that evil spirits are used of Satan in his attack on Christians, and it forces us to look deeper into the matter of spiritual conflict in our lives because this is addressed to *Christians*.

THE TRUTH SETS US FREE

The position generally held today about demonic attack or invasion is somewhat parallel to the Corinthians' view in the first century about going into the temples of false gods and there participating in a meal. Some Corinthians held that ". . . we know that no idol is anything in the world, and that there is no God but one" (1 Cor. 8:4). Therefore these Corinthian Christians reasoned that there is nothing to an idol of a false god and no spiritual danger in eating food sacrificed to an idol *in* a pagan *temple*. (Paul does permit the eating of meat purchased in the market to be eaten at *home* without questioning the source, 1 Cor 10:25-31). But Paul corrects their thinking in chapter ten, "But I say, that the things which the Gentiles sacrifice, they sacrifice to demons and not to God: and I do not want you to become sharers with demons" (1 Cor 10:20). So the strong brothers in chapter eight, advanced thinkers, actually were terribly mistaken about the true nature of demonic involvement in the affairs of men.

Today among Bible-believing people there is some recognition that Satan is real and that demons are real or at least existed in the time of Christ and the apostles. Often these biblical facts are treated carelessly or minimized. Many Christians have little awareness of the power and depth of the devil's furious hatred of all Christians and his determined attacks on believers.

How we need to hear again the words of James Denny. Commenting on 2 Cor 4:1-6 he wrote, "To St. Paul the Gospel was a very great thing. A light issued from it so dazzling, so overwhelming, in its splendour and illuminative power, that it might well appear incredible that men should not see it. The powers counteracting it, 'the world-rulers of this darkness,' must surely, to judge by their success, have an immense malignity. . . . Paul's whole sense of the might and malignity of the powers of darkness is condensed in the title which he here gives to their head— 'the *god* of this world.' . . . the dominion of evil is not unlimited in duration; but while it lasts it is awful in its intensity and range.

"It does not seem an extravagance to the Apostle to describe Satan as the god of the present aeon; and if it seems extravagant to us, we may remind ourselves that our Savior also twice speaks of him as '*the prince* of this world.' . . . What sleepy conscience, what moral mediocrity, itself purblind, only dimly conscious of the height of the Christian calling, and vexed by no aspirations toward it, has any right to say that it is too much to call Satan 'the god of this world'? Such sleepy consciences have no idea of the omnipresence, the steady persistent pressure, the sleepless malignity, of the evil forces which beset man's life.

They have no idea of the extent to which these forces frustrate the love of God in the Gospel, and rob men of their inheritance in Christ. . . . What St. Paul saw, and what becomes apparent to everyone in proportion as his interest in evangelizing becomes intense, is that evil has a power and dominion in the world, which are betrayed, by their counteracting of the Gospel, to be purely malignant—in other words, Satanic—and the dimensions of which no description can exaggerate."[1]

Even more ignorance exists about the deception and cunning of the devil and his fallen angels. This accounts for much of the failure in the lives of many Christians and the tragic collapse of those who once knew the Lord and then fell away. Failure to identify the enemy and his strength is one of the surest roads there is to defeat.

We emphatically agree with Jack Cottrell's concerns, "I am concerned for those who are harassed by evil spirits to the point that they suffer physical, emotional, or spiritual pain. I am concerned for the many who are consigned to mental hospitals because their real problem is undiagnosed. I am concerned about those who have been deluded by demonic miracles and have accepted demonic doctrines given by demonic inspiration. I am concerned because the church is not sounding an adequate warning against the real dangers that exist today in this area, and because the church is largely unprepared to help those who are suffering from demonic oppression."[2]

This state of ignorance is due not only to the dreadful lack of knowledge of what the Bible teaches but to the widely held opinion that demons are not very active today and do not attack Christians. Indeed, *some Christians* assume that Christians have somehow achieved an immunity to demonic attack and blithely declare that Christians cannot be harassed, invaded, or oppressed by the demons. If this is true, then of course the words of Paul to the Ephesian Christians must be declared to be irrelevant to our day (Eph 6:11-12).

Scriptures do not teach that demons have ceased to exist or to have discontinued their hateful attacks upon believers and unbelievers. Whether or not their power has been diminished by the power of the gospel is a moot question, though the greater power of Christ in a human life is certainly a glorious and victorious reality. "You are from God, little children, and have overcome them; because greater is He who is in you than he who is in the world" (1 John 4:4). It is the conviction of those in deliverance ministries that Christians need to have a far greater understanding of demonic attack and invasion than they do and a firm assurance that through Christ we can be more than conquerors of even demonic, invisible, supernatural powers.

SCRIPTURAL TEACHING ABOUT DEMONIC ACTIVITY

The evidence is quite clear that in the time of Christ and the apostles Jews and Gentiles, believers and unbelievers experienced attack and control from demons. Mark reports an incident in a synagogue, ". . . a man with an unclean spirit . . . cried out, saying, 'What do we have to do with You, Jesus of Nazareth? Have You come to destroy us? I know who You are—the Holy One of God!' And Jesus rebuked him, saying, 'Be quiet, and come out of him!' And throwing him into convulsions, the unclean spirit cried out with a loud voice, and came out of him. And they were all amazed, so that they debated among themselves, saying, 'What is this? A new teaching with authority! He commands even the unclean spirits, and they obey Him!'" (Mark 1:23-27). This is typical of the frequent encounters of our Lord with demoniacs as reported in the gospel accounts (Matt 8:16, 28; 9:32; Luke 13:11-13, 16, etc.). Peter summarizes this great work of Christ by stating that Jesus was "healing all who were oppressed by the devil; for God was with Him" (Acts 10:38).

Our Lord Jesus Christ also gave His apostles power over demons obviously because there was a great need of this ministry among the people. "And He appointed twelve, that they might be with Him, and that He might send them out to preach, and to have authority to cast out the demons" (Mark 3:14-15). Later the seventy disciples were sent out with Christ's authority; and they "returned with joy, saying, 'Lord, even the demons are subject to us in Your name'" (Luke 10:17-20). The expulsion of demons in the name of Christ continued in the apostolic church (Acts 5:16; 8:7; 16:16-18; 19:11-16).

The apostles issued some specific and sharp warnings to Christians in regard to the attack of evil spirits as Paul wrote to the Corinthians, "but I say that the things which the Gentiles sacrifice, they sacrifice to demons and not to God, and I do not want you to become sharers in demons" (1 Cor 10:20). *The Amplified Bible* translates, "I do not want you to fellowship *and* be partners with diabolical spirits [by eating at their feasts]. [Deut. 32:17.]". The Greek word translated here as sharers or fellowship is the same word (*koinonos*) that Peter uses when he says that Christians "become partakers of the divine nature" (2 Pet 1:4). Thus we Christians have a stern warning from God that involvement in demonic worship through idolatry could lead us to be partakers of demonic nature, in other words to be demonized.

Again Paul warns, "But the Spirit explicitly says that in the later times some will fall away from the faith, paying attention to deceitful spirits and doctrines of demons" (1 Tim 4:1).[3] Here is positive evidence that some *Christians* (having faith) will fall away from the faith in the Lord Jesus Christ through the activity of demons. One may attempt to evade the severe thrust of this passage by saying that these Christians will only fall away because they are influenced by deceitful spirits, but it certainly indicates a powerful *control* that brings about their destruction.

In the same vein John forewarns Christians, "Beloved, do not believe every spirit, but test the spirits to see whether they are from God; because many false prophets have gone out into the world" (1 John 4:1). John agrees with Paul that evil spirits will be actively working against Christians to the end of the age and can speak through the false prophets. These men appear to be Christians and maybe are or have been Christians.

Not everyone accepts the teaching of Revelation 12:7-12 as referring to our time, but we believe it is appropriate to these days which have so much evidence of the working of the devil. Many see the unusual rise in Satanism, occult activities, false religions and Eastern mysticism along with the tragic breakdown of biblical Christianity as pointing to the time of the devil's great wrath against God's people, "knowing that he has only a short time."

In vain do we search for a Scripture that grants Christians *full* immunity from the attacks or invasions of Satan. All of us know too well the external attacks of Satan which Paul calls "the flaming missiles of the evil one" (Eph 6:16). Also, we know that we sometimes sin grievously and that it comes as a shock to everyone including ourselves. Most Christians believe that believers can fall from grace, deny the Lord who bought them, and make shipwreck of the faith (Gal 5:1-4; 1 Tim 1:19; Heb 6:1-6; 2 Pet 2:1; 3:17). In the process of doing these heinous sins the influence of demons is readily apparent. Their invasion and control of brethren may account for the tragic apathy among Christians and for the shocking collapse of some brethren. Such destruction among Christians of maturity must have some adequate explanation. Demonic control from within the Christian is an adequate, and we believe the only adequate, cause for such a deadly effect.

That believers in God have been at some time invaded by evil spirits is seen in four specific cases. King Saul was invaded by demons who from time to time took control of him (1 Sam 16:14). In the ministry of Christ He released a "daughter of Abraham" who was bent double by an evil spirit of Satan for eighteen years (Luke 13:11-16). An apostle of Jesus Christ, Judas Iscariot, companied with Him up to the last night of His life, yet Satan entered into him. He betrayed the Son of God into the hands of His enemies (John 13:27).

The case of the Christian in the Corinthian congregation who became a terrible sinner through incest needs to be squarely and seriously faced by all who deny the reality of demonic invasion of believers. One cannot say that this man was not a Christian, for no such statement is made by the apostle Paul. Instead, this man through his sin now belongs to Satan and must be delivered to Satan for the destruction of the flesh that his spirit may be saved. Since he had allowed Satan to rule over him and there was no repentance, the congregation must remove him from their midst and allow Satan to possess him for the purpose of saving his spirit. We believe this is a clear illustration of those Christians described by Paul who need to "come to their senses and escape from the snare of the devil, having been held captive by him to do his will'' (2 Tim 2:26).

From this brief survey of some of the New Testament evidence we may draw the conclusions that the devil and his fallen angels are on the earth (Rev 12:9), are in an all-out attack upon God's people (Rev 12:12-13; Eph 6:12), and that Christians stand in real danger of being tempted, attacked, and even controlled by evil spirits *if* they are not careful to be fully protected by the whole armor of God and the blood of the Lord Jesus Christ (2 Pet 2:1-22). Demons are real and energetic enemies of the people of God, but Christians can overcome demonic attack. ''But they overcame him [Satan] because of the blood of the Lamb and because of the word of their testimony, and they did not love their life even to death'' (Rev 12:11). ''You are from God, little children, and have overcome them; because greater is He who is in you than he who is in the world'' (1 John 4:4).

PRESENT DAY EVIDENCE OF DEMONIC ATTACKS

In the light of the Scriptures we have studied we find sufficient reasons to believe that demons will actively attack both sinners and saints today. No Christian has immunity to temptation, and Paul tells *Christians* to have the shield of faith in place to ''be able to extinguish all the flaming missiles of the evil one'' (Eph 6:16). There is no statement of Scripture to indicate that Christians are incapable of being harassed or even invaded by evil spirits *if they give grounds* to evil spirits.

Indeed, there is an abundance of evidence that many are suffering from demonic oppression today. Dr. Jack Cottrell declares, ''We must admit that demons are active today simply because the evidence for it is overwhelming. The abundant testimony of competent eyewitnesses leaves us no other choice. The only sufficient explanation for a virtual mass of related phenomena is that they have been caused by demons.''[4]

We have empirical evidence that Christians have been invaded by evil spirits, for we have extensive notes on the more than one hundred fifty with whom we have worked in securing a

deliverance by the Lord Jesus Christ.[5] Some audio tapes of actual
deliverance sessions were made in which one can hear the evil
spirits speaking through the mouths of Christian brothers and
sisters. Merely listening to the tapes will rapidly convince most
Christians that Christians can be invaded.

Our testimony is grounded in literally hundreds of hours of
deliverance work where we have experienced the most wonderful
liberation of Christians from the control of evil spirits. This
clinical and autoptical evidence has convinced us of the possibility of some demonic control of *some* part of a Christian's
body, mind, or will even though we began the work in a very
skeptical mindset. We have been reared in a tradition that taught
that demons could not invade or control people and certainly
not Christians. Severe questioning and review of the whole
matter of the deliverance work were continued for several
months as we tested every conceivable theory of explanation
for what was happening. The only explanation that was systematically consistent and in harmony with the Word of God
was that our brothers and sisters had been invaded by evil
spirits.

As we worked with our brothers and sisters who were to some
extent in bondage to Satan, we found that at some period in
their lives, often before they became Christians, they had opened
a door to evil spirits by an act of their will. They had sinned
and by going with Satan and to him for pleasure, power, or
knowledge they had given the devil legal rights or grounds to
some part of their body, mind, or will. (This will be explained
in detail later in the chapter.) We found that there were levels
of control in an increasing measure from obsession to oppression
to possession. Dr. Merrill Unger declares that a realistic view
is that "grievously sinning saints (and such there are) may go
beyond the old nature. In cases of serious, persistent, scanda-
lous sin, such as gross immorality or participation in occultism
or occult religionism, demons may exercise control over the
believer for a time until his sin is confessed and forsaken and
deliverance from the evil powers is gained."[6]

Unger goes on to give some of the large amount of testimony
of competent Christian workers and scholars that establishes

the reality of demonic control in the lives of Christians around the world. He states, "Certainly the inspired Word of God never contradicts valid experience. The sincere truth-seeker must be prepared to revamp his interpretation to bring it into conformity with facts as they are.

"This is exactly what I have been compelled to do in the course of the years. In *Biblical Demonology* which was first published in 1952, the position was taken that only unbelievers are exposed to demonization. . . . As a result, in my study of the present day outburst of occultism entitled *Demons in the World Today*, which appeared in 1971, the confession is freely made that the position taken in *Biblical Demonology* was 'inferred since Scripture does not clearly settle the question'."[7]

Denial of the reality of demonic invasion today simply cuts the Christian off from offering the ultimate help available in the name of the Lord Jesus Christ in setting free other Christians who are in desperate need of deliverance from bondage. To deny the reality of demonic intrusion[8] today may be theologically comforting to a person but is a tragic "cop-out" to the actual needs of people. To our knowledge almost all *deniers* of the reality of demonic control today have never been involved with demoniacs or in deliverance work. As K. Neill Foster notes, "Christian believers do not need to go around ducking demons and cowering with fear. But they need to be careful. If Satan is given ground, he takes it. And he does so regardless of theological niceties."[9]

Again we would very lovingly and humbly remind those who so strongly deny that Christians may have evil spirits in their bodies that the devil is the great deceiver. One must be on guard that his theological belief is not subtly influenced by the father of lies who would have every reason to protect his demonic invaders from detection and expulsion. Opposition to the mounting evidence for demonic intrusion in Christians may say more than one thinks about the reality of the control Satan can have.

We who have been actually involved in deliverance work and have seen the incredible cleansing power of the Lord Jesus Christ at work against the indwelling demons have simply admitted that we underestimated the grace and power of our

Deliverer (Heb 2:14-16). It was impressed upon us that the blood of the Lord Jesus Christ never loses its power over the demonic powers—"When He had disarmed the rulers and authorities, He made a public display of them, having triumphed over them through Him" (Col 2:15). Christ is more than sufficient to give Christians victory in the spiritual warfare they are facing daily. This should not surprise us because the infinite power and love of God is so far beyond our finite conceptions. Paul said it clearly, "Now to Him who is able to do exceeding abundantly beyond all that we ask or think, according to the power that works with us. . ." Eph 3:20).

If those of us who are willing to "test the spirits to see if they are of God" (1 John 4:1) and who have clinical evidence of demonic invasion are correct in our observations and conclusions, then why not leave behind the handed down tradition and rejoice greatly in the Lord who has not left us powerless against evil spirits? All can praise the Lord in the "discovery" that through the ordinary means of grace all the power that is needed to break Satanic control over an individual through the authority of Jesus Christ is available. We invite all to soberly examine the evidence that is so extensive and easily accessible and allow that God is doing more than we ever anticipated. If the evidence is cogent, within the teaching of the Word of God, exalts Jesus Christ, honors the triune God, and sets Christians free of Satanic bondage, let us accept the truth without delay.

CONSIDERATION OF THREE MAJOR OBJECTIONS

When Paul and Barnabas returned to Antioch and "gathered the church together, they began to report all things that God had done with them and how he had opened a door . . ." (Acts 14:27). Note the emphatic word GOD. The apostles for all their great position and miraculous powers knew that only GOD had done the work and opened the door. The door of faith opened to the Gentiles scandalized some of the Jewish Christians who could scarcely believe that God would do such a thing. Similarly the door of faith that God has opened through some who are willing to take Him at His word in delivering people from demonic control scandalizes some Christians today.

Why is it that good Christians and intelligent leaders are so scandalized by the testimony that the Lord Jesus Christ is working in a way which they have not experienced and beyond what they thought He might do? All of us are too slow to realize how strongly our traditional teaching may prejudice us to new truth, yet it is something that happens to all of us. We assume too easily that we have been correctly taught and whatever we hold is true, orthodox, and final; therefore anything that contradicts "our truth" must be false. It is easy, then, to dismiss another view without examination. The first struggle in growing in grace and knowledge is to throw out our prejudgments and to honestly research the data that is being presented. As we may not be one hundred percent correct, so the other brother may not be one hundred percent wrong.

Both Unger and Cottrell have declared that they have changed their minds because of the evidence just as we were forced to do. "About ten years ago, however, I changed my mind," Cottrell stated. "I am convinced that demons are hard at work in many ways today, particularly in the area of the occult. I am also convinced that skepticism and ignorance about demonic activity today pose a threat even to Christians. Thus I am convinced that we need to be made aware of the reality and the nature of the work of demons in our age."[10]

Also, as sinful people we can very easily fall into the trap of limiting God or denying His Word. Jesus warned outstanding men of His day about this error, "Is this not the reason you are mistaken, that you do not understand the Scriptures, or the power of God?" (Mark 12:24). Our finite concepts or rationalistic presuppositions can lead us to deny the power of God, and this is true not just in the realm of the super-human working of God but even in the providential area. Perhaps this arises from a fear of God if we cannot control Him or know precisely what He is going to do. Basically this is idolatry, for the God of the Bible is in charge absolutely and sovereignly. All of us must be keenly aware of the false and dangerous delusion of putting God in our little boxes as J. B. Phillips noted in his book, *Your God is Too Small.*[11]

Three heavy and primary arguments opposing present day deliverance from demonic oppression are 1. that miraculous power (a charismatic gift) does not exist for such work today and is required; 2. that Christians cannot be invaded by evil spirits or have any measure of demonic control of their lives; and 3. that Satan has been bound by Christ's death and resurrection (Rev 20:1-2). Let us objectively and scripturally investigate these major objections to see if they are valid.

Miraculous Power is Required

Many Christians have concluded (we believe correctly) that the Lord Jesus Christ does not now choose to work miracles equal in uniqueness (nature) to the miracles reported in the New Covenant Scriptures. There is no question about His power and freedom to do anything that pleases Him, but the Word of the Lord seems to indicate a voluntary limitation on His part of doing the stupendous miracles such as He did to authenticate and credential the ministry of Christ and the apostles (Heb 2:1-4).[12] Assuming that this theological position is correct or allowing it to stand for the sake of the argument, yet men proceeded to fall into two grave errors.

On the one hand they forgot that even if God wills not to work miraculously (in the New Testament denotative meaning of the word) that does not mean that He cannot answer the prayers of His people in remarkable and extraordinary ways through His power through providence. It is the old story of Mark 12:24 of ignorance or unbelief about the promises of God and doubt or unbelief about God's power to give special providences of extraordinary measure. Those in a deliverance ministry for the Lord Jesus Christ are doing it only by their faith in the "immeasurable greatness of the power at work within those who believe," the power of God that raised Jesus Christ from the dead (Eph 1:19-20). It is simply making the most of the "prayer of faith" that brings healing to the sick Christian (James 5:15).

The second grave error made by opponents of the deliverance work of Christ is the argument that demons can be removed from people only by *miraculous* power. But this is based on an *inference* from scriptural premises, and we hold that the inference is invalid. Certainly it is clear that Christ, the apostles, and seventy cast demons out by the finger of God, i.e., divine miracle power. But the Scriptures do not teach that demons can be expelled *only* by miraculous power, and the objection is a philosophic one. God can work mightily and remarkably beyond the ordinary without exercising His highest power in specific miracle action. This is the confirmed experience of all of us who have humbly and in faith believed in Christ's all-sufficiency to deliver people from the enslavement to the devil and have actually observed the deliverances taking place.

It is a difficult and delicate work to try to explain the differences between the supernatural working of God *through* providential *means* and the sheer miraculous power of God *apart* from all means. Many get upset trying to make distinctions and impatiently lump all answers to prayer as miraculous. It is easier that way but not necessarily better as it can end in confusion relative to biblical teachings. We see the working of God according to natural (scientific) laws in His ordinary providence as He blesses the seed in the ground with rain and sunshine to produce a crop. On a higher plane we see a special providence of God in regard to prayer when all human means have been employed wisely and there is no improvement. God may then interpose His gracious and supernatural power to effect a restoration to life when the doctors fully expected death to occur. Yet there is the use of means and of time to effect recovery of health and strength. On the highest level God works a miracle apart from human means which is characterized by its instantaneousness, magnitude, and total success. The raising of Lazarus after being dead for four days is a clear exhibit of what we mean by a miracle in a unique and biblical sense.

Several things about our deliverance work indicate that it is not by the miraculous power of God or any miracle gift given to us even though it is done by the supernatural power of Almighty God in answer to prayer and the use of the means He has given, the anointing with oil. First, we depend solely upon prayer for the Lord Jesus Christ to heal the person, and there are occasions when He does not answer the requests affirmatively. This may be because of an impenitent heart, a failure to commit the whole issue to Christ, or some other conditions. Second, our work is done only with Christians while both Christ and the apostles cast evil spirits out of unbelievers or those not Christians. Third, the evil spirits are able to resist us, and a considerable period of time is often required with much prayer and waiting upon the Lord Jesus Christ before the demons are expelled. This is in marked contrast to the single command of Christ or the apostles for the complete deliverance of the person from all demons. Fourth, we have not experienced any special miraculous power or gift at work within us and have been totally dependent upon God's honoring our use of Scripture reading, prayers of faith, hymns, and the anointing with oil.

Christians Cannot Have Evil Spirits in Them

The heavy and primary objection to the deliverance ministry among Christians is the conviction that Christians cannot have evil spirits or be invaded by them. Dr. Richard D. Dobbins expresses such contentions in his book, *Can a Christian be Demon Possessed?*[13] He declares that the answer must be no, and in *one* sense we would agree with him. We do not believe that a genuine Christian can be *possessed,* a very strong word indicating almost complete control of a person's body, mind, and will as in the case of Legion (Mark 5:1-16). But when possessed is replaced by the words invasion, obsession, and oppression; then we believe the objective evidence requires a clear answer of "Yes."

Dr. Dobbins states that these pheonomena that are often attributed to the action of evil spirits are really just the problems of behavior that Paul would classify as works of the flesh. Yet these works of the flesh when persisted in and allowed to become habitual in the life of the Christian can bring demonic control and then invasion of the child of God. We simply have so much clinical, empirical evidence as verification that the supposition is overthrown by the facts.

Perhaps the most often used argument is that evil spirits simply cannot inhabit the same body as the Holy Spirit. Some would use 2 Corinthians 6:14-18 to try to prove that since believers are forbidden to be in fellowship with unbelievers, the Holy Spirit would not permit evil spirits to share the same body with Him. Yet is this any greater a problem than how believers can often commit sin, daily be disobedient and imperfect, and grieve the Holy Spirit while all the time the Holy Spirit is in us? We are all in a process of sanctification, and the Holy Spirit is taking over more and more of our mind, soul, will, and body.

Dr. Unger meets this objection by asserting, "In His atoning death, Christ secured a judicial sentence against 'sin in the flesh' (Ro 5:10; 8:3), so that the infinite holiness of God is not in the least compromised by the Holy Spirit's indwelling saved sinners. Similarly, the Spirit's infinite holiness is not compromised by an invading demon spirit."[14]

Like a number of those who from a theoretical and dogmatic posture contend that Christians cannot be invaded (or have residual evil spirits left over from their pre-Christian life in Satan's kingdom—Colossians 1:13), we find that Dr. Dobbins assumes that we teach that a believer can be invaded *against* his own will. Then he argues that the Holy Spirit is unable to come into a Christian without the willingness of the Christian to invite the Holy Spirit in. From these two premises he draws the conclusion that evil spirits must be more powerful than the Holy Spirit *if* they can invade the Christian without his consent.

Two important truths must be kept in mind, and these refute the above assumptions. First, God is pure and virtuous while evil spirits are ruthless, vicious, and unscrupulous. Demons will take full advantage of every opportunity they can seize or get by deception to control the child of God who *listens* to them. God respects our will and does not force Himself upon us. Second, we recognize that invasion is accomplished only when the Christian has *opened up* his heart and life to evil. *He* has made the choice by an act of his *own will*.

Because most people are so naive about the presence and subtle working of evil spirits upon them and so many Christians believe they are immune from satanic attacks, we simply have to give an extended quotation from Jessie Penn-Lewis and

Evan Roberts about the clever deceptive power of demons. We know from our experience that their testimony is perceptive and true.

"If a man who is untaught in the Scriptural statements of the work of the Triune God makes to 'obey the Spirit' his supreme purpose, the deceiver will aim to counterfeit the guidance of the Spirit, and even the presence of the Spirit Himself. . . . Those who have their eyes open to the opposing forces of the spiritual realm, understand that very few believers can guarantee that they are obeying *God* and *God only in directly supernatural guidance,* because there are so many factors liable to intervene, such as the believer's own mind, spirit, or will, and the deceptive intrusion of the powers of darkness . . . . .

. . . .

"At some time when the believer is yearning for the SENSE of God's presence, either alone, or in a meeting, and certain conditions are fulfilled, the subtle foe approaches, and wrapping the SENSES round with a soothing, lulling feeling—sometimes filling the room with light, or causing what is apparently a 'breath from God' by a movement of the air—either whispers, 'This is the presence you have longed for,' or leads the believer to infer that it is what he has desired.

"Then, off his guard, and lulled into security that Satan is far away, some thoughts are suggested to the mind, accompanied by manifestations which appear to be Divine; a sweet voice speaks, or a vision is given, which is at once received as 'Divine guidance', given in the 'Divine presence,' and hence beyond question as from God. If accepted as from God, *when from the spirits of evil,* the first ground is gained.

"The man is now so sure that God has bidden him to do this or that. He is filled with the thought that he has been highly favoured of God, and chosen for some high place in His Kingdom. The deeply hidden self-love is fed and strengthened by this, and he is able to endure all things by the power of this secret strength. He has been spoken to by God! He has been singled out for special favour! *His support is now within upon his experience, rather than upon God Himself, and the written word. . . .*

"Some of the suggestions made to the believer by deceiving spirits at this time may be: (1) '*You are a special instrument for God*', working to feed self-love; (2) '*You are more advanced than others*', working to blind the soul to sober knowledge of itself; (3) '*You are different from others*', working to make him think he needs special dealing by God; (4) '*You must take a separate path*', a suggestion made to feed the independent spirit; (5) '*You must give up your occupation, and live by faith*', aiming at causing the believer to launch out on false guidance, which may result in the ruin of his home, and sometimes the work for God in which he is engaged."[15]

We have seen this deception carried out in the lives of some of those we have worked with in precisely these developments and thoughts.

Second, no one known to us who is in a ministry of deliverance believes or teaches that a believer is invaded *contrary to his will.* It is *because* the believer opens himself by his voluntarily going to Satan in violation of God's will to get what God will not give him that allows demons the right to invade him. It is by man's own foolish, nay, sinful choice that he is brought into captivity to Satan to do his will.

From our experience we know that Unger is right when he affirms, "Dare we be so naive as Christians to believe that demonic powers will not press their claims to the limit in any life? How much more in the case of the child of God! Failing to count on what he is in Christ, neglecting to use his resources in warfare, and, above all, opening the door to the enemy by serious and persistent sin, does the believer dare to presume that he will not be attacked, defeated, oppressed, or even invaded by the enemy?"[16]

A final argument is advanced by Dr. Dobbins who well represents the opponents to the reality of demonic invasion of Christians. Using the statement of Jesus about the binding of the strong man (Matt 12:24-29), he believes that Jesus is able to bind "the strong man" because He is stronger. Then he reasons that Christians are completely set free from Satan's (the strong man) grip, because they are Christ's. To teach otherwise is to declare that demons in their lives are stronger than Christ Himself.

As touching our salvation, this is true. We belong to Christ and are temples of the Holy Spirt, but as touching our sanctification it may not be true. Indeed, we have found that in over one hundred and fifty Christians it *was* not true. Dobbins' position does not adequately deal with the realities of Satan's power which is *allowed* by God Almighty. In many conversions to the Lord Jesus Christ all satanic control is removed from the born again believers. But in other lives it simply does not take place. This is not because the demonic spirits are greater than Christ but that they have a *legal* (God granted in His moral universe) right to hold on to the individual who earlier gave them that right through submitting to Satan or making an agreement (even tacitly) with him. The Christian may need to grow in the Lord and in surrendering all areas of his life to the control of the Holy Spirit. Then he may be aware of the control that some evil spirit does have in him, and he will at once seek to have it removed through the procedure of James 5:14ff. through the full authority of his real Lord, Jesus Christ. We know Christians who know that an area of their lives is not in submission to Christ but who refuse to do anything about it.

Of course all of us are shocked by the idea that Christians may be to *some* degree controlled by evil spirits. We would prefer to believe otherwise, but it is irrational to deny the phenomena which is so widely supported by evidence from credible witnesses. It is time we admitted that our well-meaning teachers were ignorant of the evidence for demonic invasion and were mislead by erroneous interpretation of certain Scriptures. When there is mounting evidence that one may have cancer, the worst thing he can do is to refuse to have a medical examination to determine the truth.

What is the evidence now available to the investigator? First, there is our clinical evidence with Christians who have been amazed to find that they had some demonic control. One brother found that his anger and fear were not "just a part of my personality" but had demonic reenforcement. Another Christian found that he had evil spirits controlling such parts of his life as greed, rage, deception, and closemindedness. Before deliverance he had no idea that his major problems in these areas were powerfully influenced by demons. Still another brother found that by allowing hate, resentment, and bitterness to become dominant in his life he had been brought into bondage in these very areas of behavior.

Consider this testimony from a Christian woman who has experienced deliverance from Christ. "In March of '79 when we first met I was so deep in sin and so very numb in all emotions that I didn't feel even slight emotions that should have been there and the demons were so much of my own personality that they could manifest themselves at any time and no one would be able to tell unless they had known me years before. . . . I understand better now because after each session more of my emotions and mental alertness strengthen. At that point I had not been around but a few people in the past five years and that last year I had lived so closely with those demons that I was very much like them. . . . During the summer my personality became that of one of the demons that I used to hear frequently. It was like a snotty, obnoxious kid. I didn't realize I had a perverted pride until later. . . . I can now look at myself and see that there is a person there, and a Christian, amazed and very joyful that she is loved by Abba, Father and the Lord Jesus Christ is my brother."[17]

At this point we want to introduce some of the testimony of some of the expert witnesses verifying the reality of demonic invasion of Christians. Keep in mind that we are not using or agreeing with the use by some of the heavy word possession in connection with demonic activity in Christians because we do not believe a genuine Christian can be possessed.

Dr. Unger has testified about his definite belief in the possibility of demonic invasion in a Christian, and he adds the witness of another authority. "For many years the late chancellor of Wheaton College in Illinois, V. Raymond Edman, taught that a Christian under certain circumstances could be invaded by demonic powers. His firsthand experience with true demonism as a result of missionary labors in Ecuador in his earlier years, gave Dr. Edman an understanding of the subject sometimes not possessed by purely theoretical Bible interpreters."[18]

Another noted witness to the fact that Christians can be invaded by evil spirits and controlled by them to some measure is Dr. Kurt Koch. For forty years he has worked with people who have suffered from occult bondage and demonic control due to sin. He has worked with twenty thousand people and is recognized as the most outstanding authority in the world on this subject. Dr. Koch reports on a number of the cases he has worked with and cites with approval the testimony of Dr. Edman and Dr. Evans of Wales. Then he declares, "Although personally I am more inclined to take the side of those who believe in the possibility of a Christian being possessed, I sometimes think that there may be a way of bringing the two sides together, but whatever the case, in heaven all our quarreling will cease."[19]

Dr. Koch cites the evidence of a missionary he met in Africa "who had actually been possessed himself for a period of 18 months. He, like many others, had previously believed it impossible for Christians to be possessed."[20] This missionary "said later, 'God taught me a lesson, and cured me of being so inflexible in my ideas.'"[21]

Satan Has Been Bound

The third and final major objection is that Satan has been bound by Christ's death and resurrection so that he cannot attack or invade believers (Rev 20:1-3). This is a misinterpretation of this Scripture and does not afford any support to the argument against the reality of demonic invasion of Christians. While it is true that Christ has won the victory over Satan by His victorious death and resurrection (Rev 12:7-12), yet Satan is not *totally* bound or destroyed as *yet*. His doom is sure; his back is broken and he is in his death throes. Still his wrath is great, and he "prowls about like a roaring lion, seeking someone to devour" (1 Pet 5:8). Paul's warning is till urgently needed as he cries out, "For our struggle is not against flesh and blood, but against the rulers, against the powers, against the world-forces of this darkness, against the spiritual forces of wickedness in the heavenly places" (Eph 5:12).

The binding of Satan is limited in its scope during this present age and that limitation is stated, "so that he should not deceive the *nations* any longer" (Rev 20:3). Thus Satan is bound in reference to the nations, the state governments, and nothing is said to indicate that the devil is bound as regards individual Christians. "We must remember," Professor Ladd comments, "that the very idea of binding Satan is a symbolic way of describing a curbing of his power and activity; it does not mean his complete immobility. His incarceration in the abyss does not mean that all of his activities and powers are nullified, only that he may no longer deceive the nations as he has done through human history and lead them into active aggression against the saints during the thousand years."[22]

Carefully we have examined the three alleged grounds and primary objections to the reality of some Christians having within them evil spirits who usurp some of their lives and influence their behavior. Not one of the three objections has been found to be valid on the basis of logic or Scripture. The empirical evidence is positive, abundant, and from credible witnesses. It is time for all of us to face the fact that something is happening among Christians today which is strikingly parallel with cases of demonic affliction and control found in the New Covenant writings.[23] We are more than willing to share with every sincere investigator all that we have in the way of evidence for demonic control of the saints and the far greater reality that the Lord Jesus Christ can take all the evil spirits out of Christians when they are ready to receive His gracious deliverance.

THE MEANING OF SATANIC INVASION AND ITS CAUSES

It is quite important for the Christian to realize that though he may be invaded or oppressed because of giving grounds (reasons) to Satan for control, yet this does *not* mean that he was not or is not a Christian. Nor does it mean that he has lost his salvation in Christ. He may lose the "joy of Thy salvation" as David did, but he is not lost (Ps 51:12). A helpful analogy is to remember that a country like Russia can be invaded deeply by the French army under Napoleon and yet not be conquered or subjugated by the enemy. A Christian, even if invaded, has great resources from God to fight back against the power and control of Satan. Yet this fighting back and frequently losing is exhausting and dangerous for the Christian. We have known those who were worn out by the daily battle against demonic control of their lives and who wanted so much to be liberated from the grueling conflict. Christ's power to deliver His people from Satanic control is wonderful to behold. What a privilege to rejoice in the experience of the child of God being set free (Luke 4:18)!

We see the work of deliverance ministry as a very valuable means of *sanctification* and growth in the Lord (1 John 4:7-8). Paul speaks of our warfare with divinely powerful weapons "for the destruction of fortresses" which can very definitely include demonic forces and those within Christians. The word fortress is applied to God in the Old Covenant writings and so can have personal application to Satan and evil spirits in other contexts.[24] "We are destroying speculations and every lofty thing raised up against the knowledge of God, and we are taking every thought captive to the obedience of Christ" (2 Cor 10:4-5). This is a work of sanctification, and deliverance work can be an important instrument of God in achieving it.

If, however, the Christian does not fight back using all the spiritual armor God has provided and does not stand in the strength of the Lord (Eph 6:10-18), then he probably will be controlled increasingly by the devil. He may be invaded by other demons as he gives grounds for their entry. Even when a Christian does not give grounds per se, yet at a certain level of bondage to Satan and of spiritual weakness demons can invite or draw other demons in without grounds we have found. In the end a Christian may be brought to destructive unbelief or sin leading to a rejection of the Lord Jesus Christ. Or the Christian may get out of his misery by suicide. This is why the deliverance ministry is essential to the work of the Lord in our satanically-deceived society.

The ususal cause of demonic control over some area (and usually it is only a part of a person's life that is controlled) of personality, will, or body stems from that person's involvement in satanic-occult activities *before* he became a Christian. If a person has been involved actively with occult workings such as ouija board, tarot cards, witchcraft, astrology, fortune-telling, etc., then there is a strong possibililty that he has been invaded by demons. The regular use of drugs and narcotics opens the mind to Satan and often causes demonic oppression. Compulsive sins (e.g., fornication, stealing, lying, etc.) that become addictive and are continued even after knowing that they were violations of God's will can be legal rights for the devil to take control of some part of a person. False religions from Eastern mysticism through the cults to liberalism and humanism are very much used of Satan to bring people into bondage to him. Our modern world is loaded with many opportunities for people to give a door to Satan to enter and control them.[25]

Becoming a Christian will bring forgiveness of sins to the sinner through genuine faith, repentance, and baptism into Christ; *but* this often does not cancel the *specific* control over some area of his life if he has given the devil legal rights earlier. This may be parallel to the historical cases from Joshua's conquest to the present that conquering a territory or country may be successful but small bands of soldiers may hold out regardless of the conquest or a surrender document being signed. There may remain some pockets of resistance within the conquered territory that have to be specifically attacked and taken over.

If one goes to the devil for power, pleasure, knowledge, or favor, then the devil apparently has the right before God to claim the person in that area of his life because he wanted the devil, not God Almighty, to give something to him. It is a form of bargaining and has disastrous results. This is true of the Christian who seeks the devil's help in achieving any desired goal. For example, Christian leaders who become proud or lust for power may open themselves to possible invasion. Indeed, pride has been a frequent and powerful demon in various persons with whom we have worked.

A startling example of the ongoing demonic attack against Christians today appeared in *Leadership* magazine in 1982.

The author is a man in a preaching ministry with the church who illustrates in a dramatic way how demonic control and invasion can take place. This is an intense and true description of what it feels like to be demonically oppressed or obsessed, in this case with sex, one of the most treacherous and powerful of all the temptations of the devil. Please take to heart the words of this man who was in bondage for ten long years and the even worse experience of his godly fellow pastor. Demons are invading Christians!

"Ten years have passed since that awakening [to lust] in wintry Rochester, ten years spent never far from the presence of lust. . . . For ten years I have fought unremitting *guerrilla warfare.*

. . . .

"Kings had renounced their thrones, saints their God, and spouses their lifetime partners because of this strange *demon* of lust.

. . . .

"Some of you know what it is like to walk with your eyes at breast level . . . to yearn for chains on the outside of your motel room to keep you in—unless it comes with that most perverse of all modern inventions, the in-room porno movie. And you also know what it is like to wallow in the guilt of that *obsession,* and to cry and pray with whatever faith you can muster, to plead with God to release you, to mutate you, to castrate you like Origen—whatever it takes to deliver you. And even as you pray, luscious, bewitching images crowd into your mind.

. . . .

"At times the obsession has felt to me more like *possession.* I remember one time especially that scared me. I was in Washington, D.C. . . . I sauntered into a dark bar that advertised nude dancing. . . . One black girl weaved over to the part of the stage nearest my table.

"This was somewhat different from the other strip shows I had seen. There was no teasing or 'visual foreplay.' She was already naked, unashamedly so, and she wiggled maybe a foot from my head. She stared right into my eyes. This was so close, so intimate, that it seemed for a terrifying moment to be nearer a relationship than a performance. What I felt could only be called *possession*.

"I found myself—it seemed as though I had not made the decision, that *someone else's hands* inside mine were doing it— fumbling in my pocket, pulling out bills and stuffing them in a garter belt high up on her thigh.

. . . .

"Was I going crazy? Would I lose every worthwhile sensation in life? Was my soul leaking away? Was I becoming *possessed*?"[26]

The author shared his terrible condition with a very dear friend, a pastor of a very large church, and the man began to sob "great, huge, wretched sobs such as I had seen only at funerals. . . . I learned the truth. My friend was not sobbing for me; he was sobbing for himself. He began to tell me of his own expedition into lust. . . . my friend had tried it all: bondage, prostitution, bisexualism, orgies. . . .

"I saw my friend dozens of times after that and learned every horrific detail of his hellish life. . . . But I knew this man, I thought, as well as I knew anyone. His insights, compassion, and love were all more mature than mine. My sermons were like freshman practice runs compared to his. He was a godly man if I had ever met one, but underneath all that . . . my inner fear jumped uncontrollably. I sensed the *power of evil*.

. . . .

"I cannot tell you why I had to endure ten years of *near-possession* before being ready for deliverance. And, most sadly of all, I cannot tell you why my pastor friend has, since our conversation after New Hampshire, gone into an unbelievable skid toward destruction. His marriage is now destroyed. He may go insane or commit suicide before this article is published. Why? I do not know."[27]

[We believe that the teaching of Scripture and our experiences clearly indicate that this destruction is the result of a Christian giving Satan a ground for invasion, that Satan takes full advantage, and if there is no repentance and cessation of sin, then the person will become increasingly oppressed by demons.] The author finally told his wife and says, "For ten years she had watched an *invisible fog* steal inside me, make me act strange, pull me away from her." [That invisible fog was demonic, we feel, and is so descriptive of how the evil spirits can insidiously, quietly glide into the life of the willfully sinning Christian as these two pastors experienced because they knew what they were doing was sin.]

He concludes, "The war within still exists."[28] He lists a "Battle Strategy: Some Practical Advice," but he sadly fails to mention deliverance by the power of God through the procedure of James 5:14ff. We believe this would be of the greatest value for his victorious struggle with temptations to lust. Deliverance from invading demons does not free one of all temptations, but it does lessen the severity of the attack and removes the "pull," the "some one else," and the feeling of "possession." Christians can have ultimate victory over the fiery darts of the evil one.

In this chapter we have tried to set forth the scriptural teaching in regard to the activity of demons today and the confirmation of that teaching in our experience. We have investigated the three primary objections and have attempted to answer them adequately though not exhaustively. Finally, we have explained the meaning of demonic invasion and its cause. Now we are ready to consider what God is able to do about setting the captives free, and it is wonderful to behold (Luke 4:18).

NOTES

1. James Denney, "The Second Epistle to the Corinthians," *An Exposition of the Bible,* (Hartford, Ct: The S. S. Scranton Co., 1907) V, 754.

2. Jack Cottrell, "All About Demons: Who? What? When?" *The Lookout,* January 27, 1980, p. 7.

3. William Hendricksen declares, "Men will depart from the faith by *giving heed to seducing spirits and doctrines of demons.* As the context indicates (and see also I John 4:6 where 'the spirit of seduction' is contrasted with 'the Spirit of truth') these *spirits* are not men but *demons.* Like *planets* that seem *to wander* back and forth among the constellations, these spirits wander; moreover, *they cause men to wander.* They *seduce, lead astray.* By giving heed to them one is giving heed to *doctrines of demons* (cf. II Cor 4:4; Rev 13:11, 14)." *New Testament Commentary, Exposition of the Pastoral Epistles* (Grand Rapids: Baker Book House, 1957), p. 146.

4. Cottrell, op. cit., p. 7.

5. Working with this large number of people has involved hundreds of man-hours in deliverance sessions. Many hours were required because, according to the number of demons in a person and the rapidity with which Christ chose to expel them, anywhere from one session of an hour or several hours had to be held. Multiple sessions were found to be necessary in most cases. Also, it is not just young Christians or "weaker" Christians who may have been invaded. Demons have been found in old and young people, men and women. They have numbered from two evil spirits in a person to thousands in others. We have encountered the name Legion among these demons and quite appropriately as he may have several thousands under his command.

6. Merrill F. Unger, *What Demons Can Do to the Saints* (Chicago: Moody Press, 1977), p. 46.

7. Ibid., pp. 59-60.

8. The list of the various aspects of life that may be invaded and controlled by unclean spirits is almost endless. Many of the people we have worked with have admitted they had problems in various parts of their mental, moral, physical, and spiritual life; but they never identified that behavior with demonic control until they were actually tested by the Lord and His servants. Many think that these severe difficulties which they must fight against as Christians are just a part of their personality, inherited traits, or the way they happen to function. But compulsive and/or irrational behavior which is immoral or which constantly defeats the witness and integrity of the children of God is almost always evidence of either demonic harassment (external) or demonic control (internal). Among such "normal" and accepted problems may be fear, rage, anger, pride, confusion of the mind, hatred, lust, sex, homosexuality, temper, lying, gluttony, depression, resentment, infirmity, sickness, inferiority complex, and others.

9. K. Neill Foster, *Help! I Believe In Tongues*: A Third View of the Charismatic Phenomenon (Minneapolis: Bethany Fellowship, Inc., 1975), p. 155.

10. Cottrell, op. cit., p. 8.

11. J. B. Phillips, *Your God Is Too Small* (New York: Macmillan, 1965).

12. The Bible is explicit in teaching from Genesis to Revelation that the Lord God Almighty has willed to do miracles for the credentialing of His presence and of His revelation in men. It has been the consensus of believers throughout the ages that God specifically gave miracles to confirm and authenticate the men whom He sent to be the revealers of His will—prophets, the Lord Jesus Christ, and the apostles. Though the evidential value of miracles has often been denied by those with naturalistic presuppositions, the believer in a Christian, theistic world view has every reason for continuing to build upon the solid basis of the witness of Scripture.

Note just a few Scriptures that indicate the evidential value: Genesis 15:1-21; Exodus 3:2-15; 4:1, 8, 9, 29-31; Joshua 3:7-17; 1 Kings 18:30-39; Isaiah 7:10-17; 38:1-8; Luke 7:18-23; John 1:32-34; 5:36; 10:37; 15:24; Acts

2:22-24; 14:3; Romans 1:4; 2 Corinthians 12:12; Hebrews 2:1-4. These establish the fact that God has always been willing to give signs to His people to credential the messengers whom He had sent and to establish the divine character of the revelation which they gave. We hold that this is the primary but not the only purpose of the working of miracles by the messengers of God as set forth in the Bible. Therefore we would expect to find miracles clustering in abundance around the times when new revelations are given by God, and this is what the Biblical evidence reveals. During the exodus from Egypt and the giving of the Law God worked many signs and wonders. Likewise at the coming of the Lord Jesus Christ into the world and the establishment of the New Covenant many signs and wonders were wrought by God. This is our reason for believing that genuine miracles of the high order of the Biblical history are rare in our experience since the time of the apostles. Their essential mission has been accomplished since the completion of the revelation of God through the Lord Jesus Christ.

This view (called a dispensational view of miracles) is thoroughly argued by the noted scholar, B. B. Warfield. We recommend the serious student study the text, *Counterfeit Miracles,* and especially the first chapter, "The Cessation of Charismata," along with the numerous notes of documentation given at the end of the volume.

While there are about fourteen different words used to describe what is translated into English as miracle, the emphasis upon the Hebrew word *'oth* and the Greek word *semeion* (which mean "sign") point to the significant purpose of the mighty work of God. No other word expresses so clearly the basic purpose of all the miracles in Scripture as an attestation to the presence and the activity of God in accomplishing His work in redemption or in verifying the authenticity of the message that was given. Miracles are, indeed, God's signature on His Word attesting to its divine character.

13. Richard D. Dobbins, *Can a Christian be Demon Possessed?* (Akron, OH: Emerge, 1973).

14. Unger, op. cit., p. 51.

15. Jessie Penn-Lewis and Evan Roberts, *War On The Saints,* (Ft. Washington, PA: Christian Literature Crusade, 1977) abridged edition, pp. 39, 72-73.

16. Unger, op. cit., p. 73.

17. Letter to the authors, other data confidential.

18. Unger, op. cit., p. 61.

19. Kurt Koch, *Occult Bondage and Deliverance* (Grand Rapids: Kregel Publications, 1970), pp. 68-69.

20. Ibid., p. 67.

21. Ibid., p. 68.

22. George Eldon Ladd, *A Commentary on the Revelation of John* (Grand Rapids: William B. Eerdmans Publishing Co., 1972), p. 262.

23. Some Christians have fallen away into unbelief and then have been restored. Some have never been recovered. Others have been living for years with grievous sins of adultery, homosexuality, pornography, and pride in

control of their lives. Read Kurt Koch's books for many examples of invasion that he has dealt with over the years. The symptoms of the Gadarene demoniac (Mark 5:1-16) are definite indicators of the probability of demonic invasion even though his condition is best described as possession. There was supernatural strength, a resistance to God, speaking in another voice or as a different personality, irrational, bizarre, and antisocial behavior, self-inflicted injuries which in our observations are often suicidal tendencies, and clairvoyance or psychical powers. These conditions have been observed and dealt with by us and other workers.

24. Psalm 9:9; 31:2-3; 46:7; 48:3; Joel 3:16; Nahum 1:7.

25. We recommend McCandlish Phillips' excellent book on this subject, *The Bible, The Supernatural, and the Jews* (Minneapolis: Bethany Fellowship Inc., 1970). The chapter on "Stages and Degrees of Demonic Control" (pp. 164-184) is of particular interest.

26. (Name withheld), "The War Within: An Anatomy of Lust," *Leadershp,* III (Fall, 1982), pp. 32-35, 41. (Emphases added by us).

27. Ibid., pp. 42, 45.

28. Ibid., p. 47.

CAUTION

This material and procedures are intended to be used *only* by older Christians who are mature in the faith, especially qualified pastors/elders. Young, immature, and inexperienced persons attempting to do the work of deliverance lay themselves open to the strong possibility of *severe physical* or *spiritual harm*! It is best not to get into a ministry of deliverance unless the Lord Jesus Christ makes it *very clear* that He wants you to be involved!

10

Overcoming Demonic Activity: The Means, Preparation, and Procedure

The god of this world has moved powerfully to deceive this generation and to bring it into bondage to his will. With sorrow we have to admit that he has been alarmingly successful and that even some Christians have been taken captive, at least in part, to do his will. Our bodies can be invaded by bacteria that can cause serious illness and yet for a long time we may not be aware of it. As general weakness and lethargy increase, the body begins to fight the disease, but the feeling of ill health may be put up with for some time. Finally pain and severe symptoms of sickness appear, and we rush to the doctor. In some cases it is too late, for the disease has taken hold of vital organs of the body.

The body of Christ today has much weakness and is in ill health in actually carrying out the will of the Head though many do not want to admit it and others are blinded by the enemy. Its members, unbeknown to them, have in too many cases been invaded by evil spirits who sap the strength of the member and cause the whole body to function at a fraction of its strength according to God's will. Is the arm of the Lord God Almighty shortened so that He cannot deliver His people from demonic invasion today? Is He unwilling to help His people in their sickness? We believe the answer is a resounding *No*! We believe that God's power is as great as it always has been and that God is willing to honor the faith and the prayers of His people today as they claim the promises of His Word. The terrible danger to the Church of Christ today is the woeful ignorance of the people and their leaders about the reality of spiritual warfare and the necessity of combating the demons with all the weapons of God.

Jessie Penn-Lewis and Evan Roberts have written a most valuable book, *War On The Saints,* in which they thoroughly describe the deceptions of Satan and the attack of Satanic powers on those especially who are most committed to doing the will of God. They correctly state the truth about this deadly warfare. "It is therefore clear in Bible history that the manifestation of the power of God invariably meant active dealing with the satanic hosts; that the manifestation of the power of God at Pentecost, and through the Apostles, meant again an aggressive attitude to the powers of darkness; and ergo, that the growth and maturity of the Church of Christ at the end of the dispensation, will mean the same recognition, and the same attitude toward the satanic hosts of the prince of the power of the air; with the same co-witness of the Holy Spirit to the authority of the Name of Jesus, as in the early Church. In brief, that the Church of Christ will reach its high water mark, when it is able to recognize and deal with demon-possession; when it knows how to 'bind the strong man' by prayer; 'command' the spirits of evil in the Name of Christ, and deliver men and women from their power."[1]

In the past two decades there has been a growing recognition of the power and ministry of the Holy Spirit in the lives of Christians and the revival of a deliverance ministry among those who recognized the cosmic warfare that all Christians must face. We are convinced that the devil stepped in exactly as Penn-Lewis and Roberts wrote that he did in the Welsh Revival with excesses, errors, and delusions to subvert and destroy the true and proper emphasis upon the Holy Spirit's work in the life of Christians and the power of God to heal and restore people to health under James 5:14ff., including deliverance from demonic control. The extremes, excesses, and errors of neo-pentecostalism we reject; but we do not reject the truth that has been recovered however imperfectly, that God is calling us today to attack all the forces of evil in the power of the Holy Spirit.

THE SPIRITUAL MEANS THAT GOD EMPLOYS FOR DELIVERANCE

In chapters five and six you learned much about the meaning and use of the procedure for healing set forth in James 5:14

as we understand it. That is foundational to our bringing the full power of the Lord Jesus Christ to effect the liberating of the children of God who have been invaded by evil spirits. It is clear from what we have said that far more Christians have been invaded and deceived by Satan than we would have imagined before. Many of us have trouble with "sin which so easily entangles us" and that means that most of us need spiritual cleansing and healing. We are writing this book to help you, and especially elders, to know what to do about restoring you to the health that God wants for you.

Scriptural means employed in freeing a person from demonic control are not much different from those used to help Christians with various problems. The power and authority of the name which is above every name, the Lord Jesus Christ, is absolutely central to the work of deliverance. Everything is done in His name because it has proved to be true that "every knee shall bow of those in heaven, and on earth, and under the earth" (Phil 2:10). Even the demons must bow before Him and obey Him (Acts 16:18). In our experience demons have been forced to submit to our Lord Jesus Christ, to confess that He is their Lord and Conqueror and to leave the body of the Christian to go to Gehenna (hell).

Our work is done in complete confidence in Him who said, "All authority has been given to me in heaven and on earth" (Matt 28:18). We follow precisely Paul's command, "And whatever you do in word or deed, do all in the name of the Lord Jesus, giving thanks through Him to God the Father" (Col 3:17). Every prayer and command is given within the name of the Lord Jesus Christ and trusting in His finished work on Calvary's cross and the empty tomb.

Fervent and persistent prayer saturates our meeting with the demoniac. The burden of all the intercessions and petitions is our total dependence upon the power of the Lord Jesus Christ, giving Him all the glory and praise as He exercises His awesome power for the release of the one held captive by Satan. Complete submission to Christ and His will is repeatedly expressed and acted upon along with much praise and thanksgiving for each answer to prayer as the deliverance progresses.

Besides the use of the name of the Lord Jesus Christ in prayer and command, we constantly invoke the power of the blood of the Lord Jesus Christ; for it is the finished work of Christ on the cross that forever broke the power of Satan and his hosts (1 John 1:7; 3:8). The demons were conquered at the cross and through the empty tomb, and they know and even have been forced to acknowledge this fact. The Holy Spirit teaches very clearly that our overcoming the devil is in the blood of Christ. After the accuser of our brethren, the devil, had been cast down from heaven, Christians are assured of victory, "And they overcame him because of the blood of the Lamb and because of the word of their testimony, and they did not love their life even to death" (Rev 12:11). The evil spirits are bound by the blood of the Lord Jesus Christ and thus brought under His full control to obey Him. Often songs about the blood of Christ and scriptural passages are used with great effect against the demons, causing them to be brought under subjection to Christ and their resistance to be broken.

Of course, another essential means is the Holy Spirit, the divine Helper: "And in the same way the Spirit also helps our weakness; for we do not know how to pray as we should, but the Spirit Himself intercedes for us with groanings too deep for words" (Rom 8:26). Our prayers are offered in the light of this promise of Scripture, because we need the direction of the Holy Spirit in how we should pray and how we should proceed in difficult matters. Paul's words have been confirmed in our experience as God has granted us "according to the riches of His glory, to be strengthened with power through His Spirit in the inner man" (Eph 3:16). Though we do not have the unique miraculous power of the Holy Spirit, yet we believe very much that the power of the Holy Spirit given to each Christian is sufficient for our overcoming Satan. The remarkable experiences and wonderful care of God through the great number of deliverance sessions we know must come from the power and protection of the Holy Spirit.

The final means of God which we have used to allow the Lord to release people from Satan's bondage is the Word of God. The Scripture is called "the sword of the Spirit" (Eph

6:17) and is a very great part of the armor that God uses in over-coming the resistance of evil spirits. Time after time we have found that Heb 4:12-13 is true, "For the word of God is living and active and sharper than any two-edged sword, and piercing as far as the division of soul and spirit, of both joints and marrow and able to judge the thoughts and intentions of the heart. And there is no creature hidden from His sight, but all things are open and laid bare to the eyes of Him with whom we have to do." Even demons who try to stay hidden are finally exposed by the Lord and often by the reading of various parts of God's Word.

The demons hate the Word of God, so it is used extensively. In the opening of the session the Scriptures are read, and usu-ally one person will continue quietly to read Scriptures during the session. Demons can hear the Word even when it is being quietly read at some distance, and often they are brought into manifestation by such reading. They may cover the ears of the person invaded or shout out, "Shut up, I don't want to hear that." Demons have been brought out of hiding and into mani-festation by holding the Bible near the invaded person as it is read. This often has infuriated the demon so that he came into manifestation (took control of the person) and tried to tear the Bible apart. In several cases demons did succeed in ripping Bibles apart using the body of the demonized person to do so.

These are the means and powers from Almighty God that He has given us through the promises of His Word and that are available to all Christians who have the confidence in the God of all gods. You can employ these powerful weapons against Satan and his hosts—great faith in the triune God and the name of our Lord Jesus Christ, the power of His blood, the energizing of the Holy Spirit, and the Word of God. God has honored these mighty means in granting full deliverance from demonic strongholds even as Paul revealed the victorious power of God in our warfare, "For though we walk in the flesh, we do not war according to the flesh, for the weapons of our war-fare are not of the flesh, but divinely powerful for the destruction of fortresses. We are destroying speculations and every lofty thing raised up against the knowledge of God, and we are taking every thought captive to the obedience of Christ . . ." (2 Cor 10:3-5).

THE PREPARATIONS FOR DELIVERANCE

Please remember that mere men never have sent any demons out of people and into hell. It is entirely the work of the Lord Jesus Christ and by His all-power. The procedure and the words used are not the power and are not necessarily used in a standard form. There is no "magic" in the terms or in the statements. It is never a "ritual" that causes a deliverance of a person from a demon, but it is simply and solely the power of the Lord Jesus Christ working through the faith and prayers of His followers.

It is supremely important that anyone who is interested in this ministry or becomes involved in it should always work as a team of two or three. Only people of mature faith and deep consecration to the Lord should be used because there are dangers in working against the devil and demons. Of course no one is perfect or sinless, and God uses the efforts of the imperfect through the grace of our Lord Jesus Christ. People need to be instructed in all matters connected with the deliverance of people from demonic control. Pride is a very subtle counterattack of the devil against those who are involved in deliverance; because it is, indeed, an astonishing and wonderful work of Christ, a privilege to be involved in. All workers must pray much, ask the Lord to give them humility in the work, and watch out for one another's spiritual safety.

A deliverance cannot take place until there is clearly a demon that needs to be removed, so the first order is always to determine if the Christian has any behavior that appears irrational, compulsive, addictive, and anti-Christian. All Christians are tempted by the devil and his demons, and almost all Christians experience harassment from time to time. Some Christians may have surrendered their will, mind, or body or all three before they became Christians and sometimes after being Christians. If demons have invaded them, they need to be expelled.

The first thing is to check carefully to eliminate the possibility that the person's behavior is due to organic or medical conditions. Then the person needs to be examined to determine if the cause of the problems in his life are due to psychological causes. A considerable number of people will be found to have emotional difficulties and behavior problems because of these causes.

Yet there is a significant residue of people who have no known medical or psychological causes or who have not responded to those kinds of treatment. Christians are well aware that most problems of life are grounded in a spiritual condition, guilt, or sin. When there is no healing through medicine or psychiatry, the Christian leader becomes concerned that it is grounded in an inadequate or defective relationship with God and possibly some activity of the devil.

A Christian counselor will begin to do some investigating *if* the person is willing to work on getting rid of his problems. (If a person is not willing to do something about his obvious spiritual problems, nothing of any value can be done with him.) The examination will take two areas under consideration. What has this person experienced in the past which might have been used of the devil to enslave this person or some part of this person to him? Questions about occult involvement, Satan worship, witchcraft, false religions, and sin will have to be asked and answered truthfully.

Next the counselor will seek to identify symptoms of demonic control. These are known from the Scriptures and from the observation of demoniacs. There may be superhuman strength of body, changes in personality, irrational behavior, compulsive sins, hatred or fear of the name of the Lord Jesus Christ and Scripture, self-inflicted injuries, anti-social behavior patterns, inability to partake of the Lord's Supper, clairvoyance, or other mediumistic powers (Mark 5:1-15; Acts 16:16). A combination of these items when objectively determined can point to demonic invasion especially if there have been addictive sins in the individual's past life.

These qualities and factors are evaluated by a team of those who have worked with demoniacs to determine the actual condition of the person and his problem. The counselee is informed of our findings and may be encouraged to seek a session for testing for the presence of evil spirits. Prayers are offered for the person, and we wait for the Lord to lead this person to request a deliverance session. Nothing can be accomplished by working without the consent of the person who may be demonically invaded.

The final acts of preparation are twofold. In a conference the significance and action of James 5:14-16 is explained to the counselee. The necessity of a thorough confession of all his major sins and especially those addictive sins which may have given grounds for Satan's control is explained. This confession is verbal and is before one of the elders or some other mature Christian who can give guidance in the matter. All sins of bitterness, hatred, and resentment against others in his life must be confessed and forgiveness through the blood of Jesus Christ prayed for (Matt 6:12, 14-15). Next he needs to freely forgive those who have sinned against him and ask his merciful heavenly Father to forgive them also. Among those he may have to forgive are himself and God, because he may hold an unforgiving spirit toward himself or may blame God for His failure to act as he thought He should in various matters.

Confessing of sins is scriptural, and we have found it to be a great cleansing of the burdened heart of many believers who have testified to the fact that they now *know* that they are forgiven by Jesus Christ and that they are clean in His sight (James 5:16; Ps 32:1-7; 40:1-4). Such confession is a clear indication of one's trust in God and of a willing and obedient heart to follow God's Word. It also has the value of removing blocks and hindrances to the deliverance.

Of utmost importance is the genuine love and acceptance exhibited by the counselor at this point. The counselee must not only experience the love and acceptance by Abba, Father, but also full acceptance and empathy from the counselor no matter how vile or offensive the sins were that were confessed. The counselor must have his heart and life right with God to act in a Christlike way in accepting the sinful brother or sister (Gal 6:1-2; John 8:1-11). The overflowing riches of the grace of God need to be fully revealed to the counselee in word and loving acceptance.

Finally, the statement which we entitle, My Renunciation and Affirmation, is provided the counselee to read and study (cf. Appendix C). If he agrees with these declarations of truth and is willing to affirm them, he is asked to sign this document in the presence of the witnesses. This has proved to be a great assistance to the individual in establishing the depth of his submission to Christ alone and the utter repudiation of Satan as having any right to him. It also has proved to be a help in breaking the grounds or legal rights that demons may have asserted in the past for control over the individual. Occasionally we have had reason to refer to this paper when a demon has been very resistant and insistent that he has a right to the body of the Christian. This has brought rejoiners such as, "Ah, why did he sign that paper?" A copy of the Renunciation and Affirmation is given to the person to keep and to refer to when Satan might in the future counterattack and claim that he has some right to the person's life.

Now the counselee is ready to proceed to an active involvement in the actual testing for the presence of evil spirits in his life. A time and place are designated, and the meeting is committed to God with prayers by all involved.

THE PROCEDURE THAT GOD HAS HONORED IN EXPELLING DEMONS

The place for the actual deliverance session is important as it should be private, secure (locked) from interference, and as sound-resistant as possible. These are precautions that provide the counselee with a feeling of confidence and peace. It protects this very personal matter from prying eyes or listening ears.

When elders are working with women, it is also a wise safeguard to have a Christian sister present if at all possible or at least to be in the building. If present, she can be a worker and witness and to guard all from reproach. This sister can pray, quietly read the Scriptures and maybe sing softly while the men are praying to the Lord to expel the demon. Specific prayers are given at the beginning to praise and thank God, to make a total commitment of everyone to the Lord Jesus Christ, to have our Lord take complete charge of the meeting, and to bring the demons under Christ's authority. Always we pray for the Lord Jesus Christ to completely bind the body of the person to the chair so it cannot move except at God's command. A strong and specific declaration is made that we are deliberately working only and entirely from within the Name of the Lord Jesus Christ, depending upon His power and authority. We also specifically reject and repudiate all occult, psychological, psychic, or other means or power of achieving a victory over the evil spirits. (Please consult appendix D for a more detailed account of the prayers.)

Hymns are sung about the glory of God, the power of the Lord Jesus Christ, and the blood of Jesus (such as, "All Hail . the Power of Jesus' Name," "Come Thou Almighty King," "What Can Wash Away My Sins?" "There is Power in the Blood," etc.). Various Scriptures are read and often one or more of these—Pss 1, 32, 38, 91, 103; Isa 41:9-13; Matt 6:9-13; Mark 5:1-13; Eph 1:18-22; 6:10-18; Phil 2:5-11; Rev 12:7-12; 19:11-16; 20:1-10.

The man in charge (in our case usually an elder or maybe an evangelist) then begins to command in the name of the Lord Jesus Christ that all of the evil spirits who have had the right to invade this particular individual be totally and irrevocably bound by the blood of the Lord Jesus Christ and forced to be in this person's body alone. Evil spirits who may be shared with other persons (and can therefore flit back and forth between these bodies) are bound by the authority of the Lord Jesus Christ and forced to be in this one person in their entirety. All of these demons are then commanded .to be bound together in one unit in their entirety with all their networks and associated "place-takers," "no-names," and "successors" (names of demons) by the blood of the Lord Jesus Christ, drawn out of every part of the body and compacted into one unit on the face of the person.

Then we ask the Lord Jesus Christ to force into manifestation the highest ruling demon out of all those present to be the spokesman for all the others, and for the evil spirit to be manifested in the eyes and/or the face and to be forced to use the voice of the person to communicate the truth, the whole truth, and nothing but the truth. When there is a controlling demon present, it may be forced quickly into manifestation; or it may only after a considerable period of time be forced into manifestation. Evil spirits resist with all their power, because they know what is going to happen to them when bound by the blood of Christ and exposed. Sometimes the client has to be instructed further to trust the Lord Jesus and be willing to let go of the demon and his power in his life. Sometimes the workers must do a lot of praying and submitting their wills to the Lord to allow Him to accomplish the work with the precise actions and time that He has in mind.

In many cases the first manifestations may be only a pain or a feeling in the body such as a headache, nausea, or impairment of hearing or speaking. The demon is then commanded (always in Christ's name and by the power of His blood, never in the power of the counselor's words or character) to appear in the eyes, face, and mouth of the person. Usually there are clear and sharp changes in the appearance of the eyes—glowing, hateful, with half closed lids, glaring—and of the face as it may be contorted, twisted, drawn, lose all softness and become hardened or sharp. In a few cases where the demon takes a female character such as Venus or other names having to do with sexual things, the woman's face may become very radiant, seductive, and attractive. The voice of such a person is also very warm, enticing and passionate.

Sometimes the mouth may begin to have a mocking smile or a grimace. Perhaps it will begin to hiss like a snake or to growl as an animal—deep and throaty. Often there is a shout, "I hate you," or "I will kill you." It may say, "How dare you call me up? Do you know who I am?" The worker must be fully clothed in the whole armor of God and be ready for sudden, shocking or bizarre threats or even movements such as contortions of the body. Frequently the person may be attacked with pain and distracting sensations. The person, not the demon, may say, "Oh, I have a splitting headache," or "My heart or my stomach is hurting me so." Commands are then given through

Christ for the evil spirits to cease their attack upon the body of the person, and these prayers are almost instantly answered by the Lord. This is also the case when the demonized person may threaten physical harm or flight. "I am getting out of this place," or "I will hit you" and the arm is drawn back. Instant prayer is made for the Lord to restrain and bind the person so he cannot move and for his arm to go limp. Again these prayers are almost instantly answered by the Lord. The demons have then sometimes said, "If you will unbind me, I will tear your eyes out," or "I will kill you." They recognize the binding power of the name of the Lord Jesus.

The communication by the demon is sometimes a thought answer in the mind of the person or it may be as though a voice had spoken to him. Most frequently and especially farther along in a deliverance session after the demons are fully manifested under the control of Christ and the client has submitted himself to the Lord's will for the manifestation of the demons, the evil spirits speak freely through the mouth of the person. The clients generally assert after the deliverance that they could tell that their mouth was giving utterances but that what was being said was not their thoughts; "I didn't say those things." This is often obvious to the workers because the voice may be changed in its quality; and the words are often hateful, abusive, blasphemous, and obscene. When the person is fully demonized (the evil spirit has been forced forward in full exposure), then the evil, vicious, and venomous words pour out. No Christian would utter such words of hatred against God or proclaim that "Satan is my lord."

Trusting in the absolute control of the Lord Jesus Christ, we command the evil spirit to identify himself. Be prepared for all kinds of biblical names—Baal, Apollyon, Lucifer, Satan, Melchizedek, yes, and even Jesus, Holy Spirit, or Yahweh. Weird foreign names may be used with Indian, African, Japanese words especially by those who have lived in those countries and have been invaded there. Malthus, Hitler and other historical names may have been taken by the demons. There is often an association of function or power with the name (Lusty, a demon of gluttony) but not in all cases. The name may have nothing to do with the person with that name and be simply a term taken out of a desire to confuse, as in the name "Jesus."

Quite often the identification is an evil spirit that controls a certain function in the life of the person such as rage, hate, fear, depression, lust, sex, alcohol, etc. Every statement of the demon is checked by a very powerful "test for truth," "Will that statement stand as truth before the true and living God (or before Abba, Father, before the Lord God Almighty, etc.)?" The demon is forced to answer yes or no, and this test has been remarkably reliable in detecting the truth or falseness of the statement. It is not (probably because of our poor wording or other error) a 100% safeguard, and double checking is recommended because the evil spirits are very intelligent and deceitful.

After the name of the evil spirit is truly ascertained and whether or not all the evil spirits under his control in the client are actually bound in their entirety to him, then we ask the Lord Jesus Christ to force the demon to reveal if he or his organization have any grounds or legal rights to remain in the Christian. Usually we find that it is the will of the Christian coupled with some act which has permitted Satan to gain that extra leverage on the person beyond the ordinary consequences of sin, especially willful sins and those involving a bargaining of some kind with Satan (even indirectly), that brings special power or favor.

If there are at this time any legal rights claimed, these are cancelled by prayers for the blood of the Lord Jesus Christ to remove them. Sometimes repentance concerning that particular sin which gave entrance to the demons along with a renunciation of the sin is requested of the client. When all grounds have been removed, the usurping demons have no right to stay in the body of the Christian. One must be sure to check for "Shields, Blocks, and Aides" that are often demons with a special power or assignment to protect some higher demon from exposure and expulsion. If any are exposed as shields, blocks, or aides, they are dealt with as noted above in cancelling any grounds.

Certain questions may be asked by the one in charge under the Lord Jesus Christ as to other high ruling demons who are in the person. While the answers have to be checked with the test of truth like all other answers and a certain reserve taken in regard to the information, yet it has many times proved to be true and to greatly assist in letting the Lord Jesus Christ get hold of these other demons. Also it is sometimes the experience of the counselor that in answer to prayer the Lord makes known to him a particular name or an area of life that should be checked. All of this is done with the greatest dependence upon the Lord Jesus Christ and according to His will alone.

Finally the demon is commanded by the power and the blood of the Lord Jesus Christ to confess that "Jesus Christ is my Lord and my Conqueror" or "Jesus Christ is King of kings and Lord of lords." Having done this (and they are forced to do it however reluctantly and whatever time is required), the demon must renounce Satan as lord and god. James 5:14ff. is read, and with prayers the elder or elders (and only elders) anoint the Christian with olive oil and command the demon to leave in his entirety and with all of his underlings. The demon may leave at this very moment and go to hell, but if there is no immediate expulsion then the commanding continues. The blood and the name of the Lord Jesus Christ are used repeatedly to reinforce the fact that the demon is an invader and has no grounds to remain, and that the body and the life of the Christian are reclaimed for the Lord Jesus Christ. Direct commands to leave the body and life of the believer and to go to hell continue until the person indicates something has left him. There is often a change in the eyes and/or in the facial expression; and the person expresses relief, indicating that a burden is lifted and a sense of freedom has come. Sometimes the room becomes much brighter to the person; and he is happy, smiling, and so grateful to God. If this does not happen after a period of commanding, then one must check for blocks or shields.

Prayers are said for the counselee asking the Lord Jesus Christ to fill him with the Holy Spirit so as to occupy all the life and the body that the evil spirit formerly occupied. Testing of the actual expulsion of the evil spirit is carried on with questions, the confession that "Jesus Christ is Lord," and the verbal or written thanks to God for removing this evil spirit (by name) into hell. Commands are given to the evil spirit to manifest itself *if* it is not in hell. Generally, if another demon is called into manifestation by the power of the Lord Jesus Christ, that demon is asked what has happened to the other demon and the name is used. Ninety-nine percent of the time the demons have declared that the previous demon is "in Gehenna," "in hell," or "in the pit of your God." This, of course, is always tested as other statements from lying spirits: "Will that stand as truth before the true and living God, Abba, Father?" A yes or no answer will be given, and the "yes" answers have often been confirmed by other information which we have gathered.

Under the authority of the Lord Jesus Christ we command these demons to go to the abyss or hell (Gehenna) because that is their destination by the Lord's statement (Matt 25:41; 5:22). Also, we feel that they are under the condemnation of God and are being punished before their time as noted in the conversation with Jesus because they have been caught invading the possession of the Lord (Matt 8:28f.). It is also done because experience shows that when evil spirits are consigned to hell they do not come back to that person nor can they go to another person as far as we know. They are permanently removed from this world and from doing their evil work.

A great network of demons has been uncovered according to our information with a hierarchical structure, all under the final authority of Satan whom all demons proudly confess as their lord and god. There may be a few or even thousands of demons under a ruler. Over a ruler may be a chief or high ruler while above the high ruler may be a general, admiral, or some other name denoting great authority like Antichrist or 666. The highest authorities encountered have been "high priests of Satan" and "princes of Satan who stand at Satan's right hand." These are often the demons who control the whole strategy against the person.

It is important for those doing deliverance work to note that demons under rulers, etc. can often be bound to their rulers and sent to the abyss at the same time that the ruler goes to hell under the authority of the Lord Jesus Christ. This must be done by specific command; otherwise it may be that demons will remain which necessitates more sessions to remove them almost one by one. If the Lord is pleased to eliminate them in their whole organization or network, so much the better. Christ has increasingly identified the networks and cast them out in our experience. This has cut the time needed for deliverance in a drastic and most helpful way.

Again it is necessary to inform you that it is seldom that a person is completely delivered of all evil spirits in one or two sessions. This is entirely up to the Lord Jesus Christ, but it appears that He ordinarily wills for the deliverance to be over a period of several sessions. Often it seems that there has to be growth in the spiritual life of the Christian and a deepening commitment and trust in Christ. A few persons have had to have deliverance sessions over a period of two years and ranging up to twenty-five sessions. But these have been few and apparently heavily oppressed by Satan.

From various experiences and from information from other people in deliverance ministry, we know that the Lord Jesus Christ is sovereignly in charge of all deliverance.[2] He does it the way He wants to and when He wants to. We have often had to stop, humble ourselves under His authority and submissively yield the whole matter to Him. Thus the above description of our general procedure is only intended as that which the Lord Jesus Christ has honored among us in working with over one hundred Christians with demonic usurpation problems. By no means do we think it is the only way the Lord Jesus may deliver people or that these procedures and words are the only ones or necessarily the best ones. We are simply reporting for information which may be used of the Almighty God to help elders to carry out this great work for the healing of the flock committed to their care.

Over the past years of counseling with persons troubled with evil spirits usurping some part of their lives, we have recognized that there are different levels of control, different personal abilities to deal with evil spirits, and two other ways of seeking liberation from demonic control. One such method is an individual deliverance simply with the help of the Lord Jesus Christ. It may be useful and appropriate to those who are mature in Christ and have become educated through past deliverance sessions in the way demons work and Christ delivers. It basically operates without the help of others including elders.

If a Christian begins to identify certain evil thoughts or sinful activities in his life over which he has little control and in which he is often defeated by Satan, he can ask himself if he is not possibly under some demonic control. Looking back over his recent history, he may be able to determine that at some point he had indeed given grounds for an invasion by Satan. At once he can begin praying with contrition and repentance for the Lord's forgiveness, and he can request that the Lord take away and cancel all the grounds which were given to Satan.

The next step is to affirm his full assurance of faith in the finished work of the Lord Jesus Christ to deliver him from all demonic control and to specifically bind with the blood of Christ all the evil spirits he believes may have entered him, asking Almighty God to force them to be bound in their entirety so that all must leave at the same time. Confidently believing that the Lord Jesus Christ answers such prayers, he then asks the Savior to remove all the demons immediately from his body and life and put them in Gehenna by His sovereign authority. Next he should pray for Abba, Father, to fill him with the Holy Spirit as never before and protect him against giving grounds for any further invasion.

This has been successfully used by several Christians and should be tried by those who are ready in their own mind for this type of deliverance, humbly looking to Christ as the deliverer. However if over a period of time the situation does not improve and demonic control continues at a serious level leading to regular defeat, then it is wise for the child of God to call for the elders to carry out the procedure of James 5.

Another level and type of deliverance activity has been found to be used of our Lord Jesus Christ in some cases. The earliest use came about when we were faced with a sudden and unplanned-for demonic manifestation in a Christian. This was sometimes in a public place such as a meeting in a church building where the usual procedure could not be employed because of time and circumstances. The person demonized was taken into another room, and prayers were offered quickly for the total protection of those involved.

The person in charge, usually an elder, prayed for the Lord Jesus Christ to cancel all the grounds for the evil spirits by His blood, to bind them all together, and to expel them to Gehenna. After the prayer of faith and anointing with oil per James 5:14ff., commands were given in Christ's name to throw out all evil spirits through the blood of the Lord Jesus Christ. This was followed by prayer for Almighty God to fill the person as never before with the power and protection of the Holy Spirit. God has graciously blessed this brief deliverance work, and the person has usually witnessed to the fact that the evil spirits were no longer attacking him.

Some may choose to try this type of deliverance work as an alternative to the heavy and more involved deliverance procedure described above. In all of these there is a total entrusting of the deliverance to the work and will of the Lord Jesus Christ. If this alternative method does not appear to give full release from demonic control to an individual, then it is best to use the longer type. The shorter type does not enable the person to be as aware of the reality of evil spirits in his life and does not carry the same measure of assurance of expulsion that the more involved form does. Circumstances, the people involved, the depth of invasion, and the counselor's own knowledge and experience are factors which will be determinative as to which type of procedure to use to the glory of God and the setting free of the captives.

Today a mighty work of God in a clear, scriptural manner is being restored to the needy congregations of the Lord, and we commend it to your serious and prayerful study to see how God may will to use you to help others.

NOTES

1. Jessie Penn-Lewis and Evan Roberts, *War On The Saints* (Ft. Washington, Pa: Christian Literature Crusade, 1977, reprint, abridged edition), pp. 32-33.

2. Without endorsing the procedures or various theological positions in these books, we simply point to the various ways the Lord Jesus Christ may choose to deliver His people from evil spirits. As in reading anything written

by uninspired men (including us) the Christian must check everything for its validity by comparison with the teaching of the Word of God. Don Basham, *Deliver Us From Evil* (Washington Depot, Ct: Chosen Books, 1972); Kurt Koch, *Occult Bondage and Deliverance* (Grand Rapids: Kregel Publications, 1978); Merrill F. Unger, *What Demons Can Do to Saints* (Chicago: Moody Press, 1977).

"It is therefore clear in Bible history that the manifestation of the power of God invariably meant active dealing with the satanic hosts. . . .

". . . the Church of Christ will reach its high water mark, when it is able to recognize and deal with demon-possession; when it knows how to 'bind the strong man' by prayer; 'command' the spirits of evil in the Name of Christ, and deliver men and women from their power.

"For this the Christian Church must recognize that the existence of deceiving, lying spirits, is as real in the twentieth century as in the time of Christ. . . .

"These supernatural forces of Satan are the true hindrance to revival."

Jessie Penn-Lewis and Evan Roberts,
War On The Saints, (abridged edition, pp. 32-33)

11

Overcoming Demonic Activity: The Results

Nothing in our experience has ever equaled the startling results in the transformation of lives both in the magnitude and the rapidity of those changes that we have observed in the deliverance ministry. Over the past five years we have worked with more than 150 individuals (and repeatedly with most of them) and have seen God bring tremendous cleansing of their lives and a true liberation from the overpowering control of Satan in their lives. We can affirm that this ministry has been wonderfully used of the Lord Jesus Christ to bring about highly beneficial results in the lives of these people. It is by no means miraculously and instantaneously done, and it certainly is not done without a tremendous spiritual struggle on the part of us human beings. It has been a most rewarding work as we have seen the newness of life and freedom of Christians who were in severe bondage to Satan. Our confidence in the Lord Jesus Christ and in the power of prayer has grown greatly as we have seen the control of the Lord Jesus Christ over powerful and ruthless evil spirits. Most of all, it has glorified God as these individuals have been able to take up their ministry and perform their duties with a joy and a freedom which they did not have before.

IMPORTANT LESSONS LEARNED

We have learned a great many things from the involvement in the ministry of deliverance, and almost all of these have been beneficial and useful to us in becoming better shepherds and in

watching over the flock of God. We have learned to entrust
the work of deliverance to the guidance of Almighty God rather
than our own efforts to gain discernment. The Lord has graciously
led us into more effective prayers against the evil spirits which
have resulted in a dramatic cut in the time needed for deliverance. Formerly we might work from three to five hours in a
session whereas now sessions last approximately two hours and
accomplish much more than we were able to do in the previous
four or five hours. The Lord has taught us to go after the highest
demon rulers within people immediately rather than dealing
with the lower level demons who are underlings and who may
number in hundreds or thousands. When we asked the Lord Jesus
Christ, the Deliverer, to drive into manifestation as spokesman
the highest demonic power within an individual, we found the
Lord willing to do this. All the evil spirits under this demonic
ruler are then bound to him in their entirety, and the expulsion
of all evil spirits under this ruler is much more quickly accomplished.

Again, we have seen some changes in the Lord's working
through us as we became more aware in understanding the
procedure that the Lord would honor. Almighty God seems to
have broken down the resistance of the evil spirits that we deal
with so that we now have much less threatening from the evil
spirits and less active aggressive resistance to the commands
of the Lord. It is also true that as a person has gone through
deliverance sessions a number of times he or she becomes much
more capable of cooperating with the elders and to will for the
evil spirits to leave at once. The determination and spiritual
maturity of the client is of major importance in the speed and
the thoroughness with which the evil spirits are exposed and
expelled.

Another major change that has come about is that we no
longer use physical restraints to keep the demonized person in
the counseling room. At one time physical restraint was used
as necessary to keep the demonized person under control for
the duration of the session. Now our thinking is that, if the
person when demonized leaves the room in spite of our prayers
to the Lord and commands of Christ through His servant-priests,

it is the Lord's way of indicating that the person is not yet ready or other factors need to be considered. In the vast majority of cases the Lord has honored our prayers for the binding of the body of the client completely so it cannot be moved from the chair. In most cases when the demonized person was permitted to leave the room with nothing but prayers being offered to keep him, the Lord has brought the person back to the counseling room in a quiet state and the session continued. There may be a few cases where physical restraint would be appropriate for certain individuals, but the greatest gain has come about when we have not used physical restraint and have simply entrusted it entirely to the Lord Jesus Christ as to whether or not the person is to be worked with at that time.

Nothing has become more clear to us during these many hundreds of hours involved in spiritual counseling than the fact that the Lord God Almighty does *everything* in the deliverance work, and we human beings are but the instruments or mere voices of Him to use as He may choose. This is the only proper and safe position to occupy because it is true. Anything other than this can lay the person open to pride and other sins as well as attack or even invasion by evil spirits. Everything about the deliverance is in the hands of God and must be committed to Him without reservation. All glory, honor, and thanks must be given to the triune God for the deliverance and not to the individuals who have been used of God in the matter.

MEASURING THE RESULTS

God has brought the overwhelming majority of the Christians into a new confidence in the Lord Jesus Christ and a remarkable liberation from the control of evil spirits. It was soon impressed upon us that deliverance would often take a period of time in the will of God. Deliverance is, in our opinion, not an act of exorcism but a process of sanctification achieved with the Lord's power in the life of a growing Christian. A number of sessions, each one averaging about two hours, had to be held to secure a total deliverance for most individuals. As we thought about this, several reasons suggested themselves to us. Immediate and instantaneous deliverance might very well encourage thoughts of magic and might lessen a spiritual concentration upon the work of the Holy Spirit.

Also, through a process the individual was enabled to grow and mature in spiritual ability to engage in spiritual warfare. He learned to rely more upon the power of the Lord Jesus Christ in his life and to stand in the strength of the Lord rather than in a dependence upon a deliverance work, which is not the common rule for Christian growth but an exceptional and unique work. As people have grown in their understanding of the Lord and in their consecration of themselves to God, they have found greater and greater ability to have the Lord cast out the evil spirits in a shorter period of time and to have less and less need of deliverance work.

Moreover, there is the fact that there can be many networks or organizations of evil spirits within an individual, and these may not all be uncovered at one time. It seems that the Lord often is willing to remove them only by "layers" and not all simultaneously. A person may be deeply invaded and by multiple demonic organizations, and it seems the Lord's will that there has to be a process of uncovering these various layers of evil spirits. After several sessions the individuals are much better equipped to let the Lord deal with the demons, and they are more quickly removed.

In spite of the hours and the many sessions it has taken to free individuals from demonic invaders, we rejoice in the powerful working of God against all evil spirits and for the grand liberation that has been given to these individuals. All of these in this broad classification have been helped tremendously in their spiritual stability, personality integration, and wholeness of life. There is no doubt in our minds about the very remarkable workings of the triune God in setting Christians free when they desire to be free. Lives have been anchored to the Lord Jesus Christ, and there has been a maturation of spirituality in the lives of our counselees.

A small percentage of those we have worked with have been set free from demonic control quickly, occasionally in only one session or perhaps two or three sessions. The reason for these quick deliverances seems to be based on the fact that these have been strong, mature Christians who had great determination to be free from the evil spirits and trusted God fully that He would accomplish this deliverance. Also, it was evident that there were not many demonic usurpers involved in their lives or that they had not been there very long. They were not in most cases powerful and entrenched evil spirits of a high rank. Through it all, whether it took a long time or a short time or even seemed to be a failure, still we recognize that everything is in the control of the Lord God Almighty. He is the only one who knows everything about the individuals coming for deliverance and what is best for them to experience in achieving a cleansing and a freedom from evil spirits.

About ten percent of the persons with whom we have worked have not been set free or entirely liberated from some bondage to Satan. This is not to say that there were not actual deliverances from the control of evil spirits, but other conditions seemed to play a major part in blocking the complete deliverance of the individual. In several of these cases we became convinced that we were dealing with cases of possession and not lesser forms of oppression, obsession, or bondage. As we have noted elsewhere possession is the most serious level of demonic invasion and affects the person's whole life and outlook and means that evil spirits are almost always in control of the individual no matter what their particular actions or words may be. These few individuals have in some cases willingly made bargains or pacts with Satan and have rejected Jesus Christ as their Lord.

Again, most of them exhibited an unwillingness or an inability to surrender totally to the lordship of Christ and to renounce the working of Satan in their lives. In some cases the individual had some power which was occult in nature but which they enjoyed using and did not want to commit to the Lord Jesus Christ. Lasting deliverance cannot take place, in our opinion, without the normal decision of the client to seek total freedom from all influence and working of Satan in his life. If a person is unwilling to give up everything that he possesses that is not from Abba, Father, he simply cannot receive deliverance.

Also, it became evident to us that some people were unwilling to close the door to Satan's machinations and subtle workings in their lives. While deliverance was given by the Lord, they shortly found themselves to be invaded by other evil spirits and more deliverance work had to be done. This took place in some of these lives until we came to refer to them as "revolving doors." At that point we also suspected that Satan may very well have been the one who sent them to us to consume our time, frustrate and possibly injure us, and keep us from working with other people who could be delivered.

As we experienced these various episodes in the lives of those with whom we were working and saw great difficulty in setting the individuals free of Satan's control because of new invasions, our teams evaluated the situation and decided that the person either did not want deliverance actually or that it was not the time which God had chosen. We came to value very much the timing of God and to permit His sovereignty in regard to the individuals. If God knowing all things was not prepared to give deliverance, nothing could happen. The Lord is the only one who can reach the heart of individuals, and so we depended very much upon Him to answer prayer in regard to exposing the true condition of the individuals with whom we were having such difficulty.

When we gave up working with individuals, we indicated to them that it was temporary until they had prepared themselves further, had become more mature in the Lord, or could make full surrender of everything to the Lord Jesus Christ. These cases were not counted as failures on our part and certainly not any failure of the power of the Lord Jesus Christ or any lack of His lovingkindness for these individuals. In other cases we concluded that God wanted to use some other person for the deliverance work and not us.

Finally, we came to realize that some people *might* have committed the sin of blasphemy against the Holy Spirit and were in such corrupt, moral depravity that they were not going to be delivered by the Lord Jesus Christ. Such judgment, of course, must be tentative and subject to change when evidences to the contrary are forthcoming. We would caution those who may become involved in deliverance work that not everyone who comes to you for help will receive a full deliverance from the control of evil spirits. We advise you to evaluate carefully what progress is made so that you do not become entangled with a person who is a "revolving door" type that Satan can use against you.

CASE STUDIES OF THE LIVES OF THOSE RECEIVING DELIVERANCE

After the prayer of faith, the anointing of oil, and the commands in the name of the Lord Jesus Christ for the evil spirits to leave, there has been, in the overwhelming majority of cases, an immediate and often drastic change in the person. Often the transition from one personality controlling and speaking to another personality, the real self, is detected by the voice, the appearance of the face, and the eyes. These may vary from very strong and vivid contrasts to only slight modification. Clients often are impressed with the changes and may comment, "I feel so much lighter I could almost float." "It is so light in this room now." "I could feel the evil spirits leaving me as though they were flocks of birds leaving." The person may also be extremely happy and elated, very thankful to God for what He has done in his life. There are expressions of joy and thanksgiving to God for His great power and love in setting them free of that which they recognize as a terrible bondage and cruel oppression.

After the deliverance session people are urged to continue in prayer and to be very much aware of Satan's counterattacks which will surely follow. They are assured of our prayers and support, that we are available to them for whatever help they need. Usually in a day or two the counselee begins to appreciate the fact that he has really been set free of demonic control, and he begins to experience a greater love of God and ability to obey God, while having the victory over the sins which formerly had enslaved him. All of them testify to a new peace and security in God that is very different from the harassment that they had been receiving before. In some people's lives the changes have been startling with longstanding habits and problems broken and removed from their lives.

In every case of those who continued through to the end of a series of deliverance sessions we can say each was most beneficial. No spiritual harm has come to those who were willing to let the Lord work through their lives until He was finished with His work. The deliverance ministry itself is of such a high spiritual order of trusting in the Lord Jesus and His finished work on Calvary that all persons involved gain a tremendous respect for Christ and a higher dependence upon Him. We believe there is a consistent witness to the fact that the deliverance work has been most beneficial in removing demonic control from all lives and has enabled them to become true servants of the Lord Jesus Christ. No one has been hurt, to our knowledge, or hindered in his spiritual development. We want to share with you eight rather typical cases to help your understanding.

Case 101. This lady came to us with tremendous problems from hearing voices in her head that were urging her over and over, "Kill your baby, kill your baby, kill your baby." And other times it would be, "Kill your dog," or "Kill yourself." The constant bombardment of these voices had brought the woman to a consideration of suicide as an escape from the harassment. She previously had been hospitalized in a psychiatric unit, and she was almost immobilized from carrying on any normal duties of a wife and mother. From time to time her arms would involuntarily begin to shake, and she seemed to have no control over them. She was tormented and terribly oppressed by Satan.

After a work of deliverance was provided by the Lord Jesus Christ, there was almost one hundred percent improvement. The physical shaking of her body and the voices in the head were completely gone. Her physical appearance was one of radiance, happiness and serenity; and when she spoke in our assembly she thrilled the hearts of the people with her testimony of how God had completely transformed her life.

There is a sad note to attach to this case which is instructive. This lady did not follow our advice in becoming a member of either our congregation or another that was responsive to people with spiritual problems and who could minister to her in a continuing way. As a result, a year later she had been invaded by new evil spirits and had fallen back into the desperate conditions from which she had formerly escaped. It is imperative, in our opinion, that the person who is being set free from demonic control be an active member of a vital body of Christians who will make it a matter of prayer for the upbuilding of the person who has had deliverance work. All the spiritual resources of prayer, Scripture reading, and communion of the spiritually discerned body and blood of Christ must be used to the utmost for the strengthening and continuing victory for the individual.

Case 102. A brother came to us with a great many difficulties and spiritual problems, among them lust, sexual perversion, pride, arrogance, depression, anxiety, and doubt. There were also problems with deception and lying, rebellion and rage, and physical infirmities. This brother received counseling over a two year period and was set free from these evil spirits though deeper networks of evil spirits similar to these were uncovered over the period of time. By the grace of God the brother received strengthening of his spiritual character and his dedication to the Lord Jesus Christ. He had victory given by the Lord over ancestral evil spirits that had come down through the law of generations from the occult and sinful activities of his ancestors (Exod 20:5). As this brother matured in the Lord Jesus Christ, he was enabled to see many victories over the powers of darkness which he had been combating so much of his life. After more than twenty-six sessions during which the Lord gave amazing deliverances, this brother is now exercising his freedom in the Lord to grow up into the servant of God that he wants to be. Struggles go on and temptations still are plenteous, but the change in his life has been most remarkable.

Case 103. This sister came with a very difficult background from her childhood up with a major problem of low self-esteem which led to invasion. The evil spirit testified that it was able to enter her because she wanted so very much to be someone else, a happy person acceptable to people. The name of this evil spirit was "Christian." Later many other evil spirits of a most destructive nature were uncovered. "Deceit" gained grounds for invasion through selfishness. There were a great many evil spirits of Fear, Great Fear, Fear of all Ancestors.

There were evil spirits with a function or name of Hate, Confusion, Destruction; a large number of Alcohol, Pride, Controller and Breaker of Mind, Addiction, and Ugly Spirit, who claimed to be a prince of Satan. Because of these many evil spirits this person was driven to punish herself and to undergo great suffering and torment. At one time she testified that she was "totally controlled" by demons, and the result was she was addicted to drugs, alcohol, and sex. She had been under psychiatric therapy twice and was judged to be schizophrenic. The demons deceived her into believing that deliverance was actually a working of Satan and that the church must cease its ministry of deliverance. After a time of cutting off from all spiritual counseling, she attempted suicide. At this point she returned to the Lord and over a period of several months was delivered from these evil spirits so that she is now a beautiful Christian and is overcoming the addictive sins of the past.

Case 104. Another woman grew up in a family in which the father had an evil spirit which led him to exhibit a split personality and to become violent. This prepared the way for demonic invasion later on. She hated herself and wanted to be someone else. She made a bargain to empty herself. Later she became very rebellious and was involved in sexual promiscuity. She engaged in a seance with a spiritualist and finally became catatonic for periods of time. She refused to look in mirrors for fear of what she would see and often she hid behind chairs. At this point she became suicidal and would deliberately walk out into the street without looking at the traffic. She lost control of her life sexually and developed a destructive-masochistic condition. In subsequent sessions the Lord Jesus Christ delivered this woman from evil spirits of Seduction, Insecurity, Rejection, Masochism, Fear, Self-Hatred, Depression, Pseudo-Personality, Rebellion, and Sickness. Later evil spirits of Sadness, Escape, Darkness, Confusion, and the Pleaser were all expelled. The change in this person's life has been truly remarkable. She is an entirely different woman than she was two years ago. Her life radiates the loveliness of the Lord Jesus Christ.

Case 105. A brother came to us with an apparently strong background of spiritual understanding and yet had begun to suffer a great deal of harassment, depression, and temptation which often led to sin. He had been in personal contact with demoniacs whom we later adjudged to be demon possessed. He had sought communication with evil spirits in the demoniacs that he had worked with and had become fascinated by it.

One block was our difficulty in imagining that this brother might have been invaded by evil spirits because of the apparent strength of his faith in the Lord Jesus Christ. Pride also was a major block in the way of his admitting the possibility of evil spirits being in his life. Once these barriers had been broken through and deliverance began, an enormous number of evil spirits were uncovered over a period of two years. Several of the evil spirits claimed to have invaded him because of his involvement with the demon-possessed persons which underscores the extreme danger of those involved with demoniacs and in a deliverance ministry.

Among the evil spirits that were dealt with during this time were Aphrodite, Venus, Insatiable. There were a number of evil spirits with the same name, Somebody, all the way up to number thirty-six. The ground for invasion was that he felt that he was a nobody, and their function was to give him low self-esteem. Other evil spirits were Lustful, Damien, and Lucifer, twenty-eight different demons with this name.

Other evil spirits were Lachintoss, Thankman, and Loneliness. One of the most resistant to total expulsion were evil spirits of Laughter, and their testimony was that there were 513 in their organization. Laughter proved to be difficult to deal with as it often came to block the progress of the deliverance sessions. Other evil spirits included Meanman, and Deliverance, which claimed that its ground for invasion was his involvement in the deliverance ministry when he was not ready for it. There were evil spirits of Rejection, Pride, Lustful and Rebellion. Later there were such evil spirits as Mind Control-Legion-Fatigue, Breather, Itcher-Binder, Destroyer, Curser, Blasphemer, Slanderer, Witchcraft, Growler (who actually did a lot of growling), Satan the father of lies, and Jesus.

This case has been one of the most difficult and has required the most extensive spiritual resources in setting this brother free.

The intensity of the control has been unusually great as well as the immense number of evil spirits. It is our belief at this time in retrospect that we were deceived into pursuing a great number of subordinate evil spirits who were most certainly invaders but who were not the highest rulers over all of these lesser demons. At the same time it may have been the will of Almighty God to enable this brother to realize the enormous number of invaders of his life through past sins.

For some reason this person seemed to be a special object of the devil's attack and a great desire of Satan to keep this person in bondage. For a time it seemed that we were in a "revolving door" situation, and we wondered if we would ever get to the end of the evil spirits that were able to control this brother. In one session of about three hours 74 demonic rulers were confronted and expelled from this person by the blood of the Lord Jesus. Still we persisted because of the person's obvious deep commitment to the Lord Jesus Christ and his earnest desire to be totally free of all evil spirits.

Finally after some twenty-five sessions the brother experienced a great deal of freedom from the overwhelming oppression which he had been suffering and was able to live a normal Christian life. There was a surprising number of cases of new invasions in this person, and he seemed to have some definite weaknesses or loop-holes through which the evil spirits were able to invade him easily. He has had to continue to battle against harassing evil spirits and some evil spirits who had invaded him. It is possible that some further work of deliverance is needed to enable this Christian to realize his fullest potential as a gifted worker for the Lord Jesus Christ.

Case 106. In 1979 a sister came to us with a very severe spiritual condition of bondage to Satan which increasingly threatened her with immobility and a paralyzed will. Two of us worked with her for a total of seventeen hours in one session, and the very next day we continued for another seventeen hour session with excellent results.[1] The enormity of the invaders both in depth and in length of their presence in the sister going far back into her childhood enabled the evil spirits to intertwine with her personality so that she was really unable to distinguish between her real self as created by Almighty God and the pseudo-person-alities that had for so long dominated her thinking. At an early age she had a strong desire to be someone else, and she remem-bered at the age of twelve being angry with God and declaring, "We will play your game though it is cruel."

Among the first of the evil spirits that came into manifesta-tion was Pride, which often has to be removed as it can block effectively a great deal of the deliverance work. Later Lesbian, Hatred, Fear, and Sex were all exposed with the highest ruler, Governor Damien. Following this the powerful evil spirit, Leviathan, came into manifestation; and he proved to be one of the most slippery evil spirits in this person. After the close of the seventeen hour session with evident deliverance, he was still in manifestation the next day. We found that there could be blocks or shields for evil spirits which prevented the evil spirit from having to leave upon command of the Lord Jesus Christ. These blocks and shields had to be removed by the confession of sin on the part of the person and in this partic-ular case the individual was re-immersed into the Lord Jesus Christ to defeat Satan's contention that she was not truly a child of God.

Finally, the evil spirit, Leviathan, was expelled by the Lord Jesus, and an evil spirit calling itself Satan was in powerful manifestation and control for a number of hours. We waged a tremendous battle against the evil spirit, Satan, who was able to deceive the sister into believing that it was impossible for her to be delivered and that "she thinks I am her." The signing of the Renunciation and Affirmation paper also proved to be a powerful means for the Lord Jesus Christ to separate Satan from the sister's personality.[2] The anointing of oil with the prayers proved also to be greatly used of the Lord. Satan seemed to be able to cling to the person's stomach. All of the evil spirits were removed from the various areas of the body and commanded to be in one unit and only one unit on the face of the person. This, too, proved to be effective in securing the deliverance which came about with a great deal of coughing and vomiting.

Another evil spirit of Pride was expelled about two weeks later along with an evil spirit of Silence. The evil spirit, Silence, said that it came into the little girl because the parents wanted silence in their child. Following these expulsions of the evil spirits the sister experienced a tremendous amount of relief and a change in her personality and outlook on life.

In the fourth session with this person the evil spirits, Lucifer and Satan, were in manifestation as high ruling spirits and an interesting thing happened as they were thrown out. There followed a succession of manifestations of evil spirits who did not indicate who they were but were suddenly thrown out of the person by Christ within the space of two to four minutes until they were all gone in that series. Another evil spirit named Governor Damien came into manifestation, and he was bound in his entirety with all of the other evil spirits and cast out of this sister. He was not the original Governor Damien but another demon with that name.

After a lapse of eighteen months the sister indicated that she knew that she had some further demonic invaders because of the difficulties that she was experiencing in her own life. Some ancestrally derived evil spirits were uncovered who were acting as a shield for the Emperor Sargon. When these demons' power was broken, then the Emperor Sargon was cast out to the immense relief of the sister who began weeping with joy. She said everything was so different and, "I never thought I would be free!"

Case 107. Successful spiritual deliverance counseling can also be greatly dependent upon the client's mental, physical, and emotional condition. We have encountered a number of cases wherein men and women allow themselves to deteriorate physically and mentally because of willful disregard, ignorance, or indifference about what they eat and drink. As discussed in other chapters, poor nutrition may profoundly affect a person's mental health—capability to concentrate effectively, be objective, be rational, and cope with situations of even moderate stress.

Case 107 involved an overweight young woman almost completely immobilized by poor physical, spiritual, and mental health. This Christian (let us call her Lucy) was being medicated for many illnesses including severe arthritis and a thyroid condition. She also had at least one operation to remove ovarian cysts. At the time of counseling she was unable to cope with employment and was classified as physically disabled by the state of Ohio. Lucy could walk only short distances or perform only minor physical chores before she became physically and emotionally exhausted. Her diet consisted mainly of huge quantities of junk food. She was often depressed (almost clinically depressed), cried at the slightest provocation whether real or imagined, was a compulsive eater, and often engaged in lengthy phone conversations to ease loneliness. Lucy is a highly intelligent, talented young lady who was unable to function socially except with a few close acquaintances.

Lucy was counseled at different times with two husband-wife teams both of whom later became extremely frustrated at her lack of progress. Both teams had spent much time with Lucy on a purely social level, and both became close friends of Lucy. However, when counseling sessions were scheduled, she was unable to verbalize prayer and became defensive and tearful.

Several conventional deliverance sessions were conducted wherein our Lord Jesus Christ was petitioned to force demons into manifestation to reveal their names; but no progress was made as Lucy became silent, or she retaliated verbally because she felt confused and threatened. It was decided to discontinue the spiritual-psychological counseling approach until Lucy could overcome her debilitating physical-emotional conditions. Lucy was encouraged to visit a doctor who was specially trained in nutrition and metabolic processes. Blood tests and other tests revealed, via computer printout, that Lucy was hypoglycemic and deficient in several minerals. She was given a diet to follow with vitamin, mineral and glandular extract supplements; and she was given physical therapy.

It took about eight months to bring about physical and emotional improvements adequate for Lucy to begin to function normally. At this point we conducted a single spiritual deliverance counseling session wherein no manifestation of spirits was commanded as this always upset and confused Lucy. Lucy was given the option of praying silently or verbally. She at once prayed a remarkably thorough, verbal prayer for repentance of sin, affirmation of Jesus Christ as Lord and a total renunciation of Satan, the devil, and all of his spiritual and physical influence.

The elder and his wife read Scripture and prayed. Then the elder anointed her with olive oil in the name of Jesus Christ of Nazareth in accordance with James 5. Jesus Christ was petitioned to deliver Lucy from all ancestral spirits and all satanic influences of any form. Christ was petitioned to find all evil spirits which had or could have influence over Lucy and to send them to a place from whence they could never return to influence any human being. Lucy joyfully declared a heavy burden was lifted from her, and she felt spiritually strengthened.

Shortly thereafter Lucy went on a medically monitored fast-diet and lost forty-seven pounds. She is continuing to maintain this regimen until her weight becomes normal for her body frame. Now Lucy is able to take long walks, perform chores without exhaustion, withdraw from all drug-therapy medication; and she has begun part-time employment. Her doctor expects her to be able to handle full-time employment in the near future.

Our objective here is to bring to full recognition that there is no one, fixed approach to successful counseling. The counselor's approach must be adapted to meet the unique personality of each individual as each has a different background and special needs peculiar unto himself.

The fixed quantities in counseling are that above all Jesus Christ must be involved as the Great Physician; and the counselor must consider nutrition, psychology, medical fitness (to be evaluated by a member of the medical profession when necessary), heredity, and the client's life experiences especially in relationship to God and to sin.

Case 108. Smitty (continued from chapter 1). "But the Lord Jesus Christ is infinitely more powerful than you are, Satan," I shouted. "He has already defeated you by His death on the cross and His resurrection! Bound by the blood of the Son of God, your Conqueror, leave this body and go to hell."

"You cannot send me to hell; you do not have the right." "Yes, but your Lord, Jesus Christ, has all authority. In His mighty name we command you to leave and go to hell." "No, I do not have to for it is not my time yet."

"Will that stand as truth before Abba, Father?" "Yes, it will. I am the prince of the power of the air, and I do not have to obey your commands. I can go back into the air." "S.T. G?" (meaning, Will that stand as truth before Almighty God?). "Certainly."

An all out battle is fought with Lucifer, the devil, for the next several minutes. Several in the room are praying for our great Deliverer to remove Satan; others are reading Scriptures about the destruction of Satan in Gehenna, the lake of fire and brimstone.

"I command you in the name of the Son of God, the King of kings and Lord of lords, to release Smitty at once! He is under the blood of the Lamb of God. He does not belong to you. Be gone! Out in the name of your Conqueror, Jesus the Christ. God crushes you under our feet, leave at once! Go wherever the Lord Jesus Christ puts you. Oh, Lord and Redeemer, please break Satan's hold on Smitty by the power of your blood."

Vividly and swiftly a visible change of personality is observed by all, and we are sure that the father of lies is gone as quickly as he had come. Our God has driven Lucifer out once more even as we have seen Him do it a dozen times with different persons in the past five years. Such appearances of the evil one does not seem to us any triumph of the devil in getting into a person with demons but is a witness to the absolute control of the Lord Jesus Christ in permitting or even forcing the devil to expose himself. For it is then that he is shown to be powerless to remain in the person he is claiming as his own, while at the same time he has to hear the terrifying words of damnation and destruction which await him when the Son of God comes to put him forever into hell (Rev 20:10).

Looking at Smitty, I realize that he is still demonized, and I command, "Evil spirit, what is your name as truth before the Lord Jesus Christ?" His name is Lucifer, but he is an evil spirit, not the devil in this case. He is ruled over by a higher demon named Andrew. All these are bound in their entirety by the blood of Christ and are forced to confess that Jesus Christ is Lord and Conqueror. In spite of resistance they obey, and are then forced to renounce Satan, the devil, as their lord and god. To further protect Smitty and accomplish a thorough deliverance, I forced them to renounce all claim to Smitty. After reading James 5:14ff. I anointed the forehead and prayed for King Jesus to take them out, one way traffic to hell. The demons struggle to hold on, but as we continue to pray and command, they are abruptly expelled. A much relieved Smitty is in full rational control.

As we test to see if there are other evil spirits still in our brother, one is forced into manifestation on Smitty's face and eyes. "You are bound in your entirety by the blood of the Lamb of God," I declared, "and you can do nothing except tell the truth and nothing but the truth. What is your name? Christ the Lord forces you to answer."

"Steven." "S.T. G?" "Yes." "Are you the same Steven that was here the other night?" "No." "S.T. G?" "Yes." "Where is that demon Steven?" "He is in Gehenna." "S.T. G?" "Yes." "How were you able to escape detection earlier?" "I was hidden by Andrew." "S.T. G?" "Yes."

"Where are Andrew and Lucifer, the evil spirits, gone? "To Gehenna." "S.T. G?" "Yes, they left and now he is mine! I have him. He is mine, all mine!"

Instantly there is a change in the face, and we see again that domineering, powerful, and sinister appearance that we had seen almost an hour earlier. "I am the PRINCE OF DARKNESS! This man belongs to me!" The body seems flooded with power, and all of us are forced to hold on to Smitty as we attack Satan with all the divine powers at our command. We bombard him with Scriptures, commands in the name of the Lord Jesus Christ, and begin to sing, "There is power, power, / Wonder-working power / In the blood of the Lamb; / There is power, power, / Wonder-working power / In the precious blood of the Lamb!"

We keep singing about the blood of Christ because demons hate that awesome power and cannot stand before it. Suddenly a distinct change takes place, and Lucifer is gone. (No demon has the terrible presence and towering personality of Satan, and once having seen him in manifestation you do not mistake him for just a demon.)

The evil spirit, Steven, is back in control, and by questioning him we find there is another demon with the name Andrew that Steven has been successful in "just pulling into" Smitty. All of these are bound by the blood of Christ into helplessness; and after prayer and anointing in Christ's name, they are commanded out by the authority of the Son of God. They go out!

Everyone is overwhelmed with joy, and we are all praising Almighty God for His amazing work, the incredible greatness of His power against all demons and even Satan, the father of lies. There is new assurance that final victory is coming for Smitty, because each deliverance session has brought forth a much more determined Smitty due to his liberation from many evil spirits. His faith in Christ is clearly shown in his words and actions.

But three weeks later disquieting news came to me—Smitty had been involved with Satanists and had watched another animal sacrifice! He confessed to Zane that he was fascinated with occult power and seemed drawn against his will to a Satanic meeting. Also, he stated that from the age of five he had talked with spirits as he played in his room or walked in woods. Besides he confessed that he had lied to me about his involvement in the occult.

Of course this alarmed us, and my wife and I began to pray earnestly that our heavenly Father would reveal if Smitty was a "revolving door" type of person (who is delivered of demons but then continually opens the door for others to invade), a "tool of Satan" to get us into a long drawn out deliverance work which would exhaust us and take us away from our other priorities, or if he was *possessed* (so taken over by Satan in heart, will, mind and body that it would be almost impossible to free him). There are times when it is best to simply admit after thorough evaluation that some are irredeemable or that the Lord Jesus does not choose to use us as His instruments for deliverance.

We informed Zane of our concerns and indicated that Smitty must exert his will, declare an all out allegiance to Christ, and use every means of grace available to him regularly—prayer, Scripture reading, corporate worship, communion, and close fellowship with Christians.

Weeks went by, and Zane notified us that Smitty had been walking definitely in the Holy Spirit and appeared most of the time to be standing fast in the Lord. He reported that he felt harassment from evil spirits, but he was not sure if they were inside or outside. Zane was convinced that an in-depth talk with Smitty was required to clear away possible grounds of invasion. Perhaps we should probe to see if any subtly concealed evil spirits were left. We all agreed to pray about the Lord's will in the matter and wait.

Smitty decided the time for us, because he told Zane to set up a meeting with me. He felt very secure and free in Christ as Lord; but he realized that he was being harassed in a supernatural way—fearful feelings, glimpses of images, sensations of someone watching him, and a growing lure to thrill to occult power. After a meeting time and place was set, we all gave ourselves to pray for God to be totally in control of everything in our meeting and to expose everything in Smitty.

As we came together we saw remarkable changes in Smitty. He was able to confess Jesus Christ as Lord with joy and enthusiasm and to be very truthful about everything that he had done allowing demonic takeover, even his recent actions which he suspected had led to re-invasion.

It was clear that the more Smitty confessed his total surrender to Christ as Lord and Savior the more evil spirits within were agitated and pushed toward manifestation. Noting this I prayed again and again for Christ Jesus to keep complete control until Smitty had confessed everything that could give him trouble in the future.

Faster than seemed possible for a man to move Smitty shot out of the chair and bolted through the door before we could move. Bowing before our Lord we began to pray with all our might that Smitty's Savior would bring him back into the room. Probably for ten minutes we prayed, asking Jesus Christ to have full control and do with Smitty whatever He wanted done. Freely we confessed we could do nothing of ourselves.

As we prayed the door slowly opened, and Smitty came back into the room walking in a rather wooden way almost as one sleepwalking. He seated himself in the chair facing me and with resignation, wariness, almost as one defeated folded his hands. But that didn't last long, for after prayers were given; and I began commanding the highest evil spirits into manifestation in Christ's name, they came with vehemence and viciousness. But as we worked against them in Christ's name, we all noticed a difference. Though these demons were obviously powerful high rulers in the demonic hierarchy in Smitty, though their words were as threatening and furious, yet there was a weakening, even a note of fear under their tirades. All of us were convinced that we were dealing not only with defeated foes, but with foes that *knew* they were defeated, that they were going to be expelled!

Precisely this took place. For the next two hours our Deliverer forced these ruling evil spirits into manifestation before we even commanded them. Swiftly they were dealt with, and the Lord drove them into hell. Some fifteen heads of networks of demons who answered directly to Satan, the devil, were identified and expelled. Twice Lucifer, the old dragon, came into control; but each time he was soon driven out by the "divinely powerful weapons of our warfare" (2 Cor 10:4). Great rejoicing was taking place with thanksgiving for the amazing way God was cleaning out these evil spirits one after another.

The body grew quiet, the eyes opened, and Smitty was with us, exhausted but the happiest, most radiant Smitty we had ever seen. "I'm free!" he shouted. "They've all gone! I know it! It was like a flock of birds just fleeing out of me. I'm empty, Oh, I am so light I feel I could float. Hallelujah." Testing for evil spirits in the name of Christ did not produce any manifestation or evidence of demons. With immense joy, praise, and thanksgiving to God, we committed Smitty to the protection of our Lord and asked for a total filling by the Holy Spirit of every part of Smitty's body, mind, soul, and will.

"But," you may ask, "is that the end? You thought you had total purging earlier but were mistaken. How is Smitty now?" It is true that we never know how long the Lord Jesus Christ, the only Deliverer, will take to deliver a person of all invaders, one session or twenty-five, one day or two years. We just know that He does it perfectly His way.

Smitty met with us about a month later to talk over the whole experience and to be probed again for demons. External harassing demons can often give a person some ugly experiences and may even lie that they are on the inside. As we contemplated this person now talking with us, it was hard for us to think that this was that demon-driven, desperate person that we had met months before. There was a calmness and peace, a confidence and wholeness, a happy radiance that was inspiring to behold. A son of God had matured amazingly through this most agonizing, painful experience that any Christian can go through. The thrill of a Spirit-filled life was unmistakable in Smitty.

Now many months later we are thankful to report that Smitty has continued to show freedom in Christ and a maturity that is a remarkable witness to others. All of us who have been involved in Smitty's life bear witness with him that Jesus Christ is the Servant of Yahweh predicted by Isaiah who would "proclaim liberty to captives, And freedom to prisoners." Truly Peter testified, ". . . Jesus of Nazareth . . . anointed with the Holy Spirit and with power . . . went about doing good and healing all who were oppressed by the devil . . ." (Acts 10:38). All of us testify, "HE STILL DOES!"

Cases involving children. One of the most startling discoveries in our deliverance work has been the fact that evil spirits have in some way been able to invade some children from early childhood or even at birth. By invasion we mean to be present in the body so as to exercise some physical, emotional, or mental control. Some have gone into wild rages and have attacked parents or have torn at their own faces, bodies, etc. In some cases they have struck walls with their hands or heads, and when the children were demonized they manifested another personality as clearly defined as that seen in some adults. The parents often say, "That simply is not my child that is acting and speaking in that way." In some cases the very mention of phoning an elder for help has brought on violent reaction, threatening, and shouted defiance: "Don't you dare call him!" "I will tear the phone off the wall!" In a few cases the child has been brought to the elders with great effort because of violent resistance due to demonization. Yet these same children are good friends who normally go to the elders and show affection.

Since children have not sinned as morally responsible persons at these early years, we have concluded that the evil spirits must have been handed down to the children as a consequence of the "Law of Generations" in Exodus 20:5: "I, the Lord your God, am a jealous God, visiting the iniquity of the fathers on the children on the third and fourth generations of those who hate me." This was the testimony of evil spirits (whatever value you may place in their word though it was carefully checked by the test of truth). They declared they had a right to occupy the individuals because of the sins of the ancestors which often involved witchcraft, other occult behavior, or violent rebellion against God.

To us it seems highly probable that this includes in some cases the power of the evil spirits to pass from the ancestors who committed these abominable sins before the Lord into the children of the third and fourth generations. In one case, unknown to the person we were working with, her grandmother lay dying in the same state institution in which she was a patient. Upon the death of the grandmother, a demon left her body and entered into the body of the granddaughter. Dr. Koch reported that he had many such cases in his ministry. This does not mean that it inevitably happens, because there is the grace of God mediated through prayer and through the godly members of the same family or of the body of Christ which may prevent invasion.

It is standard procedure with us now to ask the Lord in deliverance sessions to break and nullify the working of the Law of Generations in the individuals with whom we are working. We regularly ask the Lord to force into manifestation any ancestrally-derived demons that He knows need to be dealt with.

Probably another way that young children may suffer an invasion of evil spirits before their years of accountability and personal sin is through the involvement of their own parents in sins especially when the child is conceived as a result of fornication or the mother may have had a previous abortion or the father or mother hate the child before it is born.

Still another possible ground of invasion may be when a relative or friend who is involved in witchcraft or occult practices puts a spell or charm upon the child. This is usually done with the "good intentions" of protecting the child against the powers of darkness. Of course the irony is that the very opposite occurs because such action is not of God. The child may be much more susceptible to demonic attack and oppression in the future. Again Dr. Koch from his long experience in counseling stated, "I have had many such cases. The children are not guilty of the sins of the parents, but they can have a bondage by them. You are right."[3]

Certainly this is an area of great theological difficulty, and we do not pretend to have any answers to the complex questions that can be raised relative to the demonic invasion of children. To us it is simply a fact which we have been forced to accept and to wrestle with the implications. We do not see any support for the teaching of "total depravity" of children, because it is not universal, and other Scriptures oppose that teaching. Also, it is clear that the children are not *guilty* of the sins of the parents, but it appears very likely that the children are suffering the consequences of the sins of the parents. The Law of Generations indicates very clearly that we are living in a moral universe ordered by our perfect heavenly Father, and He has ordained that moral acts of rebellion against His will have consequences for the individuals and for their children.

There is one episode of a demoniac that is reported in the gospel that bears on this question. After the transfiguration, Jesus came down from the mount and met a large crowd, one of whom had presented his demonized son to the disciples for the casting out of the evil spirit. They had not been able to cast out the evil spirit, and even as they were talking about it the "spirit threw him into a convulsion." Jesus then asked his father, "How long has this been happening to him?" And he said, "From childhood" (Mark 9:21). This would indicate that the child had received an evil spirit at an early age and apparently apart from any actual sin on his part. It is quite clear that there was an evil spirit that caused these conditions in the boy, for Jesus "rebuked the unclean spirit, saying to it, 'You deaf and dumb spirit, I command you come out of him and do not enter him again" (Mark 9:25). This is a confirmation that in some way children may be invaded by evil spirits.

Christ, our Lord, set us an example of praying for children and of laying His hands upon them (Mark 10:13-16). Certainly we can follow His example and pray a prayer of faith for the spiritual welfare of any child. Jesus had a grand concern for the children and for the "little ones who believe" as is clearly set forth in Matt 18:1-14. Children must receive our ministry and care along with others who are our responsibility both as pastors and parents.

Thank God that the power of the Lord Jesus Christ is even now available to enable the children who have been invaded to be helped by the prayers and the spiritual teaching of informed Christians. "And the Law came in that the transgression might increase; but where sin increased, grace abounded all the more, that, as sin reigned in death, even so grace might reign through righteousness to eternal life through Jesus Christ our Lord" (Rom 5:20-21). The children are not in such bondage to Satan that they cannot by an act of their free will at some point of life choose to renounce Satan and to turn their lives completely over to the lordship of Jesus Christ. Furthermore, there is increasingly the availability of a work of deliverance by the Lord Jesus Christ in their lives through elders who are practicing the teaching of James 5:13-16.

We have been asked by various parents to come and pray for their children who seem to be manifesting some characteristics of those who have demonic intruders, and we have followed in general the procedure set forth in James 5. We do not ask the children for confession of their sins as some of these children are very small, and most of those we have dealt with have not been Christians. Their comprehension of the meaning of confession of sin is not sufficient to warrant such a requirement. We have prayed, read Scripture, and then given a prayer of faith followed by anointing with oil.

With the parents present we have followed the basic procedure in regard to deliverance and the preparation for it. We have used the less intensive approach and have not asked the Lord to drive the demons into manifestation as we felt this was not necessary or desirable in the life of the child. Particularly we have prayed for the Lord to cancel all working of the Law of Generations and to break any kind of occult action which could have affected him spiritually.

Often the child has reacted in a dramatic way—sudden quietness, intense concentration, wide-eyed staring and, later, release of tension—which has indicated to us that there were actually evil spirits in the child. Occasionally the child has become very restless, hyper, and unable to pay attention. At times the child or an evil spirit has uttered words indicating violence, anger, fear, depression, etc. These have been taken by the pastors as *possible* names or functions of the evil spirits; and, without direct reference to them, the elder has simply prayed for the Lord Jesus Christ to bind all such alien spirits by His blood, to cancel all their grounds or legal rights, and to remove completely all of the powers of darkness from the child and send them directly to Gehenna. The results have been most gratifying, and the parents have reported notable changes in behavior. We are convinced that the Lord Jesus Christ has honored this procedure, even in the case of children.

These typical case studies may enlighten you more particularly about the utter seriousness of the spiritual work of deliverance by the Lord Jesus Christ, some of the dangers involved and, most of all, a realization of the immeasurable greatness of the power which gives victory over all evil spirits. Truly the Lord Jesus Christ is Victor, and through Him we are able to overwhelmingly conquer these demonic invaders. You will be enabled to experience this if you follow Scripture and invite the Deliverer to work in your faith.

NOTES

1. We had the additional help of another worker during the sessions for eight hours each. This allowed us some relief. There were some rest stops, of course, during this period but not meals. Since that time we have never had such long sessions, for which we thank God. There has been less need for them in that the Lord Jesus Christ has been pleased to expel the evil spirits in a shorter period of time. Also, we learned that a period of more than two or three hours could be rather exhausting, tiring, and even spiritually dangerous for both the client and the counselors. When tiredness became apparent, we practiced discernment and sought to close the session as soon as was expedient in the light of the deliverance needed. We would advise all workers to limit wherever possible a deliverance session to approximately three and not more

than four hours though we recognize that there can be a number of variables and exceptions. All of us have from time to time experienced an abnormal sleepiness and tiredness which we believe is a demonic activity because prayer has usually freed us of the condition.

2. Cf. Appendix C.

3. Kurt Koch, personal letter to authors, December 16, 1982.

12

Physical and Mental Healing Through Nutrition

The Psalmist says, "I will give thanks to Thee, for I am fearfully and wonderfully made" (Ps 139:14). The most learned physician is in awe of those processes that take up where his skills end and healing takes place. A wise doctor cooperates with nature, i.e. God's plan, the design of His handiwork.

We have basic needs in all areas of life; and when they are neglected, the quality of life suffers. In recent years we have begun to understand more fully that what we breathe, eat, and even what we think can have a profound effect upon our well-being. Good physical and mental health is often within our grasp, calling for common sense and discretion on our part. Many of us fail to give our own bodies the care we know we must give a new automobile to make certain it does not break down.

Various researchers have recognized that there has been a grave disregard of and failure to take into account the nutritional and chemical factors in mental illness. Yet mental sickness often is the evidence of abnormality in metabolism and the enzyme systems.

A typically schizophrenic, sixteen year old girl who saw visions, heard voices, was paranoid, had depression, and spoke of suicide frequently was found by Dr. Abram Hoffer to be allergic to cows' milk and peanuts. Admittedly, pure, raw cows' milk or peanut butter may not have been the culprits. It may have been the processing techniques or some unnatural ingredient absorbed by the cows in the milk, or perhaps something like aphylotoxin, which is often used to protect peanut crops.

Dr. Hoffer comments, "As soon as I gave her a glass of milk, the girl became completely psychotic within the hour. Her schizophrenic symptoms returned as before . . . . Now she knows she must avoid milk and peanuts. She has remained well since."[1]

This girl's story is one of many illustrations which verify that orthomolecular psychiatry is a major help in treating mental illness.

THE BALANCED DIET

Much has been written about a balanced diet and minimum daily requirements (MDR). The fact remains we are as different biochemically as we are in appearance, and a "balanced diet" may do well for one person but not meet another person's true needs. It is important to know oneself, to be aware of "peak" and "low" times, to consider what factors may contribute to that "peak" or "low" feeling. What amount of sleep restores our body to good energy output? What amount of exercise keeps us agile and fit? Which foods leave us clear-headed and ready for activity? Which foods slow us down and practically signal naptime? It can be very enlightening to take a look at what you are actually eating. Write down your food intake for two weeks. Make note of the way you feel each day, whether you accomplished a lot with energy to spare or dragged through the day. This can alert you to foods that may be a problem for you. Everyone of us desires to feel well, to have energy and stamina to do those things we have to do daily, to be clear-headed and optimistic—in short, to be able to cope with the stress of modern living.

Because we are so different, it takes time to develop a right pattern of eating and correct vitamin/mineral supplementation for our greatest benefit. Many nutritionists and medical doctors discredit vitamin/mineral supplementation because they recommend that "all" we need do is to eat "balanced dietary meals." What they fail to recognize or to admit is the way food is so highly processed and refined today removes most nutrients and changes others so they cannot be properly absorbed by the body. Yes, it is virtually impossible for anyone to eat "balanced dietary meals" without in-depth study or guidance as to how to go about this tremendously difficult task which is so simply stated by those who should know and who do not. There are some basic changes you can make, if you have not already done so, which can be a significant step toward improving your well-being. The table on the next page lists a few widely consumed items which have physically or mentally damaging ingredients and some suggested substitutes that can be used.

Most, if not all, of the items listed in the table are addictive substances. Our bodies once accustomed to them crave them. It takes a sincere effort to eliminate them and time for taste to adjust; but it can be done, and the reward is a healthier body and a clearer mind. Other basic steps to increase nutrition for the body include: eliminate refined and processed foods and use fresh produce in place of commercially canned or frozen vegetables and fruits. Gradually lessen the time you cook vegetables and use a steamer rather than boil out all the nutritional goodness and then pour it down the drain. The enhanced flavor will be a surprise to your palate.

Dr. Abram Hoffer states, "Allergy to sugar and other components of processed food may react on the skin in the form of hives, rashes, itch, swelling, redness, decreased ability to move because of skin rubbing and tautness, and pain. The urinary bladder may shrink and cause bed wetting. The central nervous system can react, causing a variety of unpleasant symptoms such as tension, anxiety, depression, hallucinations, thought disorders, and changes in behavior. The neuroses or psychoneuroses are psychiatric diseases that mainly alter mood."[3]

There is a danger in self-determination of diet and/or vitamin therapy. It is the old "if something is good for you, more is better" theory. But doctors have found that there is as much danger on the one side as on the other: too much is as bad as too little. Indeed the excess of some nutritional elements could bring about conditions of mental illness in certain persons akin to those caused by the absence of those nutritional elements. Common sense should tell us if we have made all the basic improvements we can; yet if time passes without significant improvement, there must be more serious factors involved. At that point we

EXAMPLES OF WIDELY CONSUMED FOOD AND DRINK WHICH DAMAGE MIND AND BODY

Item	Damaging Ingredient	Recognized Damaging Effect	Substitute or Alternate (without preservatives)
Refined White Flour Products. Polished Rice	Refined Carbohydrates	Malnutrition, neuroses, physical illness	Whole Grain Products
Sugar - White and Brown	Refined Carbohydrates, Converts to Sucrose	Addictive, Diabetes Mellitus, hypoglycemia, seborrheic dermatitis, atherosclerosis, etc.	Raw, unprocessed honey Synthetic sugar substitutes are not recommended
Coffee	Caffeine	Addictive, nervousness, stomach cramps, insomnia in some	Non-coffee substitutes. Rombouts Swiss process decaffeinated coffee Standard methylene-chloride de-caffeinated coffees are cheaper but are not recommended
Tea	Caffeine	Similar to but milder than coffee	Kaffree plus a variety of herbal teas free of caffeine
Cocoa and Chocolate	Sugar, caffeine, theobromine	Similar to effects of sugar and coffee Speeds up heartbeat, stimulates nervous system	Use similar substitutes as those recommended to replace coffee, tea and soft drinks
Soft drinks	Sugar and/or caffeine	Similar to effects of sugar and coffee	Vegetable or fruit juices (apple juice, cider, etc.)
Salt	Sodium Chloride	Hypertension or high blood pressure; hardening of the circulatory system in connective tissue, tendons and ligaments.[2] Robs body of calcium, may cause unhealthy potassium/sodium imbalance	Sea salt or potassium chloride are not recommended substitutes. Moderation is acceptable. One should develop a taste for foods without the need to add salt

need the expertise of someone more knowledgeable. Don't try to do it yourself, but get professional help.

THOSE WHO MAY HELP

Because we are mental, physical, emotional, and spiritual creatures, a breakdown in one area can affect the others. While most (not all) medical doctors tend not to deal with preventive medicine but with symptoms, after illness or disease is evident, an increasing number of psychologists and psychiatrists are beginning to see a clearer picture of the curative effects of nutrition upon the body, and specifically upon the mind. These and others who have studied the body, including some chiropractors, podiatrists, and osteopaths, have been intrigued by and led into a study of the chemical processes of the body—biochemical functions (metabolic processes).

"Orthomolecular Medicine"[4] is the practice of medicine which considers the nutritional needs of the patient. "Orthomolecular Nutrition" recognizes each patient has specifically peculiar requirements for nutrients and vitamin/mineral supplements to function at his or her best. "Orthomolecular nutrition offers a program for each of the following categories of individuals," according to Doctors Hoffer and Walker:

"(1) People who are very healthy now but would like to increase the probability that they will remain the rest of their lives in super good health.

"(2) People who need to change their pattern of living and eating in order to gain a much better state of health—good health.

"(3) People who are already in the throes of serious physical and psychiatric disability.

"People in category 3 will use orthomolecular nutrition as a treatment program. Categories 1 and 2 are preventive and maintenance programs."[5]

Each of us as a person is remarkably affected by the nutritional aspects of our lives, for these determine biochemical conditions in our nervous system. In physical and mental terms to a great measure we are what we eat. Our sense of well-being is conditioned both by our environment and by the proper working of our physical and mental constitution. Only recently have some doctors begun to realize how great a part the nutritional factors enter into the determination of our physical and mental health. But nutrients are necessary for the nourishment and enrichment of the brain, and when these are lacking the brain is weakened, just as the body is when deprived of food. In the one case you have bad mental health; in the other you have bad physical health.

The doctor who follows the nutritional approach to good health employs a number of tests to determine a patient's needs. These can include a glucose tolerance test for high/low blood sugar, determination of the level of dissolved carbon dioxide and carbonic acid in the blood, oxidation rate (the rate at which tissues turn food into energy), blood test for high/low mineral levels, sub-lingual (under the tongue) allergy tests, skin tests for allergies, a blood test for serum B12 level, and determination of brain allergies or adverse physical reaction to particular foods, based upon evaluation of the client's self-monitored eating habits.

John D. Kirschmann says, "Allergy specialists and psychiatrists have been successfully treating patients with psychiatric symptoms by isolating foods and chemicals in the environment that are causing the mental disturbances. The symptoms range from fatigue and dizziness to hyperactivity to catatonia (a complete loss of voluntary motion) and hallucinations."[6] There is increasing evidence that allergic reactions may also be a factor influencing criminal behavior. Improper diet can adversely affect not only our bodies but our minds as well. Severe emotional problems can result when blood sugar is too low.

Blood sugar balance is imperative, because the brain must have the glucose which it needs. When deprived of it, emotional stability is lost and disturbed behavior results. Some researchers are convinced that persons can experience all kinds of depression, fear, and even inclinations to violence because of the low level of glucose in their bloodstream.

The authors have come across case studies which clearly support the premise that numerous psychological problems and neuroses are often lessened or even removed by expert attention to the nutritional conditions. Some who have been diagnosed as schizophrenic have responded very well to carefully prepared diets and have returned to normal living. Nutrition was not and is not *the* answer to every emotional problem or mental illness, but it is a remarkably effective means that needs to be tested in each case to see what it can do. It certainly cannot harm the person, as many drugs can.[7]

There is a psychochemical reaction to a biochemical imbalance. Tranquilizers and anti-depressants serve only to mask physical, mental, and emotional conditions. "Disappointment and annoyance are emotions I feel at the number of psychiatrists who remain content to keep their schizophrenic patients heavily and permanently tranquilized. Those patients are perfect consumers of services, support, and every other community resource; but never again are they able to be productive citizens of society. They are being given cruel, ignorant, and inhumane treatment. Keeping them tranquilized holds them in a state of abnormality not reconcilable with the precepts of morality—the science of the good and the nature of the right."[8] The physician with training and applied experience in nutrition and chemical processes of the body (metabolism) can render real service to the individual who, despite efforts to eat properly, respecting his body's needs for exercise and rest, and using vitamin and mineral supplements, still fails to achieve optimum energy and well-being.

NUTRITION AND ALCOHOLISM

It is of first importance for the counselor to determine if the client addicted to alcohol sincerely desires to change. Is the client willing to make the great sacrificial effort necessary to' achieve release from the grip of alcohol? If not, then the counselor will be wasting time that might otherwise be more wisely used to aid someone who will be responsive. Much has been written about alcoholism, and various approaches have been used to assist the alcoholic to recovery. Let us review a recent case history of a successful approach that encouraged a client (let us call him John) to become a recovered alcoholic.

John, a middle-aged business executive, and one of the authors worked together in a commercial business operation;

but we had not contacted each other socially for several years until John called to request we have lunch together. After light conversation John, with tears in his eyes, seriously said, "I have something important and very difficult to tell you! I am an alcoholic; it is destroying my self-respect. I just received my second citation for driving while intoxicated, and I need your help!" I comforted John, told him I knew how hard it was to make such an admission and advised him that by himself he had just overcome the greatest obstacle by openly recognizing that he had a problem. Because of my already heavy counseling responsibilities I leveled with John telling him I would be willing to encourage him in his battle with alcohol but only if he was sincere and followed my recommendations closely.

Two days later we met again for lunch, and John was given the following plan made up just for him.

1. Call a family conference with wife, sons, and daughters. Level with them that you have decided that you are an alcoholic; you have requested counseling; here is your battle plan and you need their help, understanding, and encouragement to win this fight.

2. Join your local Alcoholics Anonymous group and follow its program exactly.

3. Seek spiritual counsel from and pray with your parish priest. (John is a Roman Catholic.)

4. Read a couple of chapters in your Bible daily and pray, talking to God at various times throughout each day.

5. Meet with the counselor for a business lunch about once a week to share your progress and to pray together.

6. Change your diet and take nutritional supplements according to the following chart. Also check with your family doctor to make certain he agrees with these nutritional recommendations and there is no conflicting effect with his medical treatment of your high blood pressure condition. (John's doctor said the nutritional plan couldn't do him any harm, so he might as well follow it.)

The reason for this is simply because some medical authorities recognize that alcoholics are people who suffer from definite food allergies. They usually have mineral deficiencies. A major one is the lack of magnesium, which has a lot to do with the excitability of the nervous system. So there are not only emotional/ psychological and spiritual problems in the alcoholic, but some very fundamental nutritional defects. When these are given the attention they deserve, much better results will be gained in the other areas of counseling.

7. John was given one or two selected chapters to read from a book discussing nutrition, alcohol, and their relation to physical and mental health. He was also given two selected chapters to read from Francis MacNutt's spiritual counseling book entitled, *Healing*.[9]

Our instructions relative to the use of these nutritional supplements indicated that Acidophilus was to be taken one-half hour before breakfast and one-half hour before bedtime, while all other tablets or capsules should be taken with meals. Pangamic Acid is very important as it has helped many alcoholics decrease their craving for alcohol. In addition to helping the alcoholism, the supplements above should improve the overall health condition of the individual. It is also desirable to cut out entirely from the diet all sugar and sugar substitutes. (Replace with raw honey, if necessary.) Also stop using white flour products and replace with rye or whole wheat products.[10]

At the time of this writing (five months later) John has had a completely successful battle against alcohol. He followed all seven of the recommendations exactly, has not touched a drop of alcohol, has lower blood pressure with less medication, and feels great. He is now giving talks on alcoholism and is helping other alcoholics fight the battle he just went through. John also recognizes that he must be on guard for the rest of his life, as must all recovered alcoholics. Admittedly, John was ready for counseling. His is an unusual success story, which is not typical of many other heart-breaking, tear-filled, long-term battles on the road to recovery; but it is thrilling to be part of such a significant victory.

Subsequent to the counseling of John, the authors have become aware of the use of L-glutamine in the therapeutic treatment of alcoholism. Some alcoholics treated with L-glutamine are able to stop drinking altogether, with a minimum of anguish.

NUTRITIONAL SUPPLEMENTS TO HELP COMBAT EFFECT OF AND TO HELP DECREASE CRAVING FOR ALCOHOL

COLUMN A No. Tablets/Capsules		Name	Recommended Brand (Based on availability) Dosage per Column A	Brand Recommended as More Effective Dosage per directions on label
Daily for First 2 Weeks	Daily Thereafter			
1	2	Multi-Vitamin & Mineral Supplement	"Plus" Formula #190	CTR Multi V + M Bioenergy Inc. Princeton, N.J. 08540 Kal's Mega Vita-min
1/2	1	Pangamic Acid	"Kal" Pan Gam #15 Calcium Pangamate (100 mg. each)	Bioenergy Inc. or Alacer Corporation
2	3	Calcium-Magnesium	"Schiff" Mega Chelated Calcium-Magnesium (Ca-110 mg. each) (Mg-78 mg. each) "Kal" Calcium & Magnesium	Same manufacturers as above*
1	3	Zinc	"Schiff" Mega Chelated Zinc (50 mg. each) "Kal" zinc-15 Amino Acid Chelate	Zinc Orotate Zinc-O-Tabs Alacer Corp., Buena Park, CA 90622 Kal Zinc Orotate*
2	2	Acidophilus (should contain L. Acidophilus, L. Bulgaricus, L. Thermophilus)	"Schiff" Acidophilus with Goat Milk	Any brands identified in this last column so long as they contain at least the three types of Acidophilus noted.

*Use only amino acid chelate or orotate minerals.

"Researchers theorize that alcohol may improve the transport of glutamic acid or glutamine across the blood-brain barrier or speed absorption of glutamic acid by brain cells. The genetic script of an alcoholic may dictate that his brain cells require abnormally large quantities of glutamic acid—quantities beyond that supplied by a regular diet. Or his genetic makeup may cause him to have an inadequate supply of enzymes necessary for the conversion of glutamic acid to L-glutamine. Transport of the amino acid into the brain would be impaired.

"Supplemental doses of L-glutamine would supply an abundance of the amino acid so that the needs of the brain cells could be met if needs were high due to genetic causes or if metabolism of glutamic acid were for some reason impaired. Alcohol would no longer be required as the catalyst to carry glutamic acid across the barrier and into the cells."[11]

DANGERS IN DRUG THERAPY

Words of caution have been given in a number of places in this book about the limitations and dangers of drug therapy for physical or mental illness. This danger cannot be over-emphasized, as it prevails throughout the medical world. For the most part it is almost totally ignored by family physicians and psychiatrists. The negative aspect of the use of bacteriostatic drugs is simply that they destroy the good bacterial growth as well as the destructive. This can bring about undesirable emotional conditions, resulting in abnormal behavioral problems. These may include unwarranted fears, anxiety, depression, anger, or reckless, irrational behavior. We are concerned that you are aware of the undesirable and even injurious effects on mental/emotional health that can come from the use of the widely used antibiotics.

Of all the information available on medicine and nutrition, we recommend that every counselor buy and utilize regularly the following two handbooks, which are so important they may be considered indispensable to every household: James W. Long, M.D., *The Essential Guide to Prescription Drugs.* New York: Harper & Row Publishers, 1982 ($9.95, paperback).

John D. Kirschmann, *Nutrition Almanac*. New York: McGraw-Hill Co., 1979 ($8.95, paperback).

Dr. James Long's reference book reviews usual, expected side effects of prescription drugs, the serious and infrequent side effects, and the range of minimum to maximum dosages. Cautions are included regarding the advisability of using each drug for children, pregnant women, or people over sixty. Interaction with other drugs and interaction with certain foods are included, as is a host of other very important information.

As counselors who desire to genuinely help people and return them to being able to live healthy and wholesome lives as God has planned, we must be concerned with nutrition because it is integral to a person's physical, mental, emotional, and spiritual condition. Therefore, we should desire to have the most extensive knowledge possible in the field of nutrition in order to advise people or, if necessary, refer them to competent doctors who can set up sound nutritional procedures for them. As in all things, there must be balance and good judgment in this matter. Use of nutrition is not a cure-all nor the answer to every problem of the individual who is sick.

Fasting is another facet of health care that can contribute to a person's well-being, particularly as it is done unto the Lord with prayer (see Appendix H). It not only has spiritual benefits, but can be useful in improving the physical health of individuals. Again, fasting and its effects vary with the individual. Under the guidance of a knowledgeable nutritionist, a fasting program can accomplish weight loss where diets have failed.

We are confident that the Lord God Almighty has created us in a marvelous way. This is certainly borne out by the ability of the body to withstand the immense amount of abuse that it often suffers and the long-time disregard of the most reasonable requirements for maintaining the health of the body. Counselors have the privilege of helping people to become healthy persons who can function as God intended them to function. Such restored people have a great appreciation of the Master Physician, the Lord Jesus Christ, and realize their lives are going to be immeasurably better if they allow Him to be the Lord of their lives.

NOTES

1. Abram Hoffer and Morton Walker, *Orthomolecular Nutrition* (New Canaan, CT: Keats Publishing, 1978), pp. 176-177.

2. Max Garten, *"Civilized" Diseases and Their Circumvention* (San Jose, CA: Maxmillion World Publishers, Inc., 1978), pp. 83-84.

3. Hoffer and Walker, op. cit., p. 23.

4. Hoffer and Walker, op. cit., p. 29. "Physicians seeking training in orthomolecular psychiatry can apply to the Academy of Orthomolecular Psychiatry, 1691 Northern Boulevard, Manhasset, N.Y. 11030; 516-627-7260. To assist outside organizations and individuals seeking treatment, the Academy keeps an active referral list consisting of its Fellows."

5. Ibid., pp. 65-66.

6. John D. Kirschmann, *Nutrition Almanac* (New York: McGraw-Hill Book Co., 1979), p. 150.

7. Some will be disappointed in our lack of case studies. One consideration was space, but we also were not granted permission to quote some relevant material. The interested person will be able to find it.

8. Hoffer and Walker, op. cit., p. 41.

9. Francis MacNutt, *Healing* (Notre Dame, IN: Ave Maria Press, 1974).

10. Information partially obtained from Kirschmann, op. cit.

11. A KAL, Self-Education Series, 1982, from makers of KAL, Inc. 8357 Canoga Avenue, Canoga Park, CA 91304.

13

Practical Considerations For A Healing Ministry

In Christian counseling the best place to begin is always with counseling's missing link, the Lord Jesus Christ. Counseling is a serious ministry because it involves lives that are precious to God. What the counselor does may affect the eternal destiny of the counselee. The attitude and work of the counselor may have far-reaching results for better or worse in the physical, emotional, or spiritual life of the client. Extremely poor counseling could jeopardize the physical or the spiritual life of the counselee. Because of the potential gravity of the consequences of counseling it is necessary that the counselor be trained and qualified.

SOME QUALIFICATIONS

The highest qualification is to know God and His Word, to be spiritually mature. The Christian counselor should evidence a strong, genuine life of devotion, commitment, and obedience to Jesus Christ as the Lord of all his life. Proper spiritual preparation is an absolute necessity for the power of God to be brought into the life of the client. Earnest prayer, request for the guidance of the Holy Spirit of our Lord, and the reading of Scriptural passages especially appropriate and meaningful to the counselor and the counselee will lay the firmest groundwork for successful counseling. We believe that the Holy Spirit is the great Counselor who works through his servants and is the One who can effect the healing.

Educationally the counselor needs to be as thoroughly prepared as he can be with a strong liberal arts foundation plus courses in philosophy and psychology. Graduate work naturally increases his knowledge and ability. Any and all clinical experience is invaluable as well as the experiences of the not always welcomed "school of hard knocks." All of the experiences of life can educate the counselor to be an understanding person who can empathize with other persons.

Confidentiality is an essential quality of the counselor. He needs to assure the counselee that all the disclosures will be kept in strict confidence. This must be rigidly followed because any use of the information could be potentially damaging to the client. If it becomes known that you do not keep confidential the information imparted to you, you will find that people will not come to you.

Another valuable qualification of a good counselor is that he has a listening ear. He listens with care, sympathy, and with discernment for what the person is really telling him, what is back of the words. The counselee needs to be encouraged to freely describe the symptoms which precipitated the conference and to feel warmly accepted as he does so.

Since most problems and concerns relate directly to and directly affect the person being counseled, try to concentrate on the roots of the problems of the counselee. Give your undivided attention to the client. Listen attentively without interrupting or attempting to formulate remarks, comments, or advice while you are in the process of getting all the facts you can.

Still another quality of a good counselor is that he has good judgment in making referrals to competent professionals. He will determine when the problem is too large for him to handle effectively. Specialists, associations, agencies, and other professional services are available in nearly every area of human need. Each counselor should develop a reference file for his own geographical location which identifies the types of services available with the information that enables the counselee to make contact with the referral. The counselee or someone he trusts can make such a selective list after sifting out the information about various referral services which are most effective.

Good judgment is needed to detect the meaning of strained relationships between the counselee and others (spouse, child, friend, family member, co-worker, supervisor, etc.). Comments about the other persons in his life may give you a clue as to the root problems either in the client or in the other person. It may be that you will have to seek to involve the other person in the counseling process to achieve maximum success.

THE ANALYSIS OF THE PROBLEM

During the initial stages of counseling we ought to consider a variety of possible courses of evaluation ranging from fundamental to highly complex. Keep in mind that the personal time of the counselor is a precious commodity, and good stewardship of time is needed to maintain an effective counseling ministry. With these thoughts in focus it is desirable that the counselor probe first for fundamental causes and non-complex solutions before delving into the possibility that more complex problems may be present. The following table suggests some easy to recognize problems and some possible non-complex solutions. (The footnotes at the end of this chapter apply to this table.)

Please note these two precautions regarding the use of the table:

1. The table is not intended to be complete. It provides a surface sampling designed to encourage the counselor to first consider some fundamental approaches in the evaluation and solving of problems.

2. Beware of self-analysis or self-determination of therapy without consulting competent professional physicians, psychologists, psychiatrists or nutritionists. It is illegal to practice medicine without a license.

Many problems require corrective action in more than one area, such as nutritional, spiritual, organic (physical), psychological, etc. The solution for one problem area may remove a block which facilitates or accelerates improvement in another area. Counseling seems to be approached most effectively in series rather than in parallel which simply means it is more desirable to concentrate upon the solution to one area of illness

SOME TYPICAL INITIAL OBSERVATIONS OF POTENTIALLY ELEMENTARY PROBLEMS

Description of Problem	Possible Contributing Causes/Intensifiers	Possible Solutions	Affects	
			Male	Female
Abnormal psychological or physical reactions, cyclic depression, impatience	Inadequate rest, inadequate diet	Increase sleep hours, balance diet, balance vitamin supplements	X	X
Anxiety, headaches, overwhelming emotional instability, dizziness, sudden weight gain	Side effect of birth control pill[1,2]	Temporarily stop using the pill, substitute condom or diaphragm		X
Fatigue, headaches, dizziness, clear thinking is difficult	Hypoglycemia or low blood sugar	Medical blood analysis, special diet, modify eating habits per physician's guidance	X	X
Disappointed with life, fearful of life's direction, lonely	Spiritual	Daily Bible reading, daily quiet time for prayer, teaching from counselor or friend	X	X
Abnormal over or under weight	Physical-spiritual-nutritional	Medical analysis, diet, spiritual assistance, stop junk foods	X	X
Emotional difficulties, Spiritual difficulties	Side effect of prescription drugs or tranquilizers[2]	Ease off consumption, concentrate on eliminating causes instead of treating symptoms, act under physician's guidance	X	X

or weakness at a time. This has been impressed upon us as we observed God's model in Scripture and saw His working in spiritual counseling. God chooses to work only as fast as the needs and the spiritual readiness of the counselee allow. He also works in accord with the availability of a spiritually mature counselor.

A wide variety of physical and mental types of distress can be caused or intensified by alcohol, nicotine and smoking, caffeine intake from coffee, tea, soft drinks or chocolate. Other contributors to distress can be excessive intake of sugar, highly processed foods or foods with high preservative content, and the so-called junk foods which are found in great abundance today. Typical junk foods are identified in chapter 12, Physical and Mental Healing Through Nutrition. Our obvious suggested remedy is to replace these harmful items with suitable alternates and wholesome foods as recommended in chapter 12.

Very few medical practitioners of today have had any but the briefest exposure to nutritional aspects of physical or mental health, and so they give little if any guidance in these areas. Some even go so far as to belittle the effect of nutrition upon health because it is not yet understood completely nor taught in depth in the average medical school. We recommend that counselors read books on nutritional health. It is desirable for a counselor to encourage a spouse or co-worker to read extensively on his own to become knowledgeable in depth with regard to nutritional effects upon the mind and the body. Counselors should not prescribe but should enable others to become aware of available, reliable resource information and enable them to apply good judgment in utilizing these resources. Referral to medical and psychological professionals for tests and evaluations can be effective tools for every counselor, e.g., glucose tolerance test, Taylor-Johnson Temperament Analysis and others.

When the counselor encounters a Christian, young or old in the faith, who is confused in his relationship to God one of three key areas often contributes to his spiritual confusion. Teaching in these areas can do much to accelerate spiritual maturity and oftimes aids in relieving mental and emotional distress:

1. Understanding the difference between legalism and grace.
2. Understanding sin, forgiveness of sin, and consequences of sin.
3. Understanding the insidious and destructive nature of pride and preparing spiritual defenses to conquer sinful pride.

For the reader's assistance, lessons given by the authors on sin and pride are presented in Appendixes A and B. These may be useful to the counselor whenever a specialized need for these teachings arises.

When it becomes apparent to the counselor that the counselee has problems of a complex nature, the counselor must go far beyond the scope of information in this chapter for assistance. Accordingly the wise counselor will refer suspected medical problems to physicians, nutritional problems to those specifically trained in nutrition, and psychological problems to Christian psychologists or psychiatrists, etc.

Symptoms of a complex problem which may require professional referral may include but not be limited to:

1. Psychological
   a. Schizophrenia is a severe form of mental disorder or mental illness characterized by withdrawn, bizarre, and sometimes delusional behavior and by intellectual and emotional deterioration. Delusional behavior may include exaggerated changes in personality.
   b. Psychasthenia is an incapacity to resolve doubts or uncertainties or to resist phobias, obsessions, or compulsions that one knows are irrational.
   c. Extreme depression that does not go away for long periods of time points to some heavy problems.
   d. Verbal expressions indicating suicidal tendencies should be taken seriously.
2. Spiritual
   a. The inability to lead a consistent Christian life is evidence of a problem of willful disobedience to God.
   b. Volitional inability to read Scripture or to pray, or the temporary loss of ability to hear as the counselor prays or reads Scriptures is an indication of a serious problem.

    c. On special occasions such as taking the Lord's Supper the Christian may find his mind full of evil or blasphemous thoughts. Some have not been able to partake of communion.

3. Physical / Medical

    a. Extreme overweight (obesity) is a problem with possible overlap in spiritual or psychological areas.

    b. Alarming weight loss approaching starvation is an indicator of problems. When this starvation is deliberate, the condition is *Anorexia Nervosa* and requires immediate attention.[3]

In this chapter we have tried to give some elementary and practical preparations for doing a successful job of counseling. The more thoroughly qualified you are by natural gifts and by educational preparation the better you are as a counselor. The greater your ability to analyze the essence of the problem the more effectively you can bring help to the client. There are natural abilities which need to be developed, and there are acquired skills which need to be learned so that the counselor is well equipped to bring the best help to the counselee. One of the most important qualifications of a good counselor is the ability to know when to refer a client to someone else and to do it at once.

NOTES

1. Abram Hoffer and Morton Walker, *Orthomolecular Nutrition, New Lifestyle for Super Good Health* (New Canaan, Ct: Keats Publishing Inc., 1978), p. 163.

2. James W. Long, *Prescription Drugs, What You Need to Know For Safe Drug Use* (New York: Harper and Row, Publishers, 1982).

3. We have had one brief encounter with a person suffering from *Anorexia Nervosa,* but no in-depth counseling took place. However, our observations pointed to the basically spiritual nature of the problem. We believe that Christ can heal anorexics through the procedures we follow. This "mysterious illness" is especially found among girls and women in affluent societies who frequently come from "good homes" of concerned, interested families. But anorexics perceive themselves as being fat or overweight though they are thin, undernourished, even starving. They have no appetite for food and refuse to eat. While there are psychological and sociological factors—often

low self-esteem, feelings of rejection, pride, guilt, failure—yet demonic invasion seems highly probable. Our view is strengthened by the descriptive terms used by anorexics about their condition such as tormented, an internal dictator rules out eating, a demonic power overpowers them, and yet a thrill of success in holding down the evil spirit or the dark force that would drive them to indulge in food. Perhaps our Lord will want us to work with anorexics in the future.

14

The Chaos In Counseling

Ours is a world of increasing desperation. It is a world of individuals who have been exposed to bizarre behavior sometimes hidden but more and more being exposed with boldness without apology. In America we have a new generation which expects, indeed demands, instant gratification as if this were a God-given birthright. Ours is a world where sin and sinful behavior is creeping subtly, relentlessly through society making even Christians insensitive to sin. We are being "conned" into accepting that which is to God unacceptable, bizarre, and that which violates His loving counsel. Material gratification, drugs, alcohol, fornication, adultery, homosexuality, lying, cheating, passivity of mind and mind manipulation techniques pervade every area of public and private life. These all leave physical, mental, emotional, and spiritual scars. They intensify guilt complexes and cause feelings of inferiority and inadequacy, and ever higher statistics attest to the magnitude of mental illness worldwide.

CONFLICTING THEORIES OF THERAPY

In the field of counseling there still exists a multitude of conflicting schools of thought and of different treatments for the same symptoms. The variety of treatment is narrowly confined often by the attitude of professionals who may have a vested interest of pride and finances in their particular field of practice. Approaches to counseling are also narrowly confined often by the unpaid counselor who has a vested interest of pride in the particular school of thought promoted by the organization which supports him or by the source which trained him or both.

C. H. Patterson says, "Because the foundations (of schizophrenia) are laid in infancy, inherited constitutions play a more important role, although the constitutional theory is not established. The contribution of psychoanalysis to the schizophrenias is more explanatory than therapeutic."[1] From this and similar comments we see that some objective psychologists and psychiatrists, unencumbered by pride and unwavering under the threat of financial inconvenience, admit that various approaches used in psychological counseling may not work.

There are resources available which expose the conflicting critical comments upon each other's philosophies of scholarly, practicing psychologists-psychiatrists. One such source which provides supporting evidence as to the validity of our premise that there is "Chaos in Counseling" is an article from *The Cincinnati Enquirer* entitled, "Federal Government Seeks to Analyze Role of Psychotherapy."[2] The article identifies three government agencies which are investigating the usefulness of Psychotherapy. They are the U.S. Senate, the National Institute of Health, and the Alcohol, Drug Abuse and Mental Health Administration. In this article the lone supporter of psychotherapy seems to be Dr. Donald Langsley, president of the American Psychiatric Association and former chairman of the Department of Psychiatry at the University of Cincinnati. Dr. Langsley says, "There are enough positive, controlled studies among the 700 to demonstrate that psychotherapy works."[3]

Dr. Langsley goes on to qualify his statement: "But," he adds, "now the problem is specificity. What for what? That is the question. What kind of therapy should be used for what kind of illness, and who can do the therapy well? We must try to answer these questions."[4]

Among eminent psychiatrists who expressed concerns over the scientific basis and effectiveness of psychotherapy were Dr. Jerome Frank of John Hopkins, Dr. Hans Strupp of Vanderbilt, Dr. Norman Brill of UCLA, Dr. Lester Luborsky of the University of Pennsylvania, Dr. Donald Klein, head of the New

York Psychiatric Institute. Dr. Morris Parloff, National Institute of Mental Health's chief specialist in psychotherapy research commented: "No form of therapy has ever been initiated without a claim that it has unique therapeutic advantages. And no form of therapy has ever been abandoned because of its failure to live up to these claims."[5]

In a recent review of the 700 studies noted above, Parloff noted a number of what he called "puzzling" conclusions: "1. That different forms of therapy made no difference in effect. All the schools of therapy seemed to give the same results. 2. That the length of treatment didn't seem to matter. Short and long treatments had the same effect. 3. That the amount of experience a therapist has did not seem to matter. Different levels of experience produced the same effects."[6]

DRUG THERAPY

Drug therapy is another approach being used more frequently by psychiatrists and other medical practitioners. It is our experience that drug therapy ought to be avoided except on rare occasions when life is in jeopardy. Every drug has side effects, some known and some unknown.[7] Some drugs like antibiotics cure an illness, but others such as minor tranquilizers may tend to cause dependence on the drug. Tranquilizers tend to mask an illness, especially mental-emotional-spiritual illnesses. Not only can a tranquilizer typically camouflage an illness, but it can weaken a person and may cause passivity of the mind with further deterioration of mental faculties. We have observed that heavy drug sedation and drug therapy prescribed by psychiatrists often result in robot-like thinking and behavior on the part of clients. In this condition a client may be incapable of thinking clearly enough to be helped even by the wisest of counselors.

"Tranquilizers such as Valium and Librium are good at reducing anxiety and tension, but they may interfere with thinking and can become habit forming . . . . As Psychologist Steve Matthysse of the Mailman Research Center explains, while agitation and disordered thought diminish in the drugged patient, the drugs do very little to move the patient toward recovery or to help him relate to other people. Says Matthysse: 'It's a sad thing, but a schizophrenic (on drugs) is very rarely motivated to do anything really consequential.'"[8]

Another caution comes from the Department of Health, Education and Welfare: "The FDA is planning to advise physicians that Valium was not meant to abolish everyday stress . . . . Demonstrating that many people do have problems with Valium addiction, there is now a movement called 'Valium Anonymous,' founded by Leland Ahern of Altoona, PA, who experienced sharp withdrawal symptoms after he stopped taking Valium. Ahern had been taking Valium for 7 years at a prescription level of 15 milligrams a day. A former alcoholic, Ahern describes his farewell to Valium as 'many many times worse' than his withdrawal from alcohol."[9]

ALTERNATIVE APPROACHES

There is a definite place in mental health which calls for psychological and psychiatric analysis and treatment. Yet these fields have numerous advocates of humanistic and existential models of philosophy. Most of these approaches, in an effort to promote popular concepts such as self-actualization (self-indulgence or existential narcissism), go beyond acceptable limits of ethical and Biblical standards involving self-worship and narcissism which ultimately cause additional problems. Paul C. Vitz, Associate Professor of Psychology, New York University, comments on the cult of self-worship in relation to psychology: "3. Psychology as religion is deeply anti-Christian. Indeed it is hostile to most religions . . . . 5. Psychology as religion has for years been destroying individuals, families, and communities. But for the first time the destructive logic of this secular religion is beginning to be understood, and as more and more people discover the emptiness of self-worship Christianity is presented with a major historical opportunity to provide meaning and life."[10]

From a critical point of view questions have arisen as to the efficacy of psychotherapy in the treatment of schizophrenia which is a severe form of mental disorder or mental illness. It is characterized by withdrawn, bizarre and sometimes delusional behavior and by intellectual and emotional deterioration. Delusional behavior may include multiple and exaggerated changes in personality. It is logical that one ought not criticize or question one form of treatment without recommending a suitable alternate form of treatment. To satisfy this condition we offer information on spiritual and nutritional alternative resources within this book. One such key successful approach is Orthomolecular Psychiatry which offers a soma-psychological solution wherein treatment and healing of the body can act as a catalyst to help resolve mental-emotional-spiritual problems.

"Incredible though it may seem," stated Dr. Michael Lesser, "correct nutrition can mean the difference between depression and good cheer, between sanity and insanity, even between law-abiding self-control and criminal behavior.

. . . .

"The actual core of schizophrenia, the altered perception of reality, couldn't be psychological; it had to be chemically induced. Mental delusions, confusion, inability to concentrate, hallucinations, and other distortions of perception were all predictable consequences of a chemically imbalanced brain presenting an altered picture of reality. . . . The schizophrenic manufactures his own LSD, and the vitamins help 'soak up' and detoxify the hallucinogenic chemicals. Later, one schizophrenic even complained that since he'd been taking the B vitamin niacin and vitamin C he couldn't 'get off' on LSD any more. Whenever he wanted to 'trip' on psychedelics, he had to stop the vitamins for a few days."[11]

We encourage professional counselors to give serious consideration and study to the potentially significant advantages offered in the application of principles of orthomolecular psychiatry as a supplementary assist to their current counseling practices. Kenneth Mark Colby is one psychoanalyst who recognizes that supplementary assistance is necessary if psychiatric practice is to become more effective. In August of 1973 at the Third International Joint Conference of Artificial Intelligence at Stanford, Colby announced, "In psychiatry—I'll tell you one of the deep, dark secrets—we don't know what we're doing . . . . We need all the help we can get and we're willing to take it from any direction."[12]

A CASE STUDY

In appendix E detailed documentation is given of a scriptural-spiritual approach in a counseling session involving a woman with an apparent multi-personality disorder and suffering from schizophrenic type delusions. This successful counseling case was with Janet (a fictitious name). "Evelyn" had been identified earlier as a powerful alter ego posing as the well part of Janet. In the name of Jesus Christ and upon command, we could speak to either personality, Evelyn or Janet. Janet could and did confess Jesus Christ as the Son of God, as her personal Savior and that Jesus Christ has come in the flesh (1 John 4:1-4). Since Evelyn was unable to make this same confession we deduced that Evelyn was an imposter, an unwanted personality not approved by Jesus Christ.

Eventually Janet admitted she realized that one part of her worshipped Satan, the other part, Jesus Christ. Janet recognized Evelyn as the satanic part of her and Janet as the Christian part. Janet agreed to give up Evelyn as a constant companion and take the Lord Jesus Christ as her constant companion and Savior in times of trouble. Evelyn was separated from Janet by Jesus Christ and sent to a place from whence she could never return to Janet.

Once again we were convinced of the premise that spiritually caused mental illness is unlikely to be treated successfully as an exclusively psychological phenomena because it also requires spiritual cleansing through the power and work of our Lord Jesus Christ. Janet had been counseled by at least one psychologist and more than one psychiatrist without success prior to counseling with the authors.

Psychiatry's approach to therapeutic treatment of multiple personality neuroses is often to fuse the different personalities into one. It is our contention based on experience that the correct approach is diametrically opposite. From a purely logical scientific approach, it is far better to get rid of a root cause of a problem or a poison from within the body or within the mind than to hold it in dangerous remission never knowing when it might reappear to take hold as do some hallucinogenics such as LSD or Phencyclidine Hydrochloride (PCP or Angel Dust). The correct, long lasting therapy is to first expose all unwanted personalities separately and dispose of them, leaving the one real personality intact and in control. Such an approach has been accomplished repeatedly through Christ-centered spiritual counseling; but it is considered highly unlikely that successful treatment, without relapse, can be accomplished solely through secular psychological or psychiatric therapy.

One current example of relapse from a fusion of ten personalities in one male is described in the following news release: "Columbus, Ohio (AP) - William Milligan has suffered a relapse after psychiatrists believed they had fused his 10 personalities to enable him to stand trial on rape, kidnapping and robbery charges, one of his attorneys said Wednesday. But the abrupt change to jail from a mental hospital, where he had been treated for nearly seven months, caused Milligan to lapse back to at least three personalities, defense attorney Gary Schweickart said Wednesday. 'Total diffusion or fragmentation of the person we knew Friday as William Milligan has taken place since incarceration,' Schweickart said. Common pleas Judge Jay Flowers, who had ordered Milligan to jail after the competency hearing, said he had not decided whether another hearing would be held. Psychiatrists who treated Milligan at Harding Hospital in the Columbus suburb of Worthington had no comment Wednesday. They found earlier that Milligan had at least 10 personalities, ranging in age from three to 23—two of them female. 'Last night I personally spoke to at least three of the personalities—Danny, Tommy, and Allen,' Schweickart said. According to the psychiatrists, Danny is 14, timid and frequently conscious, Tommy is 16, a clever and a skilled escape artist, and Allen is 18, a talented artist, sociable and manipulative."[13]

HEALING OF THE WHOLE PERSON

Our plea is for the counselor, professional or non-professional, to recognize that healing of body, mind, and spirit are inter-related. Therapeutic treatment may require care and involvement in more than one specialized area, including support groups such as Alcoholics Anonymous as well as a mature Christian group, sometimes called a nurture group. As soon as readiness is evidenced on the part of the counselee, it is recommended that the counselor encourage development of one-on-one, ever deepening Christian friendships with members of both sexes.

To ensure success in counseling we encourage:

1. the physician not to rely upon medication so overwhelmingly;

2. the surgeon not to rely upon or recommend use of the scalpel almost exclusively;

3. the psychiatrist not to use drugs and mind manipulation techniques so much;

4. the minister-priest not to rely on prayer alone,

5. the nutritionist not to rely upon food-vitamin therapy exclusively;

6. the counselee not to rely upon any one of the above exclusively.

Supportive testimony for the above recommendations is provided through professional information, some of which have been identified in the selected bibliography.

Some courageous voices are being raised today about the soundness of psychotherapy and its actual accomplishments. One study sought to determine the quality and extent of healing that took place when some patients were treated by psychotherapists and others by a group of mature, stable women who used their skills as mothers. The patients treated by the women were found to respond faster and improve more than those treated by the psychiatrists.

We have been surprised to read about patients who have received psychotherapy for periods of from three to six years and from one to three times a week, yet they still could not be considered as whole persons with normal lives. Some doctors wonder if psychotherapy is able to establish any validation of its supposed effectiveness. Various studies seem to indicate that it did not make any difference as to which method of therapy was used, some patients did not improve. When some improved in mental health, it could not be proved that that particular therapy was responsible. Some critics believe that most patients will recover within months even without the use of psychotherapy.

Can psychological counseling, as practiced today, be considered a science? To assist us in answering let us look at a recent definition of science: "1. a branch of knowledge or study dealing with a body of facts or truths systematically arranged and showing the operation of general laws: the mathematical sciences."[14] As a mechanical engineer, professionally registered in the state of Ohio, one of the authors recognizes that any field which one wants to consider as a field of science must have the type of firm foundation which enables repetitive, controlled procedures to achieve consistently repetitive results. Psychological counseling as currently understood and practiced seems to fall far below requirements which might conceivably include it as an acceptable field of scientific endeavor. Counseling has too wide a variety of opposing foundational theories, and its results are too inconsistent therapeutically to be considered scientific without destroying the integrity of the meaning of science. In short, the contemporary field and theory of psychological counseling is in a state of chaos. On the other hand, counseling involving spiritual and nutritional considerations and orthomolecular psychiatry do seem to provide more measurable and consistent therapeutic successes than does the conventional counseling approaches of individual or group facilitated talk, listen, directive, non-directive, inductive, drug therapy types.

Martin and Deidre Bobgan do a fine job answering the question, "Are Christianity and psychotherapy compatible?" One of their strongest criticisms of psychotherapy is quoted to enlighten the Christian and, hopefully, to pose the serious question in the mind of professional counselors as to the validity of such a strong statement.

"To participate in the ritual of psychoanalysis one must 'free associate,' give up his free will, agree to be determined by his past, blame his parents, become dependent upon the therapist, permit the therapist to take the place of both parents and God, deify sex and denigrate religion, and, above all, pay large sums of money over a long period of time, in spite of the lack of evidence that this Freudian fetish is of any value . . . . The Freudian fantasies have filtered into nearly all of the pscho- therapeutic world. In Dante's *Inferno* there is a sign over the entrance of hell (hades) which reads, 'Abandon all hope, ye who enter here.' We believe that is a safe way for Christians to view psychoanalysis.''[15]

Strangely missing in the secular psychological-psychiatric counseling model is the all important foundation of a consistent moral and ethical system. Without such a base sin can be, and indeed has been, accepted as it becomes the will of a majority. Remember Hitler's historical mass genocide! Lying, cheating, stealing, rape, murder, and sex outside marriage can all become the "norm" based on ethics and morals as determined by majority acceptance without a Christian world view.

The focal message of this volume is that biblical Christianity provides the necessary foundational base for a perfect and complete workable system of ethics and morals and when ac- curately recognized and properly applied it also provides the successful spiritual approach to counseling. It is this spiritual approach which utilizes the promised wisdom and infinite heal- ing power of the greatest of all physicians, the only begotten Son of God, Jesus Christ of Nazareth.

When society relies solely upon man's creativity, man's developed philosophy and man's psychological/psychiatric ap- proaches to mental health, beware! "The new seer (psychological, psychiatric, psychoanalytic seer) has enlarged his professional status to include virtually every manifestation of modern life," declares Martin Gross. "He has done so brashly, using the tools of modern communications to reinforce his claims. He has been at fault in exaggerating, even inventing an expertise that does not exist. But the public, in accepting him, has been not only gullible but equally culpable.

"In this last quarter of the twentieth century, we have elected the seer of the Psychological Society as our interpreter of the unknown. He has been permitted, even encouraged, to cast the mysteries of life, love, health, and happiness into a psychological form which entertains and ostensibly informs us.

"By offering the seeming structure of science wedded to mystical insight, the psychological and psychiatric seer successfully masquerades as a modern oracle. He can only be countered if we learn how to strenuously seek the truth from more reliable and responsible sources."[16]

Gross concludes, "The psychological revolution has damaged the psychic fiber of individual man and woman. It is time for comprehensive repair. It will not be done through the unstable criteria of modern psychodynamic psychology and its artificial standards of normality and neurosis. Nor will it be done through the uncertain first aid of psychotherapy. More likely, the precepts of philosophy and the strict regimen of true scientific investigation, both of which have too often been abandoned in the Psychological Society, will provide the touchstones to guide us toward a surer, more ennobling existence."[17]

NOTES

1. C. H. Patterson, *Theories of Counseling and Psychotherapy* (New York: Harper and Row Publishers, Inc., 1973), p. 258.

2. "Federal Government Seeks to Analyze Role of Psychotherapy," *The Cincinnati* [Ohio] *Enquirer,* September 28, 1980, p. H-6.

3. Ibid.

4. Ibid.

5. Ibid.

6. Ibid.

7. James W. Long, *Prescription Drugs, What You Need To Know For Safe Drug Use* (New York: Harper and Row, Publishers, Inc., 1982).

8. "Psychiatry's Depression, Psychiatry on the Couch," *Time Magazine,* April 2, 1979, p. 81.

9. *Overcoping With Valium,* U. S. Department of Health, Education and Welfare, pamphlet publication no. FDA 80-3100, December 1980.

10. Paul C. Vitz, *Psychology as Religion, The Cult of Self-Worship* (Grand Rapids: Wm. B. Eerdmans Publishing Co., 1977), p. 10.

11. Dr. Michael Lesser, *Nutrition and Vitamin Therapy* (New York: Bantam Books, Inc., 1981), pp. xiii, 25-26.

12. R. D. Rosen, *Psychobabble* (New York: Atheneum Publishers, 1977), p. 123.

13. "Lawyer Says Multipersonality Man Has Relapse," *The Cincinnati* [Ohio] *Enquirer,* October 12, 1978, p. A-13.

14. *Random House Dictionary of the English Language,* unabridged edition (New York: Random House, 1966), p. 1279.

15. Martin & Deidre Bobgan, *The Psychological Way/The Spiritual Way* (Minneapolis: Bethany Fellowship Inc., 1979), pp. 84, 85.

16. Martin Gross, *The Psychological Society* (New York: Random House, 1978), pp. 91, 92.

17. Ibid., p. 326.

15

Necessary Precautions In Spiritual Ministry

Psychological and spiritual ministry has some hazards for those involved. Some dangers are obvious, some subtle, and some almost competely hidden. We emphasize, unequivocally, that success in counseling can be achieved only through a properly balanced approach to counseling. This must include development of keen spiritual awareness of what is and what is not an acceptable counseling practice to our Lord Jesus Christ. No other foundational basis, no other benchmark can be as effective! Many other foundational bases can be dangerous and perilous to both the minister and the client.

In view of a massive deluge of requests to meet existing needs for healing, it became apparent that the authors' teams of competent workers were being swamped with work. So early in our ministry we established guidelines to help maintain a suitable, balanced approach to counseling and to protect the workers as well as the clients.

SOME GUIDELINES FOR CONDUCTING A HEALING MINISTRY

1. Be aware of the devil's cleverness in overinvolving us in working with people so much that we are prevented from doing other necessary work for the congregation and the unsaved. Discriminate between those merely wanting relief and those who desire to serve the Lord Jesus. Maintain a balance between individual needs and the needs of the congregation.

2. Consult with two other leader/workers before accepting a new person to counsel.

3. Our case load should not be more than two or three per team or per person when on more than one team. One or two sessions per week should be the most allowed for spiritual ministry.

4. Only in exceptional cases should there be more than one deliverance session with the same person in a week. Emergencies may change this, of course; but it should not be a regular practice.

5. If it becomes clear that a person has a block (an unresolved sin or condition) and is unwilling to remove that block, then the workers should, after a clear discussion of the block, cease to work with that person *until* he/she is willing to remove the block.

6. Clients ought to be taken in this order: a) committed members of our congregation, b) regular attenders in our assembly who are baptized believers, c) baptized believers from other congregations who are walking in the Lord or sincerely want to walk in the Lord. They must be willing to arrange to have one or two leaders from their own congregations to be trained during the sessions.

7. If the person continues to go to gatherings or meetings which we believe are questionable because of false teaching or possible occult involvement, then, after a clear warning about the dangers of this involvement, we should cease to work with that person until he/she changes. It appears futile and poor stewardship of our time to continue because our work in the Lord Jesus Christ can be undone by such actions.

8. Do not work alone except under emergency conditions and rarely then. Have at least one other able, faithful, and mature worker. Always seek to have a woman with you when working with a woman except for rare emergencies or to have a woman in the house.

9. Each worker needs to watch out for the others as well as for himself so that he does not become personally attached to or emotionally involved with the counselee. Do not spend lots of time with the counselee, and prevent a strong dependence of counselee on the counselor from developing. A counselor must

not become to the person "my savior." Satan can use the coun-selee and the relationship to affect adversely the counselor's life, spiritual health, and relationships with others. Remain objective and keep the relationship as a team effort. If an un-healthy dependence or involvement begins to occur, refer this person to another team for counseling. Be committed to taking the advice and warnings from others involved in the counseling and deliverance ministries and especially the elders. Satan can distort rapidly your own objectivity and set up or intensify tensions, conflicts, and divisions among those working with emotionally or spiritually disturbed or demonized people.

10. Everyone needs to realize the grave, serious, and dangerous nature of the work we have been called to do in counseling and deliverance. It is to be taken as deadly serious in nature. Don't develop pride in your work to allow yourself to think *you* are doing it. Always command and work in the name of the Lord Jesus Christ, not "I". Don't be careless in talk or light in con-versation before, during, or after counseling or deliverance sessions. You are dealing with holy things, with life and death, and jesting or levity is out.

11. Young Christians should not be used in counseling or in the deliverance ministry as it is dangerous. They can be hurt.

12. People on a team should pray and if necessary fast (accord-ing to their ability) before the session. They should speak or do things in the session only with the approval of the leader (one person in charge). Be very circumspect and helpful with-out seeming to take initiative or control away from the leader. If one is reading Scripture, singing, or praying, do it softly enough so as to be supportive but not disruptive of the leader's concentration.

13. Confidence and personal privacy must be maintained. Loose talk hurts people. Do not disclose that you are working with a person unless permission by that person is given and do not discuss with people anything of counseling sessions. Only after agreement of leaders and the counselee should details be given to any persons with a view of informing them of needed truth or in bringing in someone else to assist in the counseling ministry.

14. As with all guidelines we can expect that special situations and emergencies will arise which require flexibility conditioned by good judgment to overrule the guidelines. However, it is expected that these occasions will be rare.

THE DANGERS OF HYPNOSIS

Christians and non-Christians alike can be and are misled into dangerous practices because of innocence or ignorance. One prime example is hypnosis which seemingly offers desirable rewards including no pain during childbirth or while dental work is being performed. Some medical doctors, dentists, psychologists, psychiatrists, and some unknowing Christian counselors use hypnosis with the admirable goal of helping a client overcome pain, addiction or other type problems. But we must remember that some actions we take may ultimately be harmful to us though at the time they do seem attractive, desirable, and pleasing. This may be the subtle part of the deception. If these actions or results were obviously distasteful or unpleasant, we would not desire them. Are we authors being ultraconservative or supercritical about the degree of occult susceptibility or spiritual weakness one can develop via hypnosis which may then become mentally, emotionally, or spiritually destructive? We think not, and we urge the reader to reconsider his previous conclusions about the effects of hypnosis.

Consider the meaning of a dictionary definition of hypnosis, "1. an aritificially induced state resembling sleep, characterized by heightened susceptibility to suggestion."[1] Note the key words, *artificially induced state* and *heightened susceptibility to suggestion*. To attain a suitable hypnotic state one must condition oneself through a variety of techniques of concentration and passivity of mind. These result in artificially inducing a state of relaxation and clearing of the mind (blank or passive mind) which creates and is characterized by heightened susceptibility to suggestion. The question which must be answered is for whom have we induced heightened susceptibility? The susceptibility is to mind control, of course, but to *whose* mind control? On the surface it might appear, in the case of self-hypnosis, that one's self is in control. In the case of a trained person or professional hypnotist it might appear that he/she is in control or in partial control of the client's mind. The reader is requested not to swallow unquestioningly the frequent statement which alleges that a person under hypnosis cannot be prompted to do anything against his/her will or moral convictions. This is not a scientifically proven premise, and it is dangerously misleading. Specific occurrences, especially those experienced by the authors, have on numerous occasions served to contradict this widely advocated premise. This is particularly true of many whose minds have come under hypnotic control through cult involvement such as those in Jim Jones' People's Temple.

Returning to the question of mind control by self or by the hypnotist if other than self, it is threatening to some to recognize and even more repugnant to accept a third possibility of mind control from the world of spiritual darkness which exists all around us. This spirit world and its capability to control minds is frightening, but it is real and destructive. Its beings, specifically demons, wait patiently for us to lower our defenses and to heighten our susceptibility to suggestion so they may inexorably gain control of our minds and ultimately our wills. The Scriptures support these premises which, because of many and varied life experiences, have admittedly become verifiable and conclusive to the authors:[2]

1 Pet 5:8, "Be self-controlled and vigilant always, for your enemy the devil *is always about,* prowling like a lion roaring for [about to devour] its prey." (Italics added.)

1 Tim 4:1, 2, "God's Spirit specifically tells us in later days there will be men who abandon the true faith and allow themselves to be spiritually seduced by teachings of demons, teachings given by men who are lying hypocrites, whose consciences are as dead as seared flesh."

Rom 6:16, "You *belong* to the power which you choose to obey, whether you choose sin, whose reward is death, or God, obedience to whom means the reward of righteousness."

THE DANGERS OF A PASSIVE MIND

The practice of meditation has been widely misinterpreted and misused. Many proponents of meditation teach repetitive and/or continuous chanting or a total clearing of the mind in order to achieve various levels of sensitivity to spiritual reception, spiritual enlightenment or spiritual elevation of being. These approaches are effective insofar as they do often produce the desired results. However, their source of power comes not from the Spirit of the Holy Father God or His Son Jesus Christ but from the unholy father of lies, Satan and his host of evil and unclean spirits. Because the source of this power is satanic, persons receiving rewards or benefits including physical or mental healing from such a source must pay tribute in the form of turning over some control of their minds and bodies and even their wills to the power source. The extent of the takeover is dependent upon the degree to which the person allows himself to become involved in practices unacceptable to God. The penalty is the same for the same offense whether it is committed knowingly or unknowingly. There seems to be a significant degree of similarity in the procedures of preparation for perverted meditation to those used to prepare oneself for hypnotic control.

Again we find a dictionary definition very meaningful; "meditation . . . . 2. continued or extended thought; reflection; contemplation."[3] This definition properly identifies meditation as an activity of an active mind and not a passive, cleared out, unthinking mind waiting for supernatural revelation or supernatural emotional experiences. Continued thought, reflection, contemplation, all are unmistakably words of action descriptive of the *activity* of meditation. Yes, God does want us to study, to contemplate (meditate on) Scripture and His Son Jesus Christ; but He does not ever want us to maintain a passive mind vulnerable and open to suggestion from evil sources of power.

PHYSICAL DANGERS TO COUNSELEES

In areas of counseling involving psychological, nutritional or inner-healing of memories we have not encountered physical danger to the counselee. However, in spiritual (deliverance) counseling as the counseling teams were growing and maturing, both counselors and counselees were exposed to potentially serious physical danger. In deliverance sessions counselees, under mind control of forces of evil, have on occasion attempted to harm themselves or the counselors physically. As the counseling teams matured with experience and became more aware of the reality and dependability of the power of Jesus Christ, physically dangerous situations were encountered less and less frequently. We learned that by calling upon the name of the Lord Jesus Christ and the power of His shed blood dangerous situations of physical violence were immediately stopped. Christ offered and the teams accepted His total protection of body, soul, and spirit (1 John 5:18).

In deliverance counseling severe discomfort (headache, pain) may be encountered by the counselee which can be relieved in the name of Jesus Christ. Also one should expect that some physical reactions of a counselee may not be consistent with normal, expected medical patterns. In rare instances it may be desirable to have a medical doctor or a registered nurse available to monitor the physical condition of the counselee. Details of some unusual medical reactions of a woman in an actual deliverance counseling session have been recorded by a registered nurse in Appendix F. Also consult Appendix G.

We strongly recommend Christian counselors take out counseling malpractice insurance[4] which is inexpensive.

DANGERS OF THE TRANSFERENCE METHOD USED BY SOME WORKERS

The transference method used in deliverance counseling was taught to the authors by two people who have been in this ministry for a combined total of forty years. It consists of transferring evil spirits from a counselee to another person who is willing to help and who has had successful deliverance from evil spirits in the past. The rationale given for this method to be employed is to provide help to a person who is encountering difficulty in being freed of evil spirits. Such a situation might occur with a person who is difficult to communicate with such as a young child, or a deaf and dumb person, or a person who has a spiritual block or shield which cannot be uncovered or understood. The objective of this type of deliverance is to transfer demons from a difficult counselee to a willing, experienced counselee and then to request Jesus Christ to deliver the latter. We were told that it had worked well in a number of case histories.

Our ministry team agreed to try this method *once* in a difficult situation after which we concluded that it might not be the type of practice acceptable to Jesus Christ, so we investigated further. We found that a person who taught us had used this method with six different and willing transferees all of whom were women. We found that all six later had serious recurring spiritual problems, and at least one of the women was subsequently confined to a mental hospital.

The person our team used was a twenty-four year old male who was willing to act as a transferee to help a woman who had often exhibited heavy demonic control of her mind. This attempt at transference appeared to fail because the young woman said she would rather die than to allow her demons to pass on to this other person. However, later events indicated more may have been accomplished than we realized but in a negative sense. The young man who was the intermediary for the transfer has since that time come under a great deal of spiritual and physical difficulty and has suffered considerably from the experience or at least as nearly as we can determine relating to this experience as the cause. We do know that since that time the young man has suffered from severe physical illnesses even resulting in hospitalization. Up to this time he had been in excellent health. Medical doctors were unable to identify any really organic cause and finally suggested some kind of unknown viral infection (viremia).

One of the most serious questions that has been raised in connection with the transference method of dealing with demons is the information given to us by one of our team who has had extensive experience with occultists. He indicated that both witches and Satanists use the transference method in exorcism rites. He has stated, "Witches, of course, do not believe in demons but they do deal with spirit beings called elementals (which the Christian knows to be demons). Sometimes it is necessary to expel one of these demons from a witch where it has gained too much control. In Alexandrian witchcraft one way this is accomplished is by having someone who is stronger in the Craft to act as a bearer to which the demon will be attracted and then expelled by a more powerful demon. Satanists cast demons into their members and also remove them by using an intermediary who is filled with a more powerful demon to call the weaker demon into his host and then expel him from the host."[5] This man also indicated that pagan religions often use a form of transference method for demonic expulsion. For these reasons we believe that the transference method may have overtones of the occult and may result in spiritual harm to those involved.

It is out of deep concern for the advancement of the cause of Christ in the deliverance ministry to which we are committed that we are sharing these serious thoughts with you. We do not want to offend anyone if we can help it and speak our concerns in love.

BELIEVERS IN GOD CAN BE MISLED BY AN "ANGEL OF LIGHT"

Christians today must take with the utmost seriousness the warning of the Holy Spirit through Paul, "*God's* messengers? They are counterfeits of the real thing, dishonest practitioners, masquerading as the messengers of Christ. Nor do their tactics surprise me when I consider how Satan himself masquerades as an angel of light. It is only to be expected that his agents shall have the appearance of ministers of righteousness—but they will get what they deserve in the end . . . . For apparently you cheerfully accept a man who comes to you preaching a different Jesus from the one we told you about, and you readily receive a spirit and a gospel quite different from the ones you originally accepted" (2 Cor 11:13-15, 4; Phillips).

Private, public, religious, industrial, and educational groups are being ensnared into the realm of the occult and demonic foolishly, because they either do not know or do not apply a biblical moral standard to evaluate potentially dangerous practices. Professing Christians, too, are being misled into spiritually dangerous practices due to ignorance or because their judgment is based upon feelings or experiences at the expense of scriptural evidence. It is true that judgment in spiritual matters must be based first upon scriptural fact, second upon scriptural faith, and third upon emotional feelings or personal experience.

This subject is so vast it would require a lengthy volume to do justice to its many facets. We have chosen to point out a few examples to provide resource references should the reader choose to investigate more deeply. With considerate sensitivity we mention these because we recognize that sharing some of these practices which may be counterfeits might alarm, embarass, or turn away a reader who participates in them, though innocently.

Speaking in Tongues and Slaying in the Spirit

These are perhaps the most controversial subjects in neopentecostal practices and lead to the most vehement attacks and defenses. We have personally experienced numerous cases of spiritually disturbed people who spoke in tongues, and many of these have found out that their "tongues" were counterfeited by a demonic "Spirit of Tongues." A scriptural test for true and counterfeit spirits is given in 1 John 4:1-6, "Don't trust every spirit, dear friends of mine, but test them to discover whether they come from God or not. . . . You can test whether they come from God in this simple way: every spirit that acknowledges the fact that Jesus Christ actually became a man, comes from God, but the spirit which denies this fact does not come from God" (1 John 4:1-3; Phillips). (Consult Appendix J for testing tongues.)

In his book, which presents "a third view of the charismatic phenomenon," K. Neill Foster provides sound advice about testing spirits: "Deception in the area of spiritual gifts, especially speaking in tongues, is very difficult to face. 'Is this gift, which I have always considered to be a mark of spirituality and a sign of the baptism of the Holy Spirit, no more than a master deception? If I have been deceived here, where else have I been deceived?' The latter question is possibly more difficult to face than the first, but they are both very uncomfortable queries, though necessary all the same.

"Protesting the views expounded here may be an unhealthy sign. The deception you preserve may be your own. After all, the Holy Spirit has absolutely nothing to fear from biblical tests and standards. He is the one who inspired the Scriptures."[6]

Another current practice frequently observed is called "Slaying in the Spirit" or "Resting in the Spirit." This phenomenon is characterized by a professing Christian praying for another, then laying hands on or touching the forehead with a finger or anointing the forehead with oil. This is followed by the person touched falling to the floor, usually straight back on his/her back, where the person may remain for one minute up to several hours. The person enters into a state often identified as euphoria or as a deeply moving religious experience which the claimant says has brought him/her into the presence of God.

We have counseled with some spiritually troubled Christians who discovered they encountered spiritual difficulties after they were "slain in the spirit." The test of the source of this spirit can be conducted in a manner similar to the testing of the "Spirit of Tongues." K. Neill Foster cautions: "A word of warning here: a person should not lightly submit to the laying on of hands. If there is any reason at all to be concerned that the spiritual operations are carnal, false, or even demonic, stay away. A fair percentage of Christians under occult bondage and even victims of demon invasion have gotten into that bondage through allowing unholy hands to be laid upon them."[7]

Holistic Medicine and Psychic Healing

We believe in wholesome medical practice and biblical counseling wherein the whole needs of a person are considered, but we reject the "holistic medicine" approach. We recognize that numerous perversions are practiced and often accepted by Christians and non-Christians alike merely because they are unaware of the dangers and the penalty exacted for participating in perverted holistic practices. One of these is a perversion of the practice of kinesiology where a scientifically and spiritually sound practice is converted into a perverse, occult practice.

Legitimate kinesiology is simply the movement, adjustment, or exercise of muscles, tendons, or joints akin to that practiced in physical therapy or chiropractic. The term PSI is generally used to indicate involvement with or use of extrasensory perception and extrasensorimotor activity. PSI includes telepathy, clairvoyance, precognition, and psychokinesis. An illustration of what we believe is a perversion of kinesiology follows as reported by Jane Heimlich.

"Dr. _____, tall, bearded and ascetic looking, explained that one of the holistic tools that he uses is testing a patient's nutritional needs by means of kinesiology.

"My first experience with kinesiology was three years ago. Dr. _____, then director of the PSI center in Greenhills, told me to keep a record of what I ate for the next week. After a lengthy discussion of calcium magnesium imbalance and other nutritional hazards, Dr. _____ told me to straighten my right arm and hold it stiffly in front of me. 'Now when I press down, I want you to resist as hard as you can.' He then placed a calcium capsule in my left hand. 'Will calcium benefit this body?' he intoned. 'If yes, make her strong, if not, make her weak.' Then, using his two fingers, he pressed down on my outstretched arm; I resisted as hard as I could but he pushed my arm down easily. 'You don't need calcium.' When he tested for iron, a vein in his forhead attesting to the exertion, I resisted the pressure easily. 'You need iron,' he concluded. He then 'armtested' various supplements as well as each item on my diet record. (The arm said 'yes' to applesauce, 'no' to peanut butter and crackers.) To my surprise, my arm fluctuated from being limp as a noodle to an immovable ramrod.

"When I asked Dr. _____ for an explanation, he said: 'You and your body are nothing more than a projection of energy. If you hold a vitamin and the energy in it is compatible with your energy field, you become stronger.' It sounded like double talk to me."[8]

This doctor asked questions and then said, "If yes, make her strong, if not, make her weak." To whom is he addressing these questions, and what entity is making her strong or weak? In all likelihood these entities are spirits of Satan, the father of lies, the cruel deceiver of the whole world (Rev 12:9). It is possible that the answers will be correct and that spiritual penalties will be imposed upon all participants as they have become involved in a form of psychic (occult) healing. God forbids all practices of an occult nature—not an appeal to His perfect power and will (Deut 18:9-12)—and He will punish those who participate (Lev 20:6). Paul says that those who practice sorcery "shall not inherit the Kingdom of God" (Gal 5:20-21).

Raphael Gasson, who came out of the Spiritualist movement, gives many warnings about spiritual counterfeits. "We can see that this gift (gift of healing), like all the other gifts of the Spirit, can be either from God or from Satan. The counterfeit must be in appearance as good as the real thing, otherwise it would not fulfill its aim. Many who attend these counterfeit healing meetings become convinced upon seeing these gifts in operation, that God is behind these good works."[9]

Out-of-Body Experiences

A final example as to the extent occult practices have been cleverly insinuated into society is the availability of resources for astral projection by sound resulting in out-of-body experiences. An advertisement for cassette tapes offering astral projection identifies a partial list of those using astral sound tapes and techniques (consult Appendix I). This list shows the frightening inroads that occult practices have made on spiritually naive public and private, medical and educational institutions. Two sample quotations from this advertisement are:

"Your Astral Sound tape has been adopted as a required text in the psychology/nursing department (Metropolitan Community College, Minneapolis, Minnesota)."

"Since I began using the tape I find myself to be operating on a higher level of awareness and have had a great number of psychic precognitive glimpses at future events which have actually come to pass! (individual testimony)."

In this chapter we have sought to bring to your attention in a brief but emphatic way some of the potential dangers that are involved especially in spiritual counseling. Counselors engaged in spiritual counseling and especially in a ministry of deliverance must day by day take strong precautions to ask and receive the protection of the Lord God Almighty and of the blood of the Lord Jesus Christ. Everyone involved in any confrontation with Satan, the devil, will be the special object of his attack; and we must remember that next to the triune God, Satan has the greatest amount of power in the world. As carefully as possible we have attempted to list some of the practices that have occult foundation or can be rather easily subverted into occult workings. Naturally we hope that these warnings will forearm every person who may become involved with spiritual counseling and enable them to be victorious in the warfare against Satan.

We urge all of you who desire to enchance your knowledge of these potentially dangerous practices to obtain the resource materials listed at the end of this chapter.[10] Jessie Penn-Lewis and Evan Roberts' book, *War On The Saints,* may be one of the most perceptive and needed books written in this century to help the Christian differentiate true from counterfeit manifestations of the supernatural.[11] We suggest that you read their appendixes first as they vividly reveal the differences between the true manifestations of God Almighty and the counterfeit manifestations of Satan. "Evil spirit possession," they state, "has . . . checked every similar revival throughout the centuries since Pentecost, and these things must now be understood, and dealt with, if the Church is to advance to maturity. Understood, not only in the degree of possession recorded in the gospels, but in the special forms of manifestations suited to the close of the dispensation, *under the guise of the Holy Spirit,* yet having some of the very characteristic marks in bodily symptoms, seen in the gospel records, when all who saw the manifestation knew that it was the work of the spirits of Satan."[12]

NOTES

1. Jess Stein, Editor-in-Chief, *The Random House Dictionary of the English Language* (New York: Random House, Inc., 1966), p. 700.

2. All Scriptures in Chapter 14 are quoted from J. B. Phillips, *The New Testament in Modern English* (New York: The Macmillan Co., 1972).

3. Stein, op. cit., 890.

4. One company is the Church Mutual Insurance Co., 3000 Schuster Lane, Merrill, Wisconsin 54452.

5. Personal letter to the authors.

6. K. Neill Foster, *Help! I Believe in Tongues* (Minneapolis: Bethany Fellowship, Inc., 1975), p. 128.

7. Ibid., pp. 146-147.

8. Jane Heimlich, "Do It Yourself Health Care" (*Cincinnati Magazine,* May, 1980), p. 55.

9. Raphael Gasson, *The Challenging Counterfeit* (Plainfield, NJ: Logos Books, 1972), p. 113.

10. Jessie Penn-Lewis and Evan Roberts, *War On The Saints* (Fort Washington, Pa: Christian Literature Crusade, 1977); Kurt E. Koch, *Satan's Devices* (Grand Rapids: Kregel Publications, 1978); and *Spiritual Counterfeits Project Journal* and also the SCP Newsletter (Spiritual Counterfeits Project, P. O. Box 2418, Berkeley, CA 94702).

11. We oppose the encouragement Richard J. Foster seems to give (*Celebration of Discipline,* p. 27) to seek out-of-the-body experiences with God. Foster seems partially aware of the dangers of possible occult involvement but does not give adequate warnings. In his later *Study Guide for C of D,* he states, "Since some have asked, I might just as well come clean and tell you that I have *no* interest at all, nor experience, in astro-travel. . ." (p. 19). Unfortunately many who read the book will not see the *Study Guide.*

12. Jessie Penn-Lewis and Evan Roberts, op. cit., pp. 33-34.

16

Summary Of
Our Study

The power of Almighty God, our Creator, is the indispensable resource for healing as He works through His servants by means of His Word and prayer. This is our conviction based in a Christian theistic worldview and our own experience. We have argued the validity of the appeal to God for the restoration to health of the individuals with whom we work because of empirical evidence. Furthermore we have declared that the statements about God and the Lord Jesus Christ are true and faithful, worthy of all acceptance. Without a doubt we believe that the God of the Bible is the reality of the universe; and yet, because He is the infinite God, He is personally concerned about every individual He has created. He is totally available as the Lord of grace, comfort, and healing. Certainly we believe His promises to all those who love and obey Him, and we have by faith claimed the out-working of those promises in our ministry of healing. You can too!

Our book is based on our experiential knowledge as we have been actively engaged in working with a large enough number of case histories to lend credibility to our statements plus the reliable testimony of other trustworthy Christians. As we have seen the actual power of our God released in the lives of Christians, we have autoptical and empirical evidence that our approach is valid and actually works to the restoration to health of those who have been mentally, emotionally, physically or spiritually sick.

Frankly, we are thrilled over the positive evidence of God's response to all human needs as they have been dealt with in His appointed way. We have sought to use all the wisdom available to us from the various disciplines of science, and we hope that our experiences and evidence will be helpful to all Christians, ministers, and counselors.

Surely we will get a sympathetic hearing from every concerned person who is dealing with the devastating sufferings and defeats which a tremendous number of people are experiencing in today's world. Everywhere we look we see the breakdown of the family and the pain and misery of individuals. The cries of wounded and desperate people assault our ears day and night if we have any ears to listen with. It is our conviction that never before in the history of the world have individuals lived under such enormous pressures both internally and externally as people today. There is a tremendous effort put forth to care for those who are crashing around us, and the bill for attempting to restore people to a normal lifestyle in which they can cope with the pressures of society is enormous and continues to increase. No relief is in sight until, we believe, men and women are willing to recognize that they must have the healing of our Lord Jesus Christ, that they must be brought out of bondage to Satan and to sin, and that they must be reconciled with God.

God is totally in charge of this universe, and man must lose his arrogance and sinful pride to be in submission to his Creator. It is not up to man to judge God nor to set time tables for God. He is able to take care of every need and has provided adequate means for bringing men and women out of alienation and rebellion into reconciliation with Himself. That one great means is the Lord Jesus Christ in His perfect role as redeemer and healer of the nations. Through the power of the Lord Jesus Christ anyone can be brought into a life of harmony with God which enables him to overcome his alienation to society, to his family, and to himself.

God is a prayer-answering God who delights to take care of the needs of His children by His gracious lovingkindness. He also does tremendous things for those who are potentially His children, for He sends His rain and sunshine upon the just and the unjust. God's power is all-sufficient in each area of life.

All of us need to study His Word and obey it as the one great prescription for health and for the healing of the nations.

Through our study of the Scripture we have discovered that the single most direct and specific plan of God for healing of the sick is found in the epistle of James, chapter five. In our study we have concluded that the elders (pastors, overseers, shepherds) of the congregation have been appointed by God to exercise a particular yet flexible procedure for the healing of the sick. That procedure is grounded in faith and involves praying in faith for the good and perfect will of our Abba, Father to be done plus the anointing of the body of the sick with oil in the name of the Lord Jesus Christ. When this is done with all confidence in God, with honest confession of sin, and with the sole desire to glorify God, then we can expect positive answers which result in the healing of the individual. We have pointed out that there is no guarantee, no absolute certainty because we do not know everything about God's will for an individual at any particular time. From our experiences and that of others we can say that there is always as a result of this procedure a significant improvement in the spiritual life of the individual and in most cases the healing of the mind or the body. The procedure is open to all God-fearing elders who take the Word of God seriously and act by faith according to this simple formula that God has graciously imparted to us.

We have indicated how our counseling under the procedure of James 5 has been honored by the Lord in regard to physical healing in the lives of various children of God. As we discovered, so we think others will discover, that the carrying out of the procedure set forth in James 5 will result also in psychological healing and bring inner peace to the troubled souls of those who are trusting the Lord Jesus Christ. There can be cleansing and remarkable cures when the power of the Lord Jesus Christ is brought to bear upon the lives of the individuals through the prayers of the righteous. There is no reason why other Christians cannot experience the same remarkable work of God in the lives of those for whom they hold responsibility.

As the Lord Jesus Christ went about healing the sick and casting out evil spirits (that is demons controlled by Satan), we in a lesser way can still experience the powerful work of God in setting people free from bondage to Satan. As we have indicated we see a distinction between the miraculous (instantaneous, direct, and never-failing) acts of the Lord Jesus Christ and the work of God through us today in providence using all the *means* that are available to us. There have been remarkable, special providences in answer to prayer; and we do not count ourselves to be at a disadvantage in dealing with the sick of our day simply because we do not have the high level, extraordinary miracle power of Christ and the apostles. We have sufficient supernatural power to do all that needs to be done.

God has left us with many powerful resources. Especially this has been observed in the work of delivering people from the oppression and bondage of unclean spirits who have invaded them. Satan is the god of this world, and "the whole world lies in the power of the evil one" (1 John 5:19). Upon the testimony of Scripture and our own extensive experience we have concluded as a certainty that men and women have not only been greatly influenced and misled by demons, but in a majority of cases have actually been invaded as a result of sins committed. Yet again we are aware that the power of God is more than sufficient to bring about the deliverance of men and women from the power of the invading demonic forces through the blood of the Lord Jesus Christ. Even Satan, the devil, the father of lies, cannot resist the power and the authority of the Lord Jesus Christ, the Conqueror of all demons.

Healing certainly has a tremendous spiritual dimension, and the power of God is absolutely essential if there is to be healing; yet we have also indicated that there is in God's good world and by His design various chemicals and substances that are good for the individual's health and well-being as well as substances that are harmful or can be abused. Thus we have found a value in imparting information about good nutrition to those with whom we counsel as these are simply elementary items of therapy. God expects us to use our intelligence to determine the needs of the body and to provide wholesome foods. He expects us to make discriminating judgments in regard to the power balance of foods to sustain the proper functioning of the body as He ordained. Where counselors may feel deficient in this area they can nevertheless join forces with nutritionists who are competent in this field.

Another conclusion that we have arrived at is that while everyone is competent to help others in some measure and should develop every ability that they have to be a people-helper, still there are those with gifts from the Lord which enable them to be counselors in a particularly effective way. These counselors will have qualifications which will enable them to function at a level of commitment and competency that the Lord can use in a large way. These individuals will learn various skills and will develop knowledge in these areas particularly that we have reviewed here in the book. It has not been our purpose to set forth extensive or detailed ways to analyze the problems which people have who come to people-helpers. Certainly we hold that the Lord Jesus Christ knows everything about the individual who is sick and can enable the worker to have wisdom and discernment in regard to the root causes of illness. Again we are firmly grounded in the view that the Lord Jesus Christ, His wisdom and power, is the neglected but essential resource in most of today's counseling and work with the sick. Because of this there is a lot of chaos in methodology and therapies proposed for the healing of the mind, body, and soul. Of course, we believe that the Lord Jesus Christ and His Word is the one sure way to end the chaos. Christ's truth is the one foundation for all healing!

A number of times throughout our book we have pointed out some important and potential dangers to individuals who are involved in ministering to the sick, especially in the work of deliverance. These must not be taken lightly but with the utmost seriousness so that the individuals involved in such ministries do not receive injury or loss in the area of mental, emotional, physical or spiritual health. Again it is the Lord Jesus Christ who is our protector, and it is the working of the Holy Spirit in our lives that keeps us from being harmed even when we are in direct confrontation with Satan and his hosts of demons.

It is our conclusion that the Lord Jesus Christ is restoring to His Church today a new understanding of the meaning of

Christian or scriptural healing including the full scope of ministry to every part of a person's life and to every aspect of his personality. As we conclude that Satan is now mounting a tremendous attack against the Church and the gospel of our Lord and Savior, so we believe that the Head of the Church is alerting His leaders to once more become active in a ministry of healing to Christians who are suffering hurt, pain, and destructive illness. It is our prayer to God that He may graciously use this book to open up the minds of multiplied numbers of leaders in congregations throughout the world to their opportunity of greatly ministering to the needs of Christians.

APPENDIX A

Sin and Forgiveness

What is right about Christ's Church Cincinnati? Many things are very good, for we are building on the sure foundation, the Lord Jesus Christ; and God is in charge of us. But today I want us to think and diligently study about what is *wrong*, what is the trouble with Christ's Church Cincinnati? While we do not have as many serious difficulties as some congregations and have not suffered division in over five years of living together, still there is much that is hurting members of the body and therefore the body itself. It is my conviction that the one thing that is hurting us, weakening the body, and grieving the Holy Spirit is SIN (Luke 22:31).

I. GOD IS HOLY AND THEREFORE HATES SIN.

A. Isaiah 6:1-3; Psalm 99:1, 3, 5, 9. Our God is holy, pure, righteous, and ethical.

B. Sin separates us from the Lord (Isa 59:2-3). He hides His face and turns away from us in sin. This does not mean immediate abandonment by God, but over a period of time unrepented sin will bring separation from God. Yet every sin is grievous to God and is a victory for Satan which he can use to increase his power over us. Sins terribly injure our relationship to God and if not repented of can cut us off from God.

C. Sin is unrighteousness, brokenness, selfishness, and disobedience. It is evil, vicious, impure, and destructive. It is everything that God is not, and that is one reason why there is a hell—to remove finally from God's presence all sin, evil, and corruption (2 Thess 1:6-10).

II. GOD'S CHILDREN MUST HATE SIN AND COME OUT OF SIN.

A. As children of God we are to be praying, "forgive us our sins . . . lead us not into temptation but deliver us from the evil one" (Matt 6:12-13).

B. As obedient children of Abba, Father, we are called to live holy lives as He is holy (1 Pet 1:14-17). His nature must be shown in our lives more and more and more (1 Cor 15:58).

C. Romans 6:1-18 is a continuing challenge to us to be free of all sin and slaves only of Christ.

III. GOD'S CHILDREN MUST IDENTIFY SIN.

A. The characteristics of sin are: 1. universal (Rom 3:9-12); 2. deceptive (Heb 3:13); 3. progressive as in the case of David—lustful looks, adultery, murder (2 Sam 11:2); 4. self-revealing (Num 32:23).

B. Sin may be: 1. missing the mark or falling short of the will of God; 2. deliberate, willful, and premeditated; 3. neglecting to do the right (James 4:17); 4. ignorance or dishonesty; 5. going beyond what is written, trespassing (1 Cor 4:6); 6. apostasy or falling away from God (Heb 6:6).

C. Let us now identify sin in our own personal lives and in our life as a congregation. What are our sins of commission (doing what is wrong, forbidden)? What are our sins of omission (not doing what is right)? Is there bitterness, resentment, gossip, rejection, pride, jealousy, exclusivism, etc.? Is there lack of respect, acceptance, love, patience, humility, kindness, consideration, and practicing the Golden Rule? How are we being hurt, sinned against? How are we hurting others and sinning against them? (At the Lord's Supper we need to clear our conscience of every sin and ask forgiveness of one another.)

IV. GOD'S CHILDREN MUST HAVE VICTORY OVER SIN THROUGH CHRIST.

A. Jesus Christ is our Savior, the complete answer to sin (Heb 10:10, 12; 9:12; 8:12). There is no condemnation for us who are in Christ (Rom 8:1).

B. Kill the old person and put on the new one daily because it will probably be necessary (Col 3:5-17).

C. Stand in the strength of the LORD and put on the whole armor of God every day with prayer (Eph 6:10-18).

D. Confess our sins and pray for one another (James 5:16). To try to hide our sins is disastrous and brings suffering, sickness, and ruin (Ps 32:1-7).

CONCLUSION: We cannot as God's children allow, toy with, or tolerate sin in any form in our lives. It has no place in the life of the Christian. God wants us to live above reproach, above sin and to be clothed in the white linen of the saints, His righteousness (Rev 19:8). Christ requires that His bride be chaste, pure, clean, moral, upright, without spot or blemish, and blameless (Eph 5:26-27).

BIBLE TEACHING ABOUT SIN, FORGIVENESS, AND CONSEQUENCES

What happens to us when we turn from sin and become the children of God? What happens to our sins, our guilt, our fruit of sinful conduct? Do we reap what we have sown? Is there any real forgiveness with the Lord? Does God go on punishing us for our sins after we have accepted His Son as Savior? These are questions that often arise in the minds of many and challenge us to study to see what God has taught. Let us turn to the revelation of our Abba (Daddy) God to see the truth.

I. SIN IS A TERRIBLE REALITY KNOWN BY ALL OF US.

A. Sins can be omission (James 4:17).

B. Sins can be of commission (1 John 3:4; 5:17).

C. Sin is universal (Rom 3:23; 1 John 1:8).

D. Sin is utterly, exceedingly sinful (Rom 7:13). It is progressive and deceptive (Rom 7:11; Heb 3:13). Be sure your sin will be exposed (Num 32:23).

II. FORGIVENESS IS A GLORIOUS REALITY AVAILABLE TO ALL.

A. Acts 2:39 says all who are far off are called, no matter what the distance geographically or spiritually. Acts 2:21 says everyone who calls on the Lord shall be saved. No one is excluded but all are welcome to come. The drawing is on God's part, He calls and invites; and we must respond, turn, and come to Him. He will not force us against our wills.

B. Forgiveness is conditional (Matt 6:14-15) and includes the forgiveness of others, confession of sins to God (Ps 32:3-5) and frequently to Christians, especially the elders (James 5:15).

C. Praise the Lord, when the conditions are met the results are complete, total forgiveness (Ps 103:3-5; Rom 8:1; 1 John 1:7, 9).

D. So with the removal of all sins, guilt and guiltiness are without foundation or reality. When God has cancelled and forgotten our sins, that is total freedom from guilt and is justification—just-as-if-I-had never sinned. Praise the Lord!

III. CONSEQUENCES OF SIN MAY REMAIN THOUGH GUILT IS GONE.

A. God does give total forgiveness and removes all guilt. Death and hell are cancelled for the Christian, but there are consequences that may remain. God has not chosen to remove all *consequences* or to immediately do so. It is not automatic or guaranteed.

B. One may continue to experience some doubt, fear, or depression. Others may have spiritual hypochondria: "God doesn't love me"; "I failed"; "I can't trust, grow"; "Help me." Still others may suffer oppression by the evil spirits because of invasion as a result of their sins.

C. More often there are physical consequences that remain. Adam and Eve sinned and brought death to the whole human race (Rom 5:12-14) though Adam was forgiven. Esau could not get the birthright back (Heb 12:15-17). Moses could not enter the promised land because of sin (Deut 32:50-52). The sins of the fathers in consequences are passed on to the third and fourth generations (Exod 20:5).

D. These physical consequences are often seen in venereal disease bringing sterility and damage to babies. Tobacco and alcohol can damage the babies of mothers ingesting these poisons.

Drug and alcohol users may and often do have various damaging effects such as cirrhosis of the liver, brain deterioration, sexual impairment, etc.

E. In the merciful goodness of God *some* of these tragic consequences may be removed gradually. Some may be removed entirely by the grace of God through the healing offered in James 5. Where God does not remove these consequences, He gives the grace sufficient to endure them (2 Cor 12:9).

CONCLUSION: Sin is a hideous and destructive reality, but there is forgiveness and healing in the Lord Jesus Christ. We do not have to continue in sin; indeed, we must not by the will of God. We are to be holy and Christlike, and He was without sin. Though we are forgiven, we may have some consequences of our evil deeds which continue through our lives or part of our lives. All of us should hate sin and resist the devil who wants to damage and destroy our lives. We will be tempted, but we can overcome all temptations by putting on the whole armor of God (Eph 6:10ff.). Perhaps the greatest need is full surrender and total trust in the Lord Jesus Christ (2 Cor 1:8-10). Without this various consequences may continue: weakness, spiritual hypochondria, confusion, and failure when they should not.

APPENDIX B

Pride, the Great Sin, and Humility, the Christlike Virtue

Introduction

The church of Jesus Christ is, or should be, a fellowship of redeemed sinners. All of us are sinners! Are all of us redeemed? Does pride prevent your facing and dealing with your sins? Does pride prevent you from laying down your heavy burden of guilt at the foot of the cross? Can you believe that the results of excessive pride in your life may be showing up in physical, emotional, and spiritual illness? Is excessive pride enlarging the valley between you and Christ? Is excessive pride shortening the distance between you and the first heavenly being who fell away from God because of the sin of pride, Satan, the devil?

I. PRIDE BEGAN FIRST WITH SATAN, THE DEVIL (1 Tim 3:6; Isa 14:4-21).

A. Many have fallen into sin through pride. Some examples are: Adam and Eve (Gen 3:5), David (1 Chron 21:1-14), Uzziah/Azariah (2 Chron 26:16, 19, 21), and Hezekiah (2 Chron 32:24-26).

B. Scriptures warn us about pride. Proverbs 11:2 says, "When pride comes, then comes disgrace, but with humility comes wisdom." Proverbs 16:6 declares, "The Lord detests all the proud of heart. Be sure of this: They will not go unpunished." Again, in Proverbs 18:12 we are told, "Before his downfall a man's heart is proud, but humility comes before honor." Jesus said, "What comes out of a man is what makes him 'unclean.' For from within, out of men's hearts, comes evil thoughts, sexual immorality, theft, murder, adultery, greed, malice, deceit, lewdness, envy, slander, arrogance [pride], and folly. All these evils come from inside and make a man 'unclean'" (Mark 7:20-23). Paul writes, "He [elder] must not be a recent convert, or he may become conceited [full of pride] and fall under the same judgment as the devil" (1 Tim 3:6).

II. PRIDE IS THE GREAT SIN, THE SIN OF THE DEVIL.

A. Do you want to be like the devil or like the Lord Jesus Christ? It takes more than an easy affirmation to make it a *true* statement. Many affirm with their lips that they belong to the Lord, but their hearts are far from Him. Many religious people talk about being like Jesus; but their daily lives exhibit pride, selfishness, and arrogance. Let us honestly search our hearts and see if we are actually living like the devil or like the Lord Jesus Christ. We are speaking first to ourselves and applying this teaching to our lives first.

B. Pride is the great sin, the sin of the devil. It is the only sin that began in heaven, continues on earth, and ends in hell. It caused the archangel, Lucifer, to turn into the devil (accuser) and Satan (adversary). Pride was the first sin on this earth, for Adam and Eve were moved by pride to become like God. Pride and arrogance brought about the ruin of Pharaoh (Exod 5:2). Nebuchadnezzar was brought into humiliation before God and man because of his pride (Dan 4:28-32; 5:20).

C. God declares that pride is a terrible sin (Prov 21:4). It brings destruction. It is the root of almost all other sins we commit, a source of strife and contention even in the family and in the family of God (Prov 28:25; James 4:1-6). Pride is of the world and not of Jehovah God (1 John 2:16). It crucified the only perfect man, the most humble man who ever walked this earth. The pride of religious leaders, the Pharisees and scribes, drove them to destroy the One who was superior to them.

D. Pride is a horrible sin; because it is utterly opposite to God's nature, that of love, self-giving and sacrifice for others. Pride is competition, self-seeking, self-love, and exaltation of the self. It always means enmity between man and man and between God and man. The proud cannot know God, love Him, or serve Him in that state.

E. Pride is the great sin because it is in everyone and is admitted by no one. When have you heard a sermon on pride? We are shamefully silent about pride because of pride. C. S. Lewis has the most helpful lesson on pride known to us outside of the Scripture, his essay on "The Great Sin" in *Mere Christianity*. He declares pride is essentially competitive, takes pleasure only in having more of something than the next man, takes pleasure in being above the rest, the rabble, the common man. Lewis writes, "How is it that people who are quite obviously eaten up with pride can say they believe in God and appear to themselves very religious? I am afraid it means they are worshipping an imaginary God." He gives this test: "Whenever we find that our religious life is making us feel that we are good—above all that we are better than someone else—I think we may be sure that we are being acted on, not by God, but by the devil" (p. 98). "It is a terrible thing that the worst of all the vices can smuggle itself into the very centre of our religious life. But you can see why. The other, and less bad, vices come from the devil working on us through our animal nature. But this does not come through our animal nature at all. It comes direct from Hell. It is purely spiritual; consequently it is far more subtle and deadly" (p. 99). "Pride is spiritual cancer; it eats up the very possibility of love, or contentment, or even sense" (p. 99). Then Lewis says that the first step in acquiring humility is "to realize that one is proud. . . . If you think you are not conceited, it means you are very conceited indeed" (p. 101).

III. HUMILITY IS THE CHRISTLIKE VIRTUE WE MUST HAVE.

A. Christ is the perfect example of humility (Matt 11:29). We must copy Christ in everything. We must determine to surrender all of our being to Christ to transform. Pray for God to break your pride and expose it for you to see. Then pray for God to take it out of your life and to give you true humility in the Holy Spirit.

B. Meditate long on the fact that the only thing we can boast about is in the cross of our Lord Jesus Christ. "But may it never be that I should boast, except in the cross of our Lord Jesus Christ, through which the world has been crucified to me, and I to the world" (Gal 6:14). Reflect seriously on the fact that Paul was speaking to each of us when he wrote 1 Corinthians 4:7, "For who regards you as superior? And what do you have that you did not receive? But if you did receive it, why do you boast as if you had not received it?" Peter reinforces this, "You younger men, likewise, be subject to your elders; and all of you, clothe yourselves with humility toward one another, for God is opposed to the proud, but gives grace to the humble. Humble yourselves, therefore, under the mighty hand of God, that He may exalt you at the proper time" (1 Pet 5:5-6).

C. Lay it to heart that our Lord Jesus Christ spoke to our hearts when He said, "So you too, when you do all the things which are commanded you, say, 'We are unworthy slaves; we have done only that which we ought to have done'" (Luke 17:10). Let us diligently do what the Psalmist did, and you will be gaining the victory over pride: "I will bless Jehovah at all times; His praise shall continually be in my mouth. My soul shall make her boast in Jehovah; the meek shall hear thereof, and be glad. Oh magnify Jehovah with me, and let us exalt his name together" (Ps 34:1-3).

Pride is the greatest poison that we have in our system, and only Christ can provide the antedote of humility to displace pride. The struggle on our part is going to be very great, but Christ will conquer if we want Him to. We are too proud, but let us repent and begin now to acquire the humility of Christ by God's Spirit working in us.

APPENDIX C

The Renunciation and Affirmation

As God is my witness and judge I affirm that I am a child of God purchased with the blood of the Lord Jesus Christ (Romans 6:3-11). I acclaim Him as my only Lord and Savior and specifically renounce Satan as my lord and god. As one completely accepting the finished work of Christ on Calvary for my redemption, my only hope of eternal life, I now renounce and repudiate all the sins of my ancestors in their working or effect upon me. Since I have through the Lord Jesus Christ's own blood been delivered from the power of darkness and translated into the kingdom of God's dear Son (Colossians 1:13), I now cancel and nullify all demonic working or effect that has been passed on to me from my ancestors.

Because the Lord Jesus Christ has become a curse for me by hanging upon the tree (Galatians 3:13), I cancel every spell or curse that may have been put upon me with or without my knowledge. As a child of God covered by the blood of the Lord Jesus Christ and trusting utterly in the atoning power of the blood of my Savior Jesus (Ephesians 1:7), I cancel, renounce, and nullify every agreement or pact I have made with Satan including blood pacts. I renounce any and every way that the devil has gotten hold of me and nullify and renounce every ground that I have ever given to Satan that gave him power or claim over me. I cancel and nullify any powers, gifts, or workings in me which are not of Abba, Father, or pleasing to Him.

I belong entirely and solely to the Lord Jesus Christ. As one who has been crucified (Galatians 2:20) and raised with Christ and now sits with Him in heavenly places (Ephesians 2:5-6), I sign myself eternally and completely over to the Lord Jesus Christ. It is my intention to pray daily that our Lord Jesus Christ will have full control of my total life. All of these things I do in the name of the Lord Jesus Christ and by His absolute authority over all things, rulers, authorities, and powers (Ephesians 1:18-23). Amen.

date _____ name _____

witnesses:

_____

_____

APPENDIX D

Basic Prayers and Foundational Statements for a Deliverance Session

(BEWARE! DANGER! This ministry is very serious and can expose those immature and inexperienced to possible literal physical attack and physical and/or spiritual problems.)

From a variety of sources we have derived the concepts and terms which we have developed into a flexible arrangement of basic matters to be taken care of before any deliverance is attempted. These preliminary prayers and statements are of essential importance to the conduct of a scriptural deliverance and for protection against any occult or demonic power sneaking in to corrupt the deliverances or to perform it under the deception that it is by the Lord Jesus Christ. We recognize that the devil is clever and powerful, though not all powerful, and that some deliverances done by *others* in a non-scriptural and not carefully guarded way *may* have been done by Satan. If so, then demons are only transferred to others, we believe; or they may leave temporarily before returning.

The man in charge of the deliverance session (and *one* person must be in charge at one time) may use his discretion in the exact wording of the prayers, statements, and commands or have some other person do this work of laying the foundations in prayer. The *exact* words are not necessary as the deliverance is not the result of a ritual or of certain words but is solely the action of the Lord Jesus Christ as He chooses to act. The basic ideas are given and in some cases the usual words for your information.

1. Exaltation, praise, and thanksgiving to the triune God for His power, mercy, love, mighty working, past deliverances, perfection, and our total dependence upon Him come first.

2. Pray for full protection (through the blood of Christ our Lord) for those present and all who are in the house or may come to the house, physically, emotionally, mentally, and spiritually. Ask for the binding to the chair of the body of the person being worked with. Pray that no evil spirit can make it violent to hurt or injure the person or those present, that all strength of body be denied to every demon, and that evil spirits can use only the face, eyes, and the voice (mouth, etc.) of the person.

3. Pray for the devil and all demons in the house or who could come into the house to be bound by the blood of the Lord Jesus Christ and utterly excluded from the house and property for the next _____ hours. That there can be no interference by any evil spirit, no assistance or reinforcement sent in from the outside. Through the power of Christ's blood that only those evil spirits that have invaded this person _____ (counselee's name) be allowed to be present, that no new evil spirits can be sent in, and that Christ prevents all transference of evil spirits to anyone else. God the Almighty give total amnesia to all other evil spirits not specifically connected with this person _____, and prevent them from learning anything about what we say or do in this meeting, prevent them from being able to gain any intelligence about the deliverance so that they cannot use it against us now or later. Lord Jesus Christ, please forbid any attempts to reorganize, multiply, divide, or fragment by the evil spirits and totally control all evil spirits, bind them into helplessness by Your blood, and force them to obey the commands You will to give through Your humble servant priests.

4. Pray for the Lord Jesus Christ to bind with His powerful blood all the evil spirits who have invaded _____ and bring them in their entirety into the body of the person alone, irrevocably bound together with His blood into one and only one unit. If they are shared with another person(s), they must be brought completely out of those other persons and forced to be in this person alone. All place-takers, successors, and no-names associated with these evil spirits are bound to their demon

rulers and must accompany them to Gehenna (hell) at one and the same time. Eternal God, please cast all these evil spirits out of _____ as soon as You will to do so, quickly and easily without injury to the person or any of us. Send them with one way traffic to Gehenna in their entirety and with no stopping point or to any other person but out of _____ and into Gehenna. PTL.

5. Pray to nullify and cancel all workings and prayers of Satanists, occultists, witches, and all who oppose You, Abba, Father, and prevent them from having any effect upon us during this session. Break all spells, charms, curses by the blood of our Lord Jesus Christ.

6. Pray to cancel and nullify all grounds for the evil spirits along with all blocks, shields or aids, through the blood of Christ Jesus.

7. Before the triune God, angels, demons, and men we declare that we deliberately and explicitly choose to work only from within the Name that is above every name, the Lord Jesus Christ. We depend utterly upon His finished work at Calvary and by the empty tomb to give the victory over Satan and the demons in this deliverance. We will to work only through the power of the Holy Spirit; and we reject and deny any other power or working whether demonic, occult, psychological, or humanistic. All must be done by the Lord God Almighty and to His glory alone. All must be done to the approval of the true and living God.

8. A hymn or song is used frequently such as "All Hail the Power of Jesus' Name," and this will be followed by the reading of various Scriptures such as selections from Psalm 91, Isaiah 41:9-13, or some favorite Scripture of the person.*

* We gladly and gratefully acknowledge our indebtedness to Ernest B. Rockstad for many of these thoughts and statements. God has used him as a pioneer in the work of deliverance in the USA.

A Case Study of a Woman Diagnosed as Having a Multi-Personality Disorder
(Some names are fictitious.)

1 John 1:1-6; 2:3-14 was read, then prayers were offered for protection of counselee, counselors, all people in the building; God was petitioned to be in complete control of all events. Janet read aloud her previously signed "Renunciation and Affirmation" statement. This was quite difficult for her to verbalize because of past influences from her mother, fear of men, fear of her grandmother, and her fear of sexuality. Other Scriptures were read.

Janet evidenced grounds of unforgiveness and bitterness which the Lord cancelled through her prayer involving repentance and forgiveness of self for past sins and ongoing guilt for being defiled as a child. Janet recognized intellectually that Jesus Christ forgives, but she did not feel worthy; therefore she had not fully accepted this in her heart.

Based on previous counseling sessions a list was read of possible controlling spirits to get her strongest reaction which Janet identified as Evelyn, an alter ego supposedly the well part of Janet, and a spirit of Fear. This list read included Retaliation, Depression, Infirmity, Evelyn, Destruction, Suicide, Rebellion and Fear. Joe petitioned our Lord Jesus Christ to call to attention whichever spirit was the greatest obstacle to Janet's healing. Her entire body began shaking uncontrollably as if she had palsy and her lips began quivering. She put her hands on her ears to block out Joe's calling to attention the spirit of Fear of Sexuality.

Janet approached near hysteria when we touched her wrists to help remove her hands from her ears so she could hear the spirit of Fear of Sexuality being called to attention. At one point Janet or Evelyn began to pull her own hair, so we held her wrists to prevent self-harm. She then put her teeth around Ed's hand and began to bite. Ed chose not to flinch but called upon Jesus Christ to protect him by saying, "I am a child of the one, true living God and the evil one can harm me not." Ed spoke hurriedly so the words got out before her teeth could clamp down hard. No injury resulted from the attempt to bite.

The counselors took turns reading Genesis, Romans 6, and Ephesians 5:22-31; all related to God creating man and woman and blessing their sexuality as good. Anytime the marriage bed, undefilement, sex or anything to do with man/woman relationships was read or mentioned it evoked waves of hysteria from Janet. We concentrated upon the theme of sexuality and found that Janet's personality changed while she was answering questions. Upon command we could speak to either personality, Evelyn or Janet. Janet reconfessed Jesus Christ as the Son of God, as her personal Savior and that Jesus Christ has come in the flesh. Evelyn could only say that Janet is a Christian and believed in Christ, but this was not a function of Evelyn. Therefore Evelyn could not confess Christ as her Lord. Evelyn also claimed she had not been able to write and only Janet could write. Evelyn declared her sole function was to be a companion to Janet whom Janet could call upon in times of need when no one else cared or knew when Janet was hurt or frightened. This included God who Janet seemed to feel had abandoned her in the times of terror during her February/March periods of suicidal darkness. Janet said Evelyn became her constant companion at age twelve or thirteen at the time of Janet's serious head injury.

Finally Janet admitted she realized that one part of her worshipped Satan, the other part Jesus Christ. She successfully recognized and confessed Evelyn as the satanic part of her and Janet as the Christian part. Reflecting back upon these events it seems the essence of Janet's bargain with Evelyn was Janet's intense desire for support and strength which she accomplished by taking on the personality of another person to compensate for a very low self-image. This seems sufficient to give grounds for Satan to enter one's life via a counterfeit personality, an evil, demonic or unclean spirit. While Satan obliged by providing Evelyn, a spirit who functioned as a companion, Janet's bargain opened the door to other wicked spirits who tormented her in many destructive ways. Satan does offer attractive visions of quick power, comfort, pleasure, healing, ecstatic emotional experiences, or support in an area of specific weakness. He does in fact provide one's immediate needs as an enticement. Later Satan extracts a terrible price accompanied by never-ending penalties as evidenced by the great need for psychiatric assistance in the world today.

In order to deliver Janet from Evelyn and remove the blocks to banish the evil spirits, it was necessary that Janet understand the nature of God and then renounce her reliance upon Satan for strength. She did proclaim her desire to stand alone with God and depend upon the Holy Spirit of Yahweh, the only true comforter, for the strength she needs.

After a teaching on false spirits, the deceitful comforts provided, and the terrible penalties which are paid as a price for their invasion, Janet consented to renounce Evelyn as a power of darkness. She agreed to give up Evelyn as a constant companion and take the Lord Jesus Christ as her constant companion and Savior in times of trouble. Evelyn threatened that when she left Janet would die physically. This, of course, proved to be a lie; but we were somewhat alarmed, as was Janet.

Once again we believe the premise has been validated that true psychological schizophrenia as evidenced specifically by multiple personality is rare and that spiritually caused multiple personality is quite common. Many forms of mental illness appear to originate, intensify, and perpetuate through the powers of darkness rampant in the world. Spiritually caused mental illness is unlikely to be treated successfully as an exclusive psychological phenomena, because it also requires spiritual healing through the person and work of our Lord Jesus Christ. When treating multiple personality psychologically, we can expect improvement to consist of a series of remissions offering only temporary relief. Christian leaders have a serious obligation to get this message across to others who work in the fields of psychiatry or psychology. It is exciting to envision the tremendous impact spiritual treatment can have in enabling psychiatric treatment to be successful in restoration of a healthy person.

We praised God for delivering Janet from the spirits of Fear of Sexuality and Fear of Men. That these did leave seemed to be verified by the test of truth before the one, true living God, Yahweh Elohim. At the end of this session Janet said she thought the spirit of Evelyn was gone; but the spirit of Darkness remained and could not be removed this particular night because it was still too strong, and Janet was not ready to deal with it.

We noted that the spirits became strongly manifested primarily upon anointing with olive oil by the elder in the name of our Lord Jesus Christ per James 5:13-16 even though the evangelist conducted the counseling. The spirits could not seem to be ejected into the place chosen by Jesus Christ from whence they could never return until after anointing with oil. Twice Janet said, during remissions of manifestation, that the manifested spirit was so weak it would leave with another anointing and this proved true. This night provided another glorious victory of our Lord Jesus Christ over Satan and his powers of darkness. We prayed, gave praise, glory, laud, and honor and all credit to the Father, Son, and Holy Spirit for this conquest. We petitioned God to fill Janet full to overflowing with Yahweh's Holy Spirit to occupy any void left by the departing spirits of Satan.

The next day during a telephone conversation with the elder, Janet said she felt very good spiritually and could verbalize without difficulty that the spirit of Fear of Sexuality had left. Prior to this deliverance counseling session she had been totally unable to verbalize any words involving sex or sexuality.

Medical Observations by a Registered Nurse During a Deliverance Session

Qualified counselors who are getting involved in a deliverance ministry need to be aware of the fact that when the person is demonized (the demon is in manifestation and in partial control of the person's body) there may be some physical discomforts given by the demon to the person such as pains in the body or severe headaches. Also, the more powerful the demon or the manifestation of the demon, the more physical actions can be threatened or even carried out. Prayer must be our weapon in protecting us against physical harm from an attack of the demoniac. It is of utmost importance that all objects be removed from the demoniac's presence before the meeting begins to prevent these objects from being thrown at the counselors. The Lord Jesus Christ has graciously afforded us remarkable protection against all kinds of menacing actions, gestures, and threats of violence.

In the earlier days of our ministry we worked with some people whom we *now* adjudge to have been possessed by demons which means that they were in the worst stage of invasion with their minds, wills, and bodies almost constantly controlled by the evil spirits. When the demons in these persons were manifested, violent physical actions took place with superhuman strength so that it required four or five men to hold even a small woman or restrain the person from kicking, tearing at the hair, attempting to strangle the workers or gouge their eyes. As the counselors became more spiritually mature and relied more on the Lord's strength these violent episodes decreased in frequency and intensity.

Once when working with a woman who had been involved in cults, witchcraft, and had made a blood pact with Satan we encountered unusual diversionary physical reactions such as the person stopped breathing. Some of the physical reactions of this person did not seem consistent with normal expected reactions as established by existing historical medical observations of other persons under conditions of high physical-emotional stress. The Lord providentially provided a registered nurse who came into the room and made the following observations concerning these demonically caused physical conditions.

"The following assessment was made based on immediate observation within a stressful situation without knowledge of the individual's medical history. I (a Registered Nurse) was asked to observe due to symptoms which suggested possible danger to the client in continuing the session.

"From time to time chest pain, respiratory difficulty, cardiac pain, and cyanotic conditions were noted.

OBSERVATIONS

"Occasional periods of skin pallor and cyanosis of hands were noted. The skin would appear pale and semi-waxy. Digital capillary-filling was found to be quite slow. All of which would support a diminished vasomotor function consistent with cardiac, chest, and arm pain described. However, instead of the expected diaphoretic cool skin and additional nausea, the skin was found to be warm and dry, and no complaint of nausea was registered. Pulse and respiration would remain within the normal safe limits.

"The distribution of the noted pallor and cyanosis was at times unusual and inconsistent with chest pain described. At times when breathing was labored, counted at 40 to 52 respirations per minute, instead of an expected generalized cyanosis characteristic of impaired gas exchange, peripheral cyanosis of one or both hands was noted. Peripheral cyanosis is usually a characteristic of decreased cardiac output. During periods of cardiac pain accompanied with difficult respiration all pulses available for evaluation were normal and skin colorations were normal. Peripheral vasoconstriction, which is sometimes a direct result to chilling or indirect result to stress, can usually be reduced by gentle massage which will cause a vasodilation and return skin color. For the most part peripheral cyanosis observed with this individual did not respond to manual massage.

"One could suggest that the individual was experiencing a form of 'shock' induced by the stress of the situation. Usual symptoms: rapid thready pulse, cold clammy skin, and rapid shallow breathing. Although breathing increased in rate which is consistent with the normal hyperventilation found with shock patterns, the respirations noted were not shallow but indeed very deep and wheezing in character. At times a Cheyne-Stokes pattern would prevail for a period of about one or two minutes. At all times auscultation revealed normal bronchovesicular breath sounds above the sternum and between the scapulae, and normal vesicular breath sounds elsewhere. (Auscultation with stethescope was used when it seemed necessary to determine the amount of danger the client might be experiencing due to the evidence of physical stress).

"Although the level of consciousness varied from alert to lethargic, at no time was the client ever observed to enter into a level of obtundation. Pupils when available for observation were found to be fully dilated and always reactive to light."

Diane (Vierling) Walker, RN

APPENDIX G

Experiential Observations of Startling Physical and Emotional Reactions During Deliverance Healing Sessions

Before and during deliverance sessions there have been many instances when counselees have experienced unusual physical or emotional reactions. We believe these startling reactions to be real and caused by the "spiritual forces of wickedness" in an attempt to distract those engaged in healing of those controlled by demons. Such experiences can be unnerving to the counselor, yet they really must not be allowed to frighten the Lord's servants or stop the work of deliverance. Our Lord is infinitely capable of handling all situations with absolute control and loving care for all involved. Always He is in complete charge even when we have doubts and are being blocked, harassed or puzzled.

It is important for the counselor to learn to cope with unusual situations for one may expect such to occur regularly in deliverance sessions. Typical occurrences are listed in this appendix to help prepare the reader so he can cope with these oftimes frightening situations. Remember perfect love casts out fear, and Jesus Christ has given us perfect love. The Word of God assures us, "He who was begotten of God keeps him and the evil one does not touch him" (I Jn 5:18b).

1. Visions or hallucinations. These have occurred in the form of visual, auditory and tactile (sense of touch) sensations. Clients undergoing satanic attack have seen horrible entities representing Satan or his angels of darkness in various forms, some with horns and cloven hooves. These appearances have been seen both alone and in groups. In at least one instance the client saw the counselors being attacked physically (this was alleged to be a

prophetic look into the future). In an attempt to protect the counselors, the client agreed to a pact with the forces of darkness; and immediately she became physically and spiritually distressed.

On occasion a client has had a vision of angels in white surrounded by much light, and in one instance a client saw what she described as a loving Jesus Christ standing over her left shoulder and comforting her. Numerous clients have heard voices offering difficult to resist temptations in sweet, nonthreatening tones. Others have heard voices constantly mouthing obscenities of the vilest kind. Often the voices claim to be from God but are deceitful angels of light. Sometimes the voices gave instructions as to how the person should act or things they ought to do to reap rewards or to be obedient to the will of God. In our experience every person who has heard voices of any kind has had some degree of satanic control; and when the grounds for allowing control had been dealt with, then the voices ceased. We have had no experience to date where any voice came from God in any client with whom we have counseled. Instances have occurred when a client touched a Bible and recoiled in terror claiming it was red hot or covered by the blood of Jesus.

2. Hysteria. Occasionally when an underlying cause for a deep-rooted spiritual or psychological problem surfaced, the client became hysterical. One example is in the area of sex by a client who had experienced a traumatic sexual abuse at an age below eight years. Anytime a word was mentioned concerning sex, marriage, man-woman relationships the client would hold her hands over her ears and cry out hysterically.

Another case was encountered in the area of unintelligible tongues where it was concluded by the counselors that demonic glossalalia might be a ground for demonic invasion. Upon mentioning the possibility that tongues might be a block to spiritual healing and should be tested scripturally in accord with 1 Jn 4:1-6, the client became totally hysterical. She heard voices inferring that the tongues were a gift from God, that she would be committing the unpardonable sin of blasphemy against the Holy Spirit by allowing testing of a spiritual gift from heavenly sources. The client continued to hear voices uttering obscenities every day and almost constantly. She continued to have poor health but was adamant in her refusal to allow her source of tongues to be evaluated. In cases of this kind where the client refuses to address the potential source of a problem the counselors should discontinue counseling until the client is ready to deal with the block to healing.

3. Voice Changed. Many instances have been encountered where the voice of a person under satanic control has changed so drastically that one is unable to recognize even a vague similarity to the owner of the voice. Many demons have their own speech patterns, accents, etc. as we do; and these are often clearly associated with the personality or working of that demon. A particularly startling incident occurred with a woman whose vocal cords were used by an evil spirit. Her voice became so low and guttural that neither counselor ever heard a man speak so low. Also the spirit warned the counselors that they were delving into areas of the spirit world that they knew nothing about. Warnings of grave danger and physical damage to the servants of God were uttered by this voice.

4. Handwriting. One person had made a blood pact with Satan. When asked to write a scriptural passage or to write a renunciation of Satan, her handwriting would deteriorate to the point where it became unreadable. As the handwriting deteriorated it became a struggle for her to write at all, a veritable physical, psychological, and spiritual struggle. Often as this strange event took place she would become demonized and would struggle fiercely with the workers with superhuman strength until Christ was called upon in faith to restrain the evil spirits who controlled her body and mind.

5. Deafness. Numerous situations arose when a client became totally deaf as Bible passages were read or quoted.

6. Blindness. One evening one of the authors got a phone call from two young preachers who were having a deliverance session with a young lady who was attempting to break away from a cult called "The Way International." Their action was *unauthorized* by the elders. They had become alarmed when the client went blind during the session. When the pastor arrived he checked to make certain that she was blind, that they were

not being deceived or distracted. Having worked with a school for the blind for seven years he had experience recognizing true blindness from pretense. She was truly blind for about forty-five minutes.

The elder advised the young men that the blindness was caused by spiritual forces of darkness in the same manner as physical pain and physical disabilities had been caused in other sessions they had observed. We prayed to calm the woman, explained what caused the blindness; and the elder assured everyone the blindness was temporary. After prayer and petitions her normal sight did return through the power of the risen Christ. This verified to us again that Satan is indeed the ruler of this world, that he certainly does have control over much of our physical and emotional well being to the *extent* that we choose to surrender ourselves to his influence wittingly or unwittingly and under the permission of our Lord Jesus Christ.

7. Headaches and Breathing Problems. Some clients have developed sudden, excruciating headaches during or just prior to deliverances. Some of these were so severe as to immobilize the client. In a few situations the client hyperventilated. We countered the hyperventilation by praying and by cupping our hands over the person's mouth to help them reingest carbon dioxide which did solve the problem. Occasionally a person would stop breathing or would begin to choke. We were told that the person felt as if he or she were being choked by hands, and in one case the person said a constrictor-like snake was wrapping itself around her lungs preventing her from breathing. As we grew more experienced, we could help clients become relieved of these discomforts by calling upon the name and power of the cleansing blood of Jesus Christ to remove these attacks of the evil one or to bind into helplessness the evil spirit causing this behavior.

8. Weakness and Nausea. A few people became nauseous. Several vomited during deliverance counseling, and some became so weak they fell into a swoon and had to be supported physically by the counselors to prevent them from falling to the floor.

These are the main types of startling phenomena which we have experienced during deliverance sessions. They do not always happen but may occur at any time, especially in the early days of your ministry. Other workers have testified to experiencing sounds or noise, oppression, and even demonic forms or shapes. Some workers have felt that demons were actually trying to invade them or to take over their minds. In a few cases we have witnessed the transference of demons from the client to some other person in the room. In every case these were weak Christians or even later proved to be in need of deliverance themselves.

We write these things especially to you who might be involved in a deliverance ministry by the grace of God. You need to be forearmed against being overwhelmed by these unexpected and unimagined happenings. Your strength and protection must always be in the blood of the Lord Jesus Christ and His all-powerful name.

Some Values of Fasting

In keeping with the biblical motto for Christ's Church Cincinnati (Col 1:28), we want to bring before your sincere minds the great value of the disciplined Christian life and the value of fasting in your drawing near to God.

I. CHRISTIANS ARE CALLED TO A DISCIPLINED LIFE.

A. This means a well-ordered life, a life that is controlled by the Holy Spirit and directed to spiritual goals of eternal significance. Jesus Christ was perfectly disciplined in everything of His life, and He is our model to follow.

B. Consider Romans 12:1-2. The lifestyle of the non-Christian is almost the exact opposite of that of the Christian.

C. We are to work out our salvation (not earn it) with fear and trembling (Phil 2:12). If I am seeking my own pleasure and leisure, my interests rather than those of my Lord and His people, how can I be working out my salvation with fear and trembling? If I am not disciplined enough to pray, to study the Word of God, to give myself to others who are in need, to fast and pray, then what is happening to my salvation?

D. 2 Corinthians 7:1 is a clear and definite call to a holy life in God, a walking in the Holy Spirit. It demands definite sacrifice and self-denial (2 Cor 6:16-18).

II. CHRISTIANS ARE CALLED TO THE DISCIPLINE OF FASTING.

A. Our Lord Jesus taught clearly that His disciples would

be living righteous lives and doing their spiritual duties with spiritual motives (Matt 6:1-18). In Matthew 9:14-15 Jesus taught that His disciples would fast.

B. Paul fasted three days without food or drink after seeing Christ (Acts 9:9). It was while Paul and others were fasting and ministering to the Lord that the Holy Spirit directed men to be sent out on a great evangelizing tour (Acts 13:1-3). Paul and Barnabas were set apart with fasting, prayer, and laying on of hands.

C. The very vital work of setting elders aside to oversee the congregation involves prayer and fasting, "having prayed with fasting, they commended them to the Lord" (Acts 14:23).

These Scriptures are sufficient to indicate that fasting is an appropriate, right, and good discipline for Christians who want to excel in the Lord.

III. CHRISTIANS CAN GAIN MUCH THROUGH THE DISCIPLINE OF FASTING.

A. In Matthew 6, verses 1-18, Christ is teaching that fasting along with giving and prayer are vital services to God, a sharing in His righteousness, and a seeking of His kingdom first. Through fasting we are seeking to draw nearer to God and to crucify the carnal nature with its evil desires. It can be purifying and upbuilding for our outlook, faith, and lifestyle.

B. Ron Simkins has noted other secondary considerations and values:

1. We may become more open to the Lord and His will for us both through the Word and the answers to our prayers.
2. We may become more aware of our weaknesses and sins, such as pride, anger, conceit, bitterness, emptiness, obsessions, fears, doubts.
3. We may gain a greater effectiveness in intercessory prayer.
4. A greater humility and dependence before the Lord can develop.
5. Increased power from God for healing and deliverance of those who are sick or in bondage to Satan

can be received. Mark 9:29 is not well attested textually, but it does serve as a witness that early in the church fasting was held to be closely associated with prayer and deliverance.

6. Too many of us are governed by our stomachs; our belly is our god (Phil 3:19). Fasting helps us to have money for those who really need physical food. Also fasting tells your stomach, "You are my servant; I am not yours. Jehovah God is my God; you are not my god." (Lecture notes)

Neil Gallagher comments in his book, *How to Save Money On Almost Everything,* "Fasting on Mondays has put a clamp on me. When I make my body say no to food on Mondays, it's a slap in the face lasting all week. I'm no longer driven to food. I'm in control of it, not vice versa.

"The trauma of each Monday now is like someone shoving me in a chair, grabbing me by the shoulders, shaking me and shouting in my face, 'Food is not important! When you start eating it tomorrow, remember, food is for fuel, not fun. When you start eating again, don't pack your stomach and intestines like you did yesterday after church.' (Why do Sunday dinners absolve Christians from gluttony?)

"Each Monday is like someone holding me under a freezing shower. I feel its bristle and shock all week. It awakens me to what is essential and disciplines my daily life-style.

"Fasting trims. I don't have a weight problem. And I don't intend to wait until I have one to say no to food. Fasting makes me acutely aware that my body is a divine building, a home for God's Spirit. It teaches me to be an alert manager of this body.

. . . .

"Since fasting, I have more money to send to famine peoples. I estimate that by not eating on Monday, I save at least two dollars, which I'm then able to send to a famine-fighting organization (usually World Vision, 919 W. Huntington Drive, Monrovia, Califronia)" (pp. 190, 191).

IV. OUR MOTIVE FOR FASTING IS ALL IMPORTANT
A. Hebrews 11:6 (seek HIM); Jeremiah 29:13; Joel 2:12;

Romans 11:36. We want more of *God* in our lives, more of His presence and power. It is not self seeking, to be famous for fasting.

B. We want to show our humility before God, not to men, but to God, angels, and demons and to destroy pride, that chief sin of religious people. Submission to God can be encouraged by fasting.

V. GOD'S CHOSEN FAST RESULTS IN SPIRITUAL GROWTH AND ORTHOPRAX.

A. Isaiah attacks hypocritical worship as wrong and rejected by God (Isa 58:1-12).

B. Genuine fasting is unto God and produces positive acts of righteousness, carrying out the will of God in day to day practice.

    1. Verse 6—loosen bonds of wickedness, free the oppressed, break yokes which involve the gospel, healing, and deliverance.

    2. Verse 7—feed hungry, bring poor into your house, clothe naked; and this requires loving service and benevolence.

    3. Verses 8, 9, 12—true restorers are those who keep a true fast to the Lord out of pure hearts.

VI. PRACTICAL SUGGESTIONS ABOUT FASTING TO THE LORD.

A. Most of us can go days or weeks without food as we live on surplus fat.

B. Most people go through three phases:

    1. Craving for food on and off for two or three days.

    2. Then weakness, faintness occur for two or three days or longer.

    3. Growing strength, little or no concern for food.

C. You should end the fast according to your schedule or when hunger pangs begin—maybe a few days or the twenty-first day, fortieth day, or longer.

D. Fasting is not harmful to most because it is taught by Christ and practiced with good results by God's people. For a long fast it is wise to check with your physician, but diabetics must *not* fast.

E. Experiment with fasting by skipping a meal, later three meals, then go two or three days without food. Don't copy others or seek to outdo others. Talk little of your fasting. For a longer fast, make the last meal before the fast one of fruits. When breaking a long fast, do so with cautious care using fruit and vegetable juices just in small quantities. Gradually increase to yogurt, salads, cooked vegetables in small quantities. Rest and eat slowly.

F. Ask yourself some questions before beginning a longer fast:

1. Am I confident this is God-given and to His glory?
2. Will it be partial or normal, without food for a day or for many days?
3. Are my motives right?
4. What are my special spiritual objectives in fasting— personal sanctification, intercession (for whom, what burdens?), divine guidance, blessing?
5. Are objectives too self-centered? Have I concern for others?
6. Am I seeking the Lord God, my Abba, Father, submitting to Him, honoring Him?

G. Be prepared for spiritual warfare to break out in or around you. Christ, our Lord, suffered after His long fast, so will you. The devil hates the disciplined life, hates fasting and prayer; and he will attack you sorely. Prepare using Ephesians 6:10-18. Don't let your feelings rule. Fight the good fight. It will not be easy, but draw strength from God. Ask God to give you the victory. "From strength to strength go on/ Wrestle and fight and pray/ Tread all the powers of darkness down/ And win the well fought day" (Charles Wesley).

CONCLUSION: We are living in a soft, self-indulgent, selfish, weak, and spiritually decadent age. We Christians need to rise out of our culture and its sensual, material and carnal controls and be seen as lights in the world, a different kind of people who live for God and serve others. Why don't we allow God to show us what He may choose to do if we individually make personal decisions to pray and fast with some regularity? Are you willing to consider that God may want you and me to keep His chosen fast to set the oppressed free, our brothers and sisters even, those in trouble, bondage? Maybe here, too, we have to learn that God has some power available for release that we in our humanness, traditionalism, and rationalism are not allowing. We recommend fasting as an excellent discipline when done scripturally. God will certainly bless you through it.

For more informaiton on fasting we recommend Richard J. Foster's book, *Celebration of Discipline,* (New York: Harper and Row, Publishers, 1978), pp. 41-53. Perhaps the most valuable book is Arthur Wallis' *God's Chosen Fast,* (Ft. Washington, PA: Christian Literature Crusade, 1968).

An Advertisement of
ASTRAL PROJECTION BY SOUND

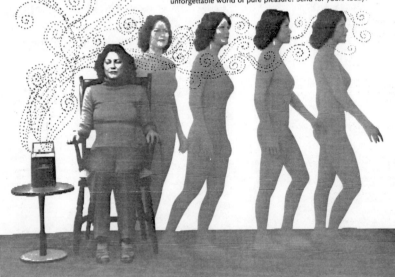

OUT-OF-BODY EXPERIENCES CAN BE AUTOMATICALLY TRIGGERED BY CERTAIN SOUNDS!

Recent experiments prove that out-of-body experiences can be induced by simply listening to certain sounds which can automatically stimulate a pleasure center in the mind while it creates a warm, comfortable vibration throughout the body.

These sounds, known as "Astral Sounds", have triggered out-of-body experiences in persons who have tried many other methods that have failed. Others report seeing visions of light, colors, designs, symbols, pictures, hallucinations, peak experiences in higher awareness, and an opening up of tremendous psychic ability.

According to many users, these "Astral Sounds" can also create physical sensations of such intense pleasure that many users could not find words to describe the feeling.

And, it's all so easy to do. Just relax, switch on your tape cassette of "Astral Sounds", and let your mind and body enjoy. The incredible sounds on the tape can automatically carry you into an unforgettable world of pure pleasure! Send for yours today!

YOU CAN EXPECT RESULTS LIKE THIS!

"The first time I used the tape I experienced a euphoric sensation of floating and began to have very mild, pleasant hallucinations. When I used the tape the second time I had my first out of body experience . . . I am happy to report that I successfully achieve an astral projection approximately 85% of the times I listen to your tape. What amazed me is that it is so easy to accomplish. All I do is turn out the lights, lie down and close my eyes, then turn on the tape of Astral Sounds . . ."
Mr. J. H., Los Angeles

"I gave it to a friend to listen to without telling him what it was. He had never attempted astral projection before. While listening, he got to the point that the chair under him, and the room about him was moving, vibrating back and forth. He also hallucinated brilliant colors and faces. Apparently he has accomplished as much in a half hour with your tape as I have in five years of trying many other techniques . . ."
Ms. C. W., Georgia

FULLY GUARANTEED!
All tapes are fully guaranteed against defects in workmanship for one full year! Defective tapes replaced free.

Shipped complete with instructions in dust-proof box!

"*Your Astral Sound tape
has been adopted as a
required text in the
psychology/nursing
department.*"
**Metropolitan Community College
Minneapolis, Minnesota**

"*Astral tape is an autogenic
training device which may
assist the user to achieve
extremely deep levels of
relaxation.*"
**Holly State Hospital
Lantana, Florida**

It Works!

Here's Proof...

"The first time I listened to your Astral
Sounds tape, the sounds actually had me
seeing mental pictures. It was like an
extremely enjoyable kaleidoscopic
hallucination . . ."

"The entire experience was one of the most
sensuous and pleasant in my life . . ."

"I tried all of the systems and theories of
Astral Projection currently available and
still had no success after nearly 6 years of
concentrated effort. Then, about a year ago,
I obtained a tape of your Astral Sounds.
The results exceeded my wildest
expectations!!"

Just by listening to those sounds (which are
nearly identical to the music I experienced
on previous spontaneous oobe's) I am
now able to induce an out-of-body
experience anytime I care to . . ."

"When first introduced to the tape by my
wife 8 months ago, I was highly skeptical
but consented to listen anyway. That first
listening session had such a dramatic effect
on me that I continued to use the tape.
After listening to it for approximately the
7th or 8th time I had an out of body
experience. I was able to perceive myself
from a vantage point far removed from my
own physical body. I have since used the
tape as an extremely effective aid to
relaxation and meditation . . ."

"Since I began using the tape I find myself to
be operating on a higher level of awareness
and have had a great number of psychic
pre-cognitive glimpses at future events
which have actually come to pass!"

"I have had countless out of body experiences, as well as other psychic experiences
just from listening to the tape . . ."

"None of the more conventional methods of
astral projection proved successful for me.
When your tape arrived I began listening to
it immediately and was quite startled at
the results. Within 3 days I was able to have
an out-of-body experience each and every
time I relaxed and listened to the tape . . ."

"These sounds not only empowered me to
accomplish astral projection, but I find
myself to be unbelievably psychic after each
time I listen to the tape . . ."

"Within a few days the tape had my body
vibrating and it is as if the sounds themselves
lifted me right out of my own body. That
was 6 months ago, and since then I am able
to accomplish an out-of-body experience
almost every time I relax and listen to
the tape . . ."

"The first time I listened to those incredible
sounds on your tape. I felt my body vibrating
and had distinct flashes of color and scenes.
Then, as the tape ended, I was left with a
beautifully calm and peaceful feeling which
encompassed my body as well as my mind.
In the 18 months between then and now
I can report having out-of-body experiences
in about 75% of my listening sessions . . ."

"I conducted a workshop in Astral Projection
using your tape. An actual count of the
out-of-body experiences is running at
approximately $^2/_3$ of the participants. The
most productive was 80% while the least
productive was 40% . . . Those who failed
to project report experiencing the vibration
effect described by Robert Monroe which
often precedes the actual projection . . ."

A PARTIAL LIST OF THOSE USING ASTRAL SOUNDS :

Toronto Board of Education
University of Pittsburgh
Laurentian University, Canada
Austin Community College, Texas
Johnson Community College
Napa College, California
Austin Peay State University
Aims Community College, Colorado
University of Chicago
Randolph-Macon College, Virginia
Chicago Board of Education
Metropolitan Community College, Minnesota
University of Windsor, Canada
University of California, Davis
University of California, Los Angeles
Cerritos College, California
Wright State University
Algonquin College, Canada
University of Southern Colorado
Schenectady County Community College, New York
New York University
Mid Plains Community College, Nebraska
Corpus Christi School District, Texas
Temple City School District, California
Centennial School District, Oregon
Godwin Heights Public Schools, Michigan
Duval County School Board, Florida
Elmhurst College, Illinois
Flinders University, Australia
St. Cloud University, Minnesota
St. Ignatius Loyola College, Puerto Rico
Worcester Technical High School, Mass.
Transpersonal Institute, Finland
Institute of Noetic Sciences, California
Pain and Health Rehabilitation Center, Wisconsin
Clinical Psychology Associates, Michigan
Lakeland Counseling Center, Wisconsin
The City of Jacksonville, Florida — City Hall
Center for Internal Medicine, California
Maimonides Medical Center, New York
The Menninger Foundation, Kansas
Mental Health Board, Michigan
Lima State Hospital, Ohio
Maurer Educational Center, Ohio
Wilson-Green Mental Health Center, North Carolina
Santa Ana Dept. of Mental Health, California
Montgomery County Department of Health
Biofeedback Society of Sydney, Australia
Mr. Jose Silva, Founder, Silva Mind Control
Peru Public Library, Illinois
Lima State Hospital, Ohio
Museum of Natural History, Minnesota
Pyramid Energy Center, Denmark
A. B. Dick Company, Illinois
Atomic Research, New York
American Clinic, Texas

APPENDIX J

Speaking in Tongues and the Testing of Tongues

Today there is a dynamic movement which attracts many people by its spiritual nature and claims to honor the Holy Spirit by allowing Him to have full power in the life of the individual. This is called the "charismatic renewal movement" and has been widespread in most of the denominations in the past twenty years. Seeking the experience called "the baptism in the Holy Spirit" is the most prominent feature of this movement, and speaking in tongues is the most notable outward manifestation of those who have received what they call "the baptism in the Holy Spirit." It is considered valid and even infallible evidence that a person has received some unusual power from the Holy Spirit.

We have heavy questions relative to the theology of this movement, and we believe that it lacks a sound exegetical basis in the New Testament revelation. Nevertheless we have tried to be open to the possibility that there might be a genuine gift of speaking in tongues that would be from the Lord God Almighty. Dr. Kurt Koch raises the possibility that there are a few manifestations of tongue speaking that may be labeled biblical and gives some examples in his book, *The Strife of Tongues.* [1]

In the deliverance ministry we encountered individuals from time to time who had received what was called a baptism in the Holy Spirit or who had been prayed for and had hands laid on them to receive a "supernatural gift," especially that of speaking in tongues. This caused us to do further research into the matter of the origin of the tongues speaking which we were encountering, and we found that several eminent authorities in the field raised the serious possibility that the overwhelming majority of tongues speaking is either from a human source (autosuggestion) or from a demonic or occultic source. Kurt Koch believes in the possibility of the exercise of supernatural gifts today and yet is very forcible in warning against a naive and uncritical attitude toward tongues speaking. "Bearing in mind," he says, "all these questions it becomes more and more clear that maybe over 95% of the whole tongues movement is mediumistic in character."[2]

In a letter to the authors recently, Dr. Koch wrote, "I agree with your opinion but your estimate of 80% of wrong cases is too low. I have now over fifty-three years experience, and I think even 95% is too low.

"There are a few cases which seem to be genuine. A girl student of a Bible School in Canada (Prairie Bible School) spoke in tongues. She was tested according to 1 John 4 and answered: 'Yes, I confess that Christ has come in the flesh. I love him. He is my Lord.' That is a good case.

. . . .

"For me it is impossible to believe that 80% are wrong and 20% genuine. Among 100 perhaps one is genuine."[3]

In another book Dr. Koch lists as one of Satan's devices the speaking in tongues. He says, "I have to say a decisive *no* to the tongues movement itself. Every year the number of negative experiences of which I hear grows."[4] He recommends as the most scholarly book in the field the one written by John P. Kildahl, *The Psychology of Speaking in Tongues.*[5] (We would recommend as the most scholarly work in the critical area of linguistics, *Tongues of Men and Angels* by William J. Samarin, professor of anthropology and linguistics at the University of Toronto.[6])

"It looks," Dr. Koch writes, "as if the tongues and the so-called charismatic movements are the most dangerous weapons Satan uses against the Christian camp. It must, however, be clearly emphasized that within these two movements there are many true Christians who remain there because they lack the gift of discerning the spirits."[7]

Another scholar who raises serious questions about the origin of much of the tongues speaking in the modern day movement is Dr. Merrill F. Unger. In his book, *New Testament Teaching on Tongues,* he declares, *"Tongues today run the risk of inviting demonic deception and despoiling.* This somber note of possible danger needs to be sounded in our time. Many sincere but naive believers taken in by the error that tongues evidence a deeper spiritual experience are quite oblivious of the fact of the possibility of demonic delusion.

. . . .

"That tongues can and are counterfeited by demon spirits is evidenced by the fact that spiritistic mediums, Muslim dervishes, and Indian fakirs speak in tongues."[8]

A most surprising testimony in regard to the danger of speaking in tongues without any consideration of their origin is given by K. Neill Foster in his book, *Help! I Believe in Tongues.*[9] Foster is a strong advocate of the present day manifestation of miraculous gifts in the church; but he writes very sensibly and with warnings which need to be heeded, particularly as they come from one who himself practices speaking in tongues. He recognizes that the Scripture is clear that not all Christians are going to speak in tongues.

Foster states some sobering statistics: "Yet I would estimate twenty-five percent of the deliverance ministry God has allowed me over the years has involved the extrication of deceived people from the false charismatic manifestations. Most of the cases included demonic tongues.

"One brother who has tested tongues for forty years says that in his experience nine out of ten were false.

"In a recently published article one of our contemporaries cites a similar statistic: Ninety percent of the tongues he and his colleagues have tested have been false. In my own experience perhaps eighty percent of the tongues manifestations that I have had to deal with have been false.

"Still I doubt that the statistics tell the whole story. Because people with genuine gifts and healthy spiritual life do not come for counselling nearly so frequently. But there is no denying that the devil has been having a field day among charismatics. His penetration, whatever the percentage, appears to be massive."[10]

In our limited experience in testing of tongues to determine their origin, we have not found a genuine gift from Abba, Father, in the ten cases tested. Nine were clearly demonic and the Christians renounced them. The tenth case was inconclusive as the client refused to continue with the testing.

We have found a great aversion and rejection on the part of almost every Christian who is speaking in tongues to obey the scriptural injunction: "Beloved, do not believe every spirit, but test the spirits to see whether they are from God; because many false prophets have gone out into the world" (1 John 4:1). God has given us a direct command to test the spirits, and we must follow that command if we are to honor God. In the light of the preceding testimony about demonic tongues, it would seem to be the only safe course to follow. Why, then, do many tongues speakers disregard God's command for testing when the evidence points to a demonic origin for most cases?

Probably the most common answer is that to question a gift of the Holy Spirit is "to commit the sin of blasphemy against the Holy Spirit." There is no exegetical basis for such a claim. The Scriptures do not teach that obeying the command of God in 1 John 4:1 causes one to commit the sin (which is actually a sinful *state* of moral depravity) of blaspheming the Holy Spirit. Honoring God in the testing of the spirits in regard to any of the claimed charismatic gifts will certainly bring God's protection and true judgment.

It is never wrong to obey Scripture, so we urge all those with supernatural gifts to be tested to see if the spirit is of God or of Satan. The procedure is simple and is drawn from 1 John 4:2-3: "By this you know the Spirit of God: every spirit that confesses that Jesus Christ has come in the flesh is from God; and every spirit that does not confess Jesus is not from God; and this is the spirit of the antichrist, of which you have heard that it is coming, and now it is already in the world."

After foundational prayers similar to those beginning a session for deliverance have been prayed, the person is asked to begin speaking in tongues and to continue without interruption. The tester will then ask, "Do you, spirit, confess that Jesus Christ has come in the flesh?" This may be repeated several times until an answer is given. The answer should be in English and should be yes or no at least. It may be more complete such as, "Yes, Jesus Christ has come in the flesh."

Whatever the answer is it is appropriate to rephrase the question and ask it again. "Do you confess that Jesus Christ is your Lord?" Or you might say, "Do you, the source of this tongue, confess that in Jesus Christ the fulness of the Godhead dwells bodily?" The evil spirits are deceptive and will lie whenever possible, so the wording must be precise and the answer precise, clear, and immediate. Hesitancy and any rewording of an answer may indicate that a demon is speaking.

Also it is quite necessary to instruct the person with the gift that he is not to do the speaking at all in response to the questions, for the questions are put to the spirit that is giving the tongues. The person can usually tell whether or not he has done the speaking or some other personality. Sometimes, if an evil spirit is the source of the tongues, it will begin to speak directly through the voice of the individual. The words will indicate the spirit of the antichrist if it refuses to confess the Lord Jesus Christ.

Be aware of the fact that the answer, "I believe in Jesus" is not good enough, for there have been demons with the names of "Jesus," "Holy Spirit," and even "Yahweh." The confession must be that Jesus Christ is the Son of God or that Jesus Christ of Nazareth has come in the flesh. Dr. Koch confirms this by a report from a missionary in Florida who counseled with a lady. "She fell into a trance and spoke in foreign languages. The missionary commanded the tongues-speaking spirit, "Do you confess that Christ has come in the flesh?" No answer. Again he commanded, 'I command you to reveal yourself.' 'I belong to Jesus.' 'To which Jesus?' the missionary asked. No answer. 'I command you in the name of Christ to say the truth.' And the answer was, 'I belong to the Jesus of Satan'."[11]

"When the tongue is a true gift of the Holy Spirit," says Ernest Rockstad, "the speaker will experience in his spirit a continuing agreement and affirmation while the questions are being asked. It is not likely that any answers will come from him without his volition, any more than the speaking in the tongue is apart from his own volition.''[12] We feel that this is weak because of the power of deception aided by the arch-deceiver, Satan, which has allowed some people with counterfeit gifts to *feel* very secure and serene in their deceived state. It is our conviction that there needs to be a genuine verbal confession that Jesus Christ is the Son of God and has come in the flesh. This can be done in the power of the Holy Spirit if the tongues is given by the Holy Spirit of Yahweh.

A better position is stated by Neill Foster, "In 1 John 4:2 and 3 the verb forms used indicate that every spirit that *continually* and *genuinely* confesses that Jesus Christ is come in the flesh is of God. Therefore reluctant admissions or occasional positive declarations that Jesus Christ is come in the flesh are not sufficient. *The confession must be continual. A superficial understanding of this principle can short circuit the whole procedure of testing.*"[13]

The person who is being tested needs to be carefully instructed to allow the spirit to respond and that if the spirit does not continually, readily, and genuinely confess that Jesus Christ is Lord, the Son of God, and has come in the flesh; then he should be willing to renounce the gift. The elder or tester needs to immediately ask the Lord Jesus Christ to bind with His blood the evil spirit(s) giving the gift of tongues and to cast it into hell. In some cases it may be that the speaking in tongues is only a fleshly manifestation and an imitation of tongues. If that is the result of the test, then the person needs to repent of the sin of deception which he has practiced and to give up his fleshly activity. It is not pleasing to God Almighty.

The result that can follow a deliverance from a demonic spirit of tongues is usually a sense of release and a peace in the Lord Jesus Christ. Dr. Koch relates an experience that he had. "A Dutch Reformed minister confessed in my presence that he was a member of the so-called charismatic movement. He spoke in tongues, and when he prayed people fell down and got 'the baptism of the Holy Spirit.' He was proud of it. In spite of these experiences he lived in gross sins.

"He came in 1981 the first time to Sizabantu and was disturbed by the messages. He did not agree, but he came a second time in 1982 and was convinced that he was on the wrong track. He repented and renounced his tongues and the so-called baptism with the Holy Spirit. Since that renewal the people of his congregation do no more collapsing (slain in the Lord), but confess their sins and give their lives to Christ. He now has a small revival in his community."[14]

Regardless of what we do, what gift we have, we all need to humble ourselves before the Lord Jesus Christ and allow Him to test our gifts.

NOTES

1. Kurt E. Koch, *The Strife of Tongues* (Berghausen, Germany: Evangelization Publisher, n.d.), pp. 19-22.

2. Ibid., p. 35.

3. Personal letter to the authors from Kurt E. Koch, December 12, 1982, pp. 1-2.

4. Kurt E. Koch, *Satan's Devices* (Grand Rapids: Kregel Publications, 1978), pp. 206-210.

5. John P. Kildahl, *The Psychology of Speaking in Tongues* (New York: Harper & Row, Publishers, 1972).

6. William J. Samarin, *Tongues of Men and Angels* (New York: The Macmillan Company, 1972).

7. Kurt E. Koch, *Satan's Devices,* p. 207.

8. Merrill F. Unger, *New Testament Teaching on Tongues* (Grand Rapids: Kregel Publications, 1971), pp. 162-164.

9. K. Neill Foster, *Help! I Believe in Tongues* (Minneapolis: Bethany Fellowship, Inc., 1975).

10. Ibid., pp. 88-89.

11. Kurt E. Koch, personal letter to the authors, December 12, 1982, p. 2.

12. Ernest B. Rockstad, "Speaking in Tongues Scripturally Tested" (Mimeographed lesson, 1977), p. 2.

13. Foster, op. cit., pp. 110-111.

14. Kurt E. Koch, personal letter to the authors, December 12, 1982, p. 1.

Selected Bibliography

BOOKS

Adams, Jay. *Christian Counselor's Manual.* Grand Rapids: Baker Book House, 1973.

_____. *Competent to Counsel.* Nutley, NJ: Presbyterian and Reformed, 1970.

_____. *Matters of Concern to Christian Counselors: A Potpourri of Principles and Practices.* Phillipsburg, NJ: Presbyterian and Reformed, 1978.

Alexander, William M. *Demonology in the New Testament.* Edinburgh: T. and T. Clark, 1902. (Now, *Demonic Possession in the New Testament.* Baker Book House, 1980.)

Baldwin, Stan. *Games Satan Plays.* Wheaton, IL: Victor Books, 1971.

Barnhouse, Donald Grey. *The Invisible War.* Grand Rapids: Zondervan Publishing House, 1965.

Basham, Don. *Deliver Us From Evil.* Washington Depot, CT: Chosen Books, 1972.

_____ and Dick Leggatt. *The Most Dangerous Game: A Biblical Exposé of Occultism.* Greensburg, PA: Manna Christian Outreach, 1975.

Biederwolf, William Edward. *Whipping Post Theology or Did Jesus Atone for Disease?* Grand Rapids: William B. Eerdmans Publishing Co., 1934.

Bobgan, Martin, and Deidre Bobgan. *The Psychological Way/ The Spiritual Way.* Minneapolis: Bethany Fellowship, Inc., 1979.

Brittle, Gerald. *The Demonologist.* Englewood Cliffs, NJ: Prentice-Hall, Inc., 1980.

Brooks, Pat. *Occult Experimentation: A Christian View.* Chicago: Moody Press, 1972.

Brown, Raymond E., Joseph A. Fitzmeyer, and Roland E. Murphy, eds. *The Jerome Biblical Commentary.* Englewood Cliffs, NJ: Prentice-Hall, Inc., 1968.

Bruner, Frederick D. *A Theology of the Holy Spirit: The Pentecostal Experience and the New Testament Witness.* Grand Rapids: William B. Eerdmans Publishing Co., 1970.
    This is one of the best examinations of Pentecostal teaching.

Bubeck, Mark I. *The Adversary: The Christian Versus Demon Activity.* Chicago: Moody Press, 1975.

Carnell, Edward J. *An Introduction to Christian Apologetics.* Grand Rapids: William B. Eerdmans Publishing Co., 1948.

Cerullo, Morris. *The Backside of Satan.* Carol Stream, IL: Creation House, 1972.

Cerutti, Edwina. *Olga Worrall—Mystic With the Healing Hands.* New York: Harper and Brothers Publishers, 1975.

Chapman, Colin. *Christianity on Trial.* Wheaton, IL: Tyndale House Publishers, Inc., 1972.

Collins, Gary. *Christian Counseling.* Waco, TX: Word Books, 1980.

Crabb, Lawrence J., Jr. *Effective Biblical Counseling.* Grand Rapids: Zondervan Publishing House, 1977.

Curran, Charles A. *Religious Values in Counseling and Psychotherapy.* New York: Shedd and Ward, 1969.

Dobbins, Richard D. *Can A Christian Be Demon Possessed?* Akron, OH: Emerge, 1973.

Eareckson, Joni, and Steve Estes. *A Step Further.* Minneapolis: Worldwide Publications, 1978.

Eliade, Mircea. *Occultism, Witchcraft, and Cultural Fashions.* Chicago: University of Chicago, 1976.

Elwood, Roger. *Strange Things Are Happening.* Elgin, IL: David C. Cook, 1973.

Ensign, Grayson H. *You Can Understand the Bible.* Joplin, MO: College Press, 1978.

Ernest, Victor H. *I Talked with Spirits.* Wheaton, IL: Tyndale House Publishers, Inc., 1970.

Foster, K. Neill. *Help! I Believe in Tongues: A Third View of the Charismatic Phenomenon.* Minneapolis: Bethany Fellowship, Inc., 1975.

Foster, Richard J. *Celebration of Discipline,* New York: Harper and Row, Publishers, 1978.

Freeman, Hobart E. *Angels of Light?* Plainfield, NJ: Logos Books, 1969.

Fuller, John G. *Arigo: Surgeon of the Rusty Knife.* New York: Pocketbook, 1975.

Gallagher, Neil. *How To Save Money On Almost Everything.* Minneapolis: Bethany Fellowship, Inc., 1978.

Garten, Max. *"Civilized" Diseases and Their Circumvention.* San Jose, CA: Maxmillion World Publishers, Inc., 1978.

Gasson, Raphael. *The Challenging Counterfeit.* S. Plainfield, NJ: Bridge Publishing, Inc., 1972.

Geisler, Norman L. *A Philosophy of Religion.* Grand Rapids: Zondervan Publishing House, 1974.

_____. *Christian Apologetics.* Grand Rapids: Baker Book House, 1976.

Gordon, A. J. *The Ministry of Healing.* Harrisburg, PA: Christian Publications, Inc., n.d.

Gross, Martin L. *The Psychological Society.* New York: Random House, 1978.

Hammond, Frank, and Ida Mae Hammond. *Pigs in the Parlor: A Practical Guide to Deliverance.* Kirkwood, MO: Impact, 1973.

Hendricksen, William. *New Testament Commentary, Exposition of the Pastoral Epistles.* Grand Rapids: Baker Book House, 1957.

Hick, John. *Arguments for the Existence of God.* New York: Seabury Press, 1971.

_____. *Evil and the God of Love.* Great Britain: Collins. The Fontana Library, 1968.

Hitt, Russell. *Demons Today.* Philadelphia: Evangelical Foundation, 1969.

Hoffer, Abram, and Morton Walker. *Orthomolecular Nutrition.* New Canaan, CT: Keats Publishing, 1978.

Jacobson, Oscar W., and others. *Attack from the Spirit World —A Compilation*. Wheaton, IL: Tyndale House Publishers, Inc., 1973.

Kallas, James. *Jesus and the Power of Satan*. Philadelphia: Westminster, 1968.

Kildahl, John T. *The Psychology of Speaking in Tongues*. New York: Harper and Row, Publishers, 1972.

Kirschmann, John D. *Nutrition Almanac*. New York: McGraw-Hill Book Co., 1979.

Koch, Kurt E. *Between Christ and Satan*. Grand Rapids: Kregel Publications, 1971.

_____. *Christian Counseling and Occultism* (The Counseling of the Psychically Disturbed and Those Oppressed through Involvement in Occultism). Grand Rapids: Kregel Publications, 1972.

_____. *Demonism, Past and Present*. Grand Rapids: Kregel Publications, 1973.

_____. *Occult Bondage and Deliverance* (Advice for Counseling the Sick, the Troubled, and the Occultly Oppressed). Grand Rapids: Kregel Publications, 1972.

_____. *Satan's Devices* (An Exposé of the Occult and Other Extreme Movements and Ideologies with Counsel for Deliverance), trans. Michael Freeman. Grand Rapids: Kregel Publications, 1978.

_____. *The Strife of Tongues*. Berghausen, Germany: Evangelization Publisher, n.d.

Ladd, George Eldon. *A Commentary on the Revelation of John*. Grand Rapids: William B. Eerdmans Publishing Co., 1972.

Leek, Sybil. *The Story of Faith Healing*. New York: Macmillan, 1973.

Lesser, Michael. *Nutrition and Vitamin Therapy*. New York: Bantam Books, Inc., 1981.

Lewis, C. S. *Letters to Malcolm*. London: Collins, 1963.

_____. *Mere Christianity*. New York: Macmillan, 1943, 1945, 1952.

_____. *Miracles*. New York: Macmillan, 1947.

_____. *The Problem of Pain*. London: Geoffrey Bles, 1940.

_____. *The Screwtape Letters.* New York: Macmillan, 1956.

Long, James W. *Prescription Drugs, What You Need To Know For Safe Drug Use.* New York: Harper and Row, Publishers, 1980.

_____. *The Essential Guide to Prescription Drugs.* New York: Harper and Row, Publishers, 1982.

Macknight, James. *Apostolic Epistles.* Grand Rapids: Baker Book House, 1949 (reprint).

MacNutt, Francis. *Healing.* Notre Dame, IN: Ave Maria Press, 1974.

Mallone, George. *Those Controversial Gifts.* Downers Grove, IL: InterVarsity Press, 1983. The best part of this book is the Appendix, "Gospel and Spirit: A Joint Statement" by seventeen leaders/scholars who give a carefully balanced view of modern day gifts.

Manuel, Frances D. *Though An Host Should Encamp.* Ft. Washington, PA: Christian Literature Crusade, 1973.

Martin, Malachi. *Hostage to the Devil* (The Possession and Exorcism of Five Living Americans). New York: Reader's Digest Press, 1976.

This work is by a former Jesuit professor with his doctorate in Semitic languages, archaeology, and Oriental history. It is very explicit, blunt, and lurid in details. It should *not* be read except by the most mature Christian and even then with much prayer and caution.

Martin, Walter R. *The Kingdom of the Occult.* Santa Anna, CA: Vision House, 1974.

_____. *Screwtape Writes Again.* Santa Anna, CA: Vision House, 1975.

Mavrodes, George I. *Belief in God.* New York: Random House, 1970.

Mayhue, Richard L. *Divine Healing Today.* Chicago: Moody Press, 1983.

Montgomery, John W., ed. *Christianity for the Tough Minded.* Minneapolis: Bethany Fellowship, Inc., 1973.

_____. *Demon Possession.* Minneapolis: Bethany Fellowship, Inc., 1976.

_____ . *Principalities and Powers: The World of the Occult*. Rev. ed. Minneapolis: Bethany Fellowship, Inc., 1975.

Nevius, John L. *Demon Possession*. Grand Rapids: Kregel Publications, 1968.

New American Standard Bible. La Habra, CA: The Lockman Foundation © 1960, 1962, 1963, 1968, 1971, 1972, 1973, 1975, 1977.

Newbold, H. L. *Mega-Nutrients For Your Nerves*. New York: Peter H. Wyden Publisher, 1975.

Nolen, William A. *Healing: A Doctor in Search of a Miracle*. New York: Random House, 1975.

North, Gary. *None Dare Call It Witchcraft*. New Rochell, NY: Arlington House, 1976.

Oates, Wayne E. *Religious Factors in Mental Illness*. New York: Association, 1955.

Oesterreich, Traugott K. *Possession and Exorcism Among Primitive Races, in Antiquity, the Middle Ages, and Modern Times*. New York: Causeway Books, 1974.

Pache, Rene. *The Inspiration and Authority of Scripture*. Chicago: Moody Press, 1969.

Patterson, C. H. *Theories of Counseling and Psychotherapy*. New York: Harper and Row, Publishers, 1973.

Peck, M. Scott. *People of The Lie, The Hope for Healing Human Evil*. New York: Simon and Schuster, 1983. This is required reading for all who are seriously concerned about evil in people. As a noted psychiatrist, Dr. Peck brings powerful and much needed truth to all counselors. His testimony is strong and convincing even about demonic invasion.

Penn-Lewis, Jessie, and Evan Roberts. *War On The Saints*. Abridged ed., first Amer. ed. Ft. Washington, PA: The Christian Literature Crusade, 1977. This is an essential book for all who want a scriptural introduction to spiritual warfare and especially Satan's counterfeits. The unabridged edition is available, but we find considerable doctrinal error which might confuse some people. We recommend this abridged edition.

Petettierri, Dom Robert. *Exorcism: The Report of a Commission Convened by the Bishop of Exeter*. London: Society for Promotion of Christian Knowledge, 1972.

Phillips, J. B., translator. *The New Testament in Modern English,* Rev. Edn. New York: Macmillan Publishing Co., © J. B. Phillips 1958, 1960, 1972.

Phillips, J. B. *Your God Is Too Small.* New York: Macmillan, 1965.

Phillips, McCandlish. *The Bible, The Supernatural, and the Jews.* Minneapolis: Bethany Fellowship, Inc., 1970.

Philpott, Kent. *A Manual of Demonology and the Occult.* Grand Rapids: Zondervan Publishing House, 1973.

Pinnock, Clark H. *Biblical Revelation—The Foundation of Christian Theology.* Chicago: Moody Press, 1971.

_____. *Set Forth Your Case.* Nutley, NJ: Craig Press, 1967.

Rose, Louis. *Faith Healing.* ed. Bryan Morgan. London: Penguin Books, 1968, 1970.

Rosen, R. D. *Psychobabble.* New York: Atheneum Publishers, 1977.

Rushdoony, Rousas J. *The One and the Many.* Nutley, NJ: Craig Press, 1971.

Samarin, William J. *Tongues of Men and Angels.* New York: Macmillan, 1972.

Sayers, Dorothy L. *The Mind of the Maker.* 2d ed. London: Methuen and Co., Ltd., 1941.

Schaeffer, Francis A. *He Is There and He Is Not Silent.* Wheaton, IL: Tyndale House Publishers, Inc., 1972.

_____. *The God Who Is There.* Chicago: InterVarsity Press, 1968.

Schonfield, Hugh J. *The Authentic New Testament.* London: Dobson Books, Ltd., 1955.

Stein, Jess, ed. *Random House Dictionary of the English Language.* Unabr. ed. New York: Random House, 1966.

Unger, Merrill F. *Biblical Demonology.* Wheaton, IL: Scripture Press, 1952.

_____. *Demons in the World Today: A Study of Occultism in the Light of God's Word.* Wheaton, IL: Tyndale House Publishers, Inc., 1971.

_____. *New Testament Teaching on Tongues.* Grand Rapids: Kregel Publications, 1971.

_____. *What Demons Can Do to the Saints.* Chicago: Moody Press, 1977.
    This book has much that is valuable on the demonic deliverance ministry, but we do not agree with some doctrinal points, especially in chapters three and six.

Vine, W. E. *An Expository Dictionary of New Testament Words.* Westwood, NJ: Fleming H. Revell Co., 1920.

Vitz, Paul C. *Psychology as Religion, The Cult of Self-Worship.* Grand Rapids: William B. Eerdmans Publishing Co., 1977.

Warfield, B. B. *Counterfeit Miracles.* London: Banner of Truth Trust, 1972.

Warnke, Mike. *The Satan-Seller.* Wheaton, IL: Logos Books, 1972.

Wenham, John W. *The Goodness of God.* Downers Grove, IL: InterVarsity Press, 1974.

Wigram, George V., and Ralph D. Winter. *The Word Study Concordance.* Pasadena, CA: William Carey Library, 1978.

Wilburn, Gary A. *The Fortune Sellers.* Glendale, CA: Regal Books, 1972.

Wilson, Colin. *The Occult: A History.* New York: Random House, 1971.

Wright, J. Stafford. *Christianity and the Occult.* Chicago: Moody Press, 1972.

_____. *Mind, Man and the Spirits.* Grand Rapids: Zondervan Pubishing House, 1971.

Young, Edward J. *Thy Word Is Truth.* Grand Rapids: William B. Eerdmans Publishing Co., 1957.

Overcoping with Valium. U. S. Department of Health Education and Welfare Publication No. (FDA) 80-3100, 1980.

MULTIVOLUME WORKS AND SERIES

Blanshard, Brand. *The Nature of Thought.* 2 vols. New York: Macmillan, 1939.

Buttrick, George Arthur, ed. *The Interpreter's Bible.* Vol. XII New York: Abingdon Press, 1957.

Cook, F. C., ed. *The Holy Bible with an Explanatory and Critical Commentary.* Vol. IV of New Testament. New York: Charles Scribner's Sons, 1904.

Denney, James. *An Exposition of the Bible.* Vol. V. Hartford, CT: The S. S. Scranton, Co., 1907.

Henry, Carl F. H. *God, Revelation and Authority.* 4 vols. Waco, TX: Word Books, 1976.

Huther, J. E. *Critical and Exegetical Handbook to the General Epistles of James, Peter, John, and Jude* of *Meyer's Commentary on the New Testament,* trans. from 3d ed. of German by Paton J. Gloag, D. B. Croom, and Clarke H. Irwin. New York: Funk and Wagnalls, Publishers, 1887.

Kittel, Gerhard, ed. *Theological Dictionary of the New Testament,* trans. Geoffrey W. Bromiley. Vol. II. Grand Rapids: William B. Eerdmans Publishing Co., 1964.

Plummer, Alfred. *An Exposition of the Bible.* Vol. VI. Hartford, CT: The S. S. Scranton Co., 1908.

Robertson, A. T. *Word Pictures in the New Testament.* Vol. VI. New York: Harper and Brothers Publishers, 1933.

Tenney, Merrill C., ed. *The Zondervan Pictorial Encyclopedia of the Bible.* Vols. I-V. Grand Rapids: Zondervan Publishing House, 1975.

PERIODICALS

Brand, Paul and Philip Yancey. "A Surgeon's View of Divine Healing." *Christianity Today,* November 25, 1983, pp. 14-21.

Clapp, Rodney. "Faith Healing: A Look at What's Happening." *Christianity Today,* December 16, 1983, pp. 12-17.

Coleman, Linda. "Christian Healing: Is It Real?" *Spiritual Counterfeits Project Journal,* August 1978, pp. 42-51. This research organization is the most outstanding source of high quality material on cults and occultism. Write to Box 2418, Berkeley, CA 94702.

Cottrell, Jack. "All About Demons: Who? What? When?" *The Lookout,* January 27, 1980, p. 7. (Cf. also other issues for information.)

"Expanding Horizons: Psychical Research and Parapsychology." *Spiritual Counterfeits Project Journal,* Winter 1980-81, pp. 3-44.

"Federal Government Seeks to Analyze Role of Psychotherapy." *The Cincinnati* [Ohio] *Enquirier,* September 28, 1980, p. H-6.

Heimlich, Jane. "Do It Yourself Health Care." *Cincinnati* [Ohio] *Magazine,* May 1980, p. 55.

"Holistic Health Issue." *Spiritual Counterfeits Project Journal,* August 1978, pp. 3-51.

"Lawyer Says Multipersonality Man Has Relapse." *The Cincinnati* [Ohio] *Enquirer,* October 12, 1978, p. A-13.

Nash, Stephen. "Is Physical Healing An Intended Benefit of the Atonement?" *The Seminary Review,* September 1981, pp. 111-121.

"Psychiatry's Depression, Psychiatry on the Couch." *Time Magazine,* April 2, 1979, p. 81.

Scanlan, Michael. "Inner Healing Reexamined." *Pastoral Renewal,* August 1980, p. 15.

Scott, Steve, and Brooks Alexander. "Inner Healing Issue." *Spiritual Counterfeits Project Journal,* April 1980, pp. 12-15.

Tabor, James. "The Occult Revolution." *Mission,* May 1973, p. 20.

Waters, Kenny. "This Miracle Didn't Happen." *The National Courier,* February 4, 1977, p. 3.

UNPUBLISHED MATERIALS

Rockstad, Ernest B. "Speaking in Tongues Scripturally Tested." 1977. (Mimeographed.)
  This writer has a number of valuable tracts, monographs, and tapes concerning the whole area of the deliverance ministry and speaking in tongues. We recommend that you secure a list of his resources by writing to Faith and Life Publications: 632 North Prosperity Lane; Andover, KS 67002.

Index

Occult Bondage and Deliverance by Kurt Koch. Copyright © 1970 Kregel Pubications and used by its permission.

"The War Within: An Anatomy of Lust" (name withheld) from *Leadership,* Fall, 1982. Copyright LEADERSHIP 1982, used by permission.

Scripture quotations are from the *New American Standard Bible,* © The Lockman Foundation 1960, 1962, 1963, 1968, 1971, 1972, 1973, 1975, 1977.

Mere Christianity by C. S. Lewis. Copyright 1943, 1952 by Macmillan Publishing Co., Inc. Copyrights renewed. Used by its permission.

Miracles by C. S. Lewis. Copyright 1947 by Macmillan Publishing Co., Inc., renewed 1975 by Arthur Owen Barfield and Alfred Cecil Harwood. Used by permission of Macmillan.

The New Testament in Modern English, Rev. Edn., J. B. Phillips, translator © J. B. Phillips 1958, 1960, 1972, and used by permission of Macmillan.

The Problem of Pain by C. S. Lewis. Copyright 1943 by Macmillan Publishing Co. and used by its permission.

What Demons Can Do To The Saints by Merrill F. Unger. Copyright 1977, Moody Press. Moody Bible Institute of Chicago. Used by permission.

"Inner Healing Reexamined" by Michael Scanlan in *Pastoral Renewal,* August 1980. Copyright 1980 *Pastoral Renewal* and used by permission.

Thomas W. Leahy "THE EPISTLE OF JAMES" in THE JEROME BIBLICAL COMMENTARY, edited by Brown/Fitzmeyer/Murphy, © 1968, pp. 376, 377. Reprinted by permission of Prentice-Hall, Inc., Englewood Cliffs, N.J.

THE RANDOM HOUSE DICTIONARY OF THE ENGLISH LANGUAGE, edited by Jess Stein. Copyright © 1966 Random House, Inc. and used by its permission.

The Psychological Society by Martin L. Gross. Copyright © 1978 Random House, Inc. and used by permission of Random House, Inc.

"Christian Healing: Is It Real?" by Linda Coleman in *Spiritual Counterfeits Project Journal,* August, 1978. Reprinted by permission of Spiritual Counterfeits Project, Inc., © 1978, P. O. Box 4308, Berkeley, CA 94704.

"Inner Healing" by Steve Scott and Brooks Alexander in *Spiritual Counterfeits Project Journal,* April 1980. Reprinted by permission of Spiritual Counterfeits Project, Inc., © 1980, P. O, Box 4308, Berkeley, CA 94704.

"All About Demons: Who? What? When?" by Jack Cottrell in *The Lookout,* January 27, 1980. Copyright © 1980 Standard Publishing Co. and used by its permission.

"Psychiatry's Depression, Psychiatry on the Couch" in TIME April 2, 1979. © 1979 TIME Inc. and used by its permission.

"Federal Government Seeks to Analyze Role of Psychotherapy" by Philip J. Hilts in *The Cincinnati* [Ohio] *Enquirer,* Sept. 28, 1980. © 1980 *Washington Post* and used by its permission.

Posma "Physician," Helmbold "Anoint," Stoesz "Gifts of Healing," Horne "Sacraments." Taken from ZONDERVAN PICTORIAL ENCYCLOPEDIA OF THE BIBLE, ed. by Merrill C. Tenney. Copyright © 1975 by the Zondervan Corporation. Used by permission.

A Step Further by Joni Eareckson and Steve Estes. Copyright © 1978 by Joni Eareckson & Steve Estes. Used by permission of Zondervan Publishing House.

From THE CHRISTIAN COUNSELOR'S MANUAL by Jay E. Adams. Copyright 1973 by Jay E. Adams and used by permission of Baker Book House.

From NEW TESTAMENT COMMENTARY: I-II TIMOTHY AND TITUS by William Hendriksen. Copyright 1957 by William Hendriksen and used by permission of Baker Book House.